SOUND AND SENTIMENT

PUBLICATIONS OF THE AMERICAN FOLKLORE SOCIETY
New Series
General Editor, Marta Weigle
Volume 5

SOUND AND SENTIMENT

Birds, Weeping, Poetics, and Song in Kaluli Expression

STEVEN FELD

UNIVERSITY OF PENNSYLVANIA PRESS
Philadelphia
1982

This work was published with the support of the Haney
Foundation.

Library of Congress Cataloging in Publication Data

Feld, Steven.
  Sound and sentiment.

  (Publications of the American Folklore
Society; v. 5)
  Based on the author's thesis (doctoral)—Indiana
University, 1979.
  Bibliography: *p.*
  Discography: p.
  Includes index.
  1. Kaluli (Papua New Guinea people)—Social life
and customs. 2. Kaluli (Papua New Guinea people)—
Rites and ceremonies. 3. Kaluli (Papua New Guinea
people)—Music—History and criticism. 4. Folk
music—Papua New Guinea—History and criticism.
5. Folk-songs, Bosavi—Papua New Guinea—History
and criticism. 6. Birds—Papua New Guinea—
Mythology. I Title. II. Series.
DU740.42.F44   306'.0995'3   81–43518
ISBN 0–8122–7829–1   AACR2
ISBN 0–8122–1124–3 (pbk.)

Printed in the United States of America

To
the boy who became a *muni* bird
and
in memory of Charlie Parker, John Coltrane,
and Charles Mingus,

ane kalu ɔbɛ mise

CONTENTS

ILLUSTRATIONS

ix

TABLES

ACKNOWLEDGMENTS

Many people helped make this study possible, and it is a pleasure to thank them here. My greatest debt is to the Kaluli people, particularly those of Sululib, for their comradery and trust. While I often think of times I spent with Kiliyɛ, Sɛlibi, Gaima, Gaso, Gigio, Hasili, Mewɔ, Ɛsiyɛ, Ganigi, Gɔbɔ, Gaso *sulɔ*, and Ulahi, I must single out Kulu and Jubi, two Kaluli intellectuals and sensitive companions whose thoughts contribute to almost every page of the text. I greatly look forward to future times we will share.

Arrival in unknown places amidst numerous technical and practical difficulties is a part of every fieldworker's experience; I was fortunate in having Antje and Bill Clarke in Port Moresby, Ivor Manton in Mount Hagen, and Keith and Norma Briggs at Mount Bosavi to help make my transitions comfortable. I appreciated their hospitality so much during the times I was most frantic.

Field support during 1976–77 was provided by the Institute of Papua New Guinea Studies, and I am grateful to its former director Ulli Beier and music archivist, Frederic Duvelle, for their interest in my research. The Papua New Guinea Bird Society and particularly Harry Bell, Bill Peckover, and John Hansen generously aided my ornithological work. I am also grateful to John for the support he arranged from the National Broadcasting Commission and its Technical Services Division. Other field support was provided by the Anthropology Film Center, the Archives of Traditional Music, and my family; my thanks to them all.

When I returned from the field, Carroll and Joan Williams made the Anthropology Film Center the right kind of environment for me to begin putting the pieces together. Performance during the same period with the Transcultural Minstrel Jass Band and Tom Guralnick gave me an important outlet to express many new things I was hearing.

Sound and Sentiment was first formulated as a dissertation in anthropological linguistics at Indiana University in 1979. For the fellowship that supported my graduate work, I am deeply grateful to the Danforth Foundation. As an undergraduate Sam Leff, Alexander Lesser, Gerry Rosenfeld, Gitel Steed, and Colin Turnbull brought me into anthropology and demonstrated its relevance to a humane and politically engaged view of contemporary life. Then Alan Merriam got me started in ethnomusicology, Carl and Flo Voegelin drew me into linguistics, Judith Friedman Hansen kept telling me that there is more to culture than structure, and Sol Worth and Robert Plant Armstrong posed some tough questions about communication and aesthetics. Ralph Bulmer and Brent Berlin helped shape my understanding of critical issues in ethnobiology and Kaluli natural history. Allen Grimshaw, Bonnie Kendall, and Charles Bird got me through the dissertation and much more; I think of them with the same fondness I usually reserve for Kaluli waterfalls.

Rewriting and condensing a dissertation has been a long process, one that has benefited considerably from Larry Gross's advice and support, John McGuigan's patience, and the careful editorial attention of Marta Weigle and Lee Ann Draud. I can't forget Charlie Keil, who came up with a list of materialist counterinterpretations at just the right moment in the revision process. The reevaluations they prompted have not changed my basic position but did aid the presentation considerably.

Finally, Buck and Bambi Schieffelin walk through these pages with me in a special way; they brought me to Bosavi as a fellow researcher and kinsman and continue to share much research and kinship with me. Other special contributions within are Janis Essner's maps and diagrams and Mary Groff's magical bird drawings. The last thank you goes to Shari Robertson, whose love and aesthetic agitation made a major contribution during the writing. This study is affectionately dedicated to the mythic figure that animates and links Kaluli sound and sentiment, and to three musicians whose sounds have had a major impact on my life.

Philadelphia
September 1981

Myth and music are like the
conductors of an orchestra
whose listeners are the silent
performers.

Claude Lévi-Strauss
The Raw and the Cooked

Abyss of the birds: The abyss is
Time, with its sadnesses and
weariness. The birds are the opposite
of Time; they are our desire for
light, for stars, for rainbows, and
for jubilant song!

Olivier Messiaen
Quartet for the End of Time

SOUND AND SENTIMENT

Introduction

This is an ethnographic study of sound as a cultural system, that is, a system of symbols, among the Kaluli people of Papua New Guinea. My intention is to show how an analysis of modes and codes of sound communication leads to an understanding of the ethos and quality of life in Kaluli society. By analyzing the form and performance of weeping, poetics, and song in relation to their origin myth and the bird world they metaphorize, Kaluli sound expressions are revealed as embodiments of deeply felt sentiments.

In both theoretical orientation and descriptive style, this book aims to be compatible with a more general ethnography of the Kaluli, Edward L. Schieffelin's *The Sorrow of the Lonely and the Burning of the Dancers.* Many points about Kaluli social life discussed in his book are omitted or only briefly sketched here. For the reader unfamiliar with this work, a short introduction will serve as an orientation.

The Ethnographic Setting

The Kaluli people live in a tropical rain forest just north of the slopes of Mt. Bosavi, the collapsed cone of an extinct volcano on the Great Papuan Plateau in the Southern Highlands Province of Papua New Guinea. They are one of four small groups who collectively refer to themselves as *Bosavi kalu* 'people of Bosavi' and to their language as *Bosavi to* 'Bosavi language'. The Kaluli, Ologo, Walulu, and Wisesi are culturally identical but linguistically marked by small, mutually intelligible differences. I lived with members of clan Bonɔ at a site called Sululib; this is in the central Bosavi area, where the people refer to themselves as Kaluli.

The total population of the Bosavi people is twelve hundred, spread

3

Aerial view of the Great Papuan Plateau and the Bosavi airstrip. Some 500 square miles of land are covered by thick forest of the kind seen here; the only clearings visible from the air are the longhouse sites of the Bosavi peoples and their swidden gardens.

out in about twenty longhouse communities, each separated by an hour or so walking distance through secondary forest. This is a small number of people in relation to the land spread of the Great Papuan Plateau. All of the Bosavi longhouses are set on lowland hill forest grounds whose elevations range between 550 and 850 meters; the Kaluli longhouses are set around 600 meters. Some Kaluli are familiar with lands higher up the mountain slopes, where they traditionally hunt. Up to 1,000 meters the forest is mixed lowland growth, and from there to about 1,500 meters this begins to merge with lower montane rain forest. From 1,500 meters to the caldera at 2,600 meters, the mountain is too cold and inhospitable in its mossy growth and fog-covered hills to invite hunting or traveling.

The Kaluli are swidden horticulturalists whose staple food is sago, derived from wild palms that grow in swampy areas throughout the forest. They also maintain large shifting cultivation gardens that produce bananas, pandanus, breadfruit, and green vegetables. Fish are abundant in numerous small streams throughout the area, and small game, as well as wild pigs, are hunted in surrounding forests. Domestic pigs are kept in small numbers and also occasionally contribute to the food supply. Compared with New Guinea Highlanders' food resources, the Kaluli diet is diverse and varied. A low population density means that forest foods are never in danger of depletion.

Each longhouse community is a residential grouping made up of the members of two or three named patrilineal descent groups—approximately fifteen families. Marriage is exogamous, the preferred arrangement being sister exchange. Residence is patrilocal. This system promotes large networks of relations between affines and matrilateral relatives across longhouse communities.

Kaluli society is highly egalitarian, lacking the "big man" social organization found in the New Guinea Highlands. Men utilize extensive networks of obligation and reciprocity in the organization of work and the accomplishment of major social transactions, such as bridewealth and hunting.

As with most Papua New Guinea cultures described in the ethno-

A Kaluli communal longhouse, *a*, is usually the home of sixty to eighty people. In earlier times longhouses were built on high ridges. The end of raiding and subsequent increase in outside contact has meant that longhouses are now being built on lower grounds surrounded by cleared forest and degrassed courtyards.

graphic literature, the theme of reciprocity as an organizing motif for daily events is highly visible in Kaluli society. The most focused and crystalized expression of reciprocity, as exchange, affection, comradery, and hospitality, is found in traditional Kaluli ceremonies. E. Schieffelin concentrated his ethnography on *gisalo,* the most important of these, showing how an analysis of its organization could serve as "a lens through which to view some of the fundamental issues of Kaluli life and society" (1976:1).

Gisalo is one of five ceremonials in Bosavi and the only one that Kaluli people maintain they originated. It takes place from dusk until dawn inside a longhouse lit by resin torches. Members of a guest community stage the singing and dancing for a host longhouse. The guests prepare costumes and newly composed songs for a period of a few weeks, and the hosts prepare food for a few days prior to the event. Occasions for these ceremonials include marriages, pork distributions, and other formal exchanges between communities.

Once it turns dark, the dancers enter the longhouse and begin their performance. They dance up and down the hall, singing with the accompaniment of rattle instruments and a chorus. The songs are sung in a plaintive voice, and the texts are sad and evocative, reflecting on loss and abandonment. They cite places and events familiar to all or specific groups of the hosts and are composed with the intention of making the hosts nostalgic, sentimental, and sad. The hosts listen intently, identifying with the map that the singers construct by weaving together place names, metaphors, and onomatopoeic devices.

At points in the songs where they become overcome with sadness and grief, the hosts burst into tears and loud mournful wails. This may set off a chain reaction of wailing throughout the house. Angered by the grief they have been made to feel, one of the hosts jumps up, grabs a torch from a bystander, and rushes onto the dance floor to jam the flickering torch into the shoulder of a dancer. The dancer continues as if unaffected by the burn and may be burned repeatedly. Hosts either sit down again and cry or move to the rear veranda of the longhouse to weep alone.

In the aftermath of the ceremonies, food prestations are made. Discussion recalls how the songs made the hosts cry and burn the dancers. For Kaluli generally, it is not the burning that is central, rather it is the extent to which the compositions and their manner of performance were effective, as judged by the extent to which they moved the hosts to tears.

Schieffelin's ethnography is dedicated to elucidating the social meaning of this particular sequence of events. The present work aims to complement that by looking at the particular dynamics of weeping, song, and poetics as sound modalities whose performed expression embodies basic premises of Kaluli ethos. Just as *gisalo* can be understood as a ceremonial crystallization of Kaluli concern about reciprocity, the structure and content of its sound modes and codes can be viewed as expressive means for articulating those same shared feelings and emotions.

The Geographical and Historical Setting

The Great Papuan Plateau was named by patrol officer Jack Hides in 1935. To anyone who has studied modern maps of the area, or walked through it, it is hardly a plateau. Hides was really more an explorer than a geographer (Sinclair 1969). The name, however, has stuck and is applied to the area (see map) bordered on the north by the Karius Range, on the south by Mt. Bosavi, on the east by the Kikori River, and on the west by the Sioa River. The area comprises more than 500 square miles. In addition to the 1,200 Bosavi people, who constitute the largest group, the plateau is populated by another 1,000 people speaking several other languages (for accounts of the distribution, see E. Schieffelin 1976:5–17, and Kelly 1977:7–17).

First contact with the peoples of the plateau occurred in 1935 when Jack Hides and Jim O'Malley made their Strickland-Purari patrol (see Hides 1973 and Sinclair 1969 for accounts). The following year the Archbold Expedition flew over Bosavi in preparation for the Bamu-Purari patrol of Ivan Champion and C. I. J. Adamson (see Champion 1940). This later patrol made the first contact with Kaluli people; the previous one had passed through the land of the Onabasulu to the north.

Thus the 1930s brought the beginnings of European goods, in the form of steel axes and cloth, to the Bosavi area. Contact continued during the 1940s and 1950s, although patrolling was sporadic for a variety of reasons, not the least of which was the fact that the nearest government station was at Lake Kutubu, a hard, five-day trek to the northeast. The first government census was taken in 1958. In the early 1960s increased contact began, and major changes took place. Under Australian colonial government pressure, the 1960s brought an end to raiding and cannibalism, enforcement of such "sanitary" procedures as latrines and burial of

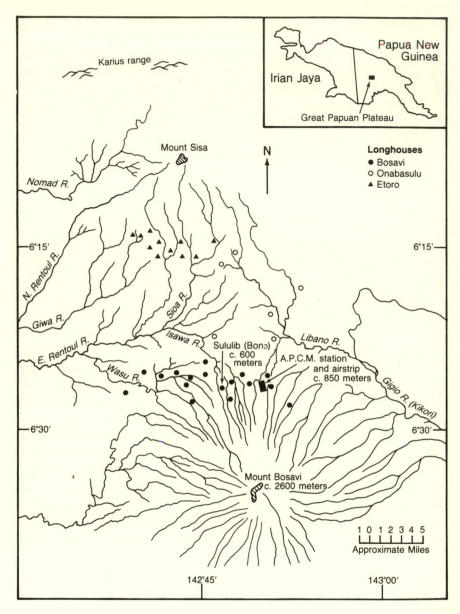

The Great Papuan Plateau

the dead, and the building of government rest houses in each longhouse community. In 1964 missionaries working in the neighboring Lake Kutubu and Fasu areas built an airstrip under the auspices of the Unevangelized Fields Mission (U.F.M.), now called the Asia Pacific Christian Mission (A.P.C.M.).

Edward Schieffelin began ethnographic research among the Kaluli in 1966 and was joined by Bambi Schieffelin in 1967. At that time the airstrip and missionary station were manned by Papuan pastors, and there was little Christian evangelization in the area. In 1970 Keith and Norma Briggs of the A.P.C.M. arrived to live at the station and do medical and teaching work; they are still in residence there.

Other ethnographers also came to the Great Papuan Plateau in the late 1960s and early 1970s. To the north, Ray Kelly worked with the Etoro (Kelly 1977) and Tom Ernst with the Onabasulu (Ernst n.d.), both concentrating on social structure and social organization. To the east Paul Freund studied social change among the Kasua (Freund 1977), and on the south side of Mt. Bosavi, Michael Wood studied Kamula social organization and ceremonialism (Wood n.d.).

Having concentrated his first research on reciprocity and ceremonialism, Edward Schieffelin returned to Bosavi in 1975 to work on history and social change, spirit mediumship and seances. Bambi Schieffelin began research on socialization, developmental sociolinguistics, and Kaluli language. I joined them in the field in 1976 to work on expressive culture in music and language and stayed on for a few months after they departed in 1977. Aside from ourselves and the Briggs family, there were no other resident outsiders on the Great Papuan Plateau during 1975–77.

Bosavi society had changed considerably by the late 1960s and 1970s, particularly under the growing internal pressures of evangelical Christianity and a simultaneous lack of government and outside influence. While the impact of these changes occasionally enters the discussion here, as in the analysis of specific events and texts, the purpose of this study is to explicate traditional Kaluli values and expressive systems, not to present them as vestiges of a former way of life. The text, then, takes 1976–77 as a historical ethnographic present and describes knowledge, understandings, beliefs, and practices that I observed, participated in, or discussed with Kaluli people between the ages of twenty and seventy. For them, whatever the ongoing changes, these events were socially real and salient.

The Fieldwork Setting

Much ethnographic reportage gives the impression, whether intentionally or not, that research takes place in a vacuum. My work was influenced
at each stage by two other people, Edward (Buck) and Bambi Schieffelin.
When we met in 1972, Buck had just finished his dissertation based on
field research among the Kaluli in 1966–68. I read a portion of the
dissertation that dealt with the music of *gisalo* and saw a selection of slides
and films. Several months later I listened to all of the tapes from this field
trip and found the music unlike anything I had heard from Oceania. At
that point my own training was as an Africanist, but my enthusiasm for
Kaluli music led me to consider working in Bosavi.

The Schieffelins returned to Bosavi in the fall of 1975. Before their
departure we discussed the possibility of some collaborative projects in
expressive culture and language. The timing was not good, however. I
was in a depressed state, alienated from academia, and had pretty much
dropped out. I was making a living as a jazz musician and was not sure
whether I wanted to finish my degree and be an anthropologist. When
I finally decided to go to Bosavi, it was because I had relistened to the
music and found it terribly moving. I wanted to learn how to make it and
how to understand it. But I had no well-worked-out theories or hypotheses to test, just the intuition that as a tropical rain forest people, Kaluli
must use sound to advantage over other sensory systems. I suspected that
the variety of sound expressions was great, and that particularly strong
relationships would exist between ecology and sounds of the natural
world and those of cultural expression. This was hardly an original intuition in any case, deriving, on the one hand, from years of conversations
with Buck and Bambi, and on the other, from the research on African
pygmy music that I had begun during undergraduate study with Colin
Turnbull.

Nevertheless, by usual standards I probably had a better orientation
to my field situation than do many young students going off to a remote
bushy place. The tape recordings, films and slides, talks with the Schieffelins, Buck's dissertation (1972) and book (1976), a missionary grammar
(Rule 1964), and correspondence before my departure gave me a pretty
good idea of where I was going and what the society would be like. I knew
that there was little pidgin or English spoken in Bosavi and that research
would have to be conducted in large part monolingually. I also knew that
I would be walking into a situation in process, with houses built, supplies

and necessities arranged, research going on, and people accustomed to outsiders asking questions, taking pictures, recording sounds, and generally hanging around.

A final letter told me that the Kaluli knew I was coming and knew that I was a "song man" in my own land. I also learned that I was to be introduced as Bambi's brother (*ao*), Buck's brother-in-law (*idas*), and their son Zachary's mother's brother (*babo*). While it seemed likely that an introduction as a kinsman of the Schieffelins would mean a certain amount of instant rapport, I had no idea that members of another village were angrily protesting to Buck and Bambi that Sululib already had two anthropologists. In all fairness I should be sent off to live with them; they would take care of me well, indeed, and our trade salt, fish hooks, razor blades, mirrors, and beads could then be more equitably distributed in Bosavi! This matter was finally resolved by the argument that since I was a member of the Schieffelin family, particularly a helpless younger brother who didn't even speak the language, it would be unthinkable to send me off alone; it was a family obligation to feed and care for me at Sululib.

It is hard to overestimate the value of this introduction as a kinsman of people the Kaluli knew and trusted, and equally hard to overestimate the benefits of working together with friends who had good control of the major linguistic and cultural details of Bosavi society. Daily interaction in a situation in which each of us pursued specific research while constantly hearing about and discussing the work of two others had a critical as well as humbling effect, minimizing simplistic reductions and interpretations. For me, the greatest impact was the continual methodological reminder that divergent routes could lead to similar answers as often as similar routes could lead to divergent answers.

Everyone who has attempted field research knows how much time it takes to scout locations, find people to work with, get set up and going. Then there is that set of basic materials that must be gathered to create a social baseline: demography, local history, genealogies, social structural details, ecological factors, economic and subsistence data, language structure and use. My work proceded differently; in some ways, it was like doing the second year of fieldwork without having had to do most of the first. I had the luxury of being able to go to other field notes any time I needed a genealogy, a village history, a social or economic detail. Even language learning, which occupies so much time in a basically monolingual situation, was much easier with other people who knew the language and could answer questions, help translate, or provide shortcuts.

The Kaluli were also comfortable with this arrangement. Often, in the first months of work, they told me not to worry about my misunderstandings because my sister or brother-in-law would help. Later, upon seeing us together, one might come over and say to Buck or Bambi, "Tell him about. . . ." Men who had worked with Buck in the past felt a particular obligation to school me. In good Kaluli fashion, others extended their sense of relationship to me, as when Gaso *sulɔ* (elder Gaso) first greeted me by saying, "I call Bage (Buck) 'brother' so I will call you 'brother-in-law.' " Thereafter I called him *bas sulɔ* 'elder brother-in-law'. And because Kaluli place particular emphasis on elder sisters helping younger brothers, Bambi was able to appeal to women to work with me when it might otherwise have been awkward for me to initiate discussions. In these ways my research and social orientation proceeded without some of the delays and frustrations many fieldworkers experience. It also pleased the Kaluli because it provided them with a culturally acceptable framework for incorporating a newcomer.

Mt. Bosavi as it appeared on most days from my porch. From the village edges, one's visual perception of depth is a function of layers of sunlight coming through the forest canopy and the ever-present soft clouds that veil the mountain itself.

My daily routine in Bosavi was quite varied. Some days were spent at Sululib, my home village, interviewing, transcribing texts, and working on musical and linguistic issues with a group of close assistants. Other days were spent in the bush, recording and observing birds and learning about forest ecology from experienced hunters. Still other days were spent at sago camps or work areas visiting Sululib people and recording songs and sounds as they went about their everyday activities. Every few months Buck and I went off to distant communities for periods of about a week, to seek out spirit mediums and record their seances. On a few occasions, I staged recording sessions for historical materials or specific elicitations, but most of my fifty hours of recordings were made at spontaneous events.

Textual materials from these tapes, including five hundred songs, several hours of sung weeping, and many myths, were all transcribed and translated in the field, first with the performers, then with regular linguistic assistants, and then perhaps with the performers again. These transcriptions and the kinds of discussions that spontaneously evolved as they were being made provided the basis for further interviewing and analysis of poetic grammar, song composition, and performance style. By the end of my research, I had enough control over the formal aspects of poetics and song to compose several of my own songs, usually manipulating one structural dimension or another in order to test several hypotheses about constraints upon form. These compositions provided additional springboards for conversations and questions, which then frequently led back to materials that had been previously transcribed and annotated.

By combining a strong component of such basic empirical procedures with less formal ones, such as the ongoing, day-to-day hanging around with people for varied periods as they ate, relaxed, socialized, or worked, I felt a certain sense of methodological balance. While controlled linguistic tests yielded quick insights into issues, it was more often the case that periods of just watching people interact and overhearing their conversations filled in the pragmatic details that made formal constructs more or less telling. The patterns revealed by this type of participant-observation data collection are mirrored in the presentation here by a continual back and forth movement between texts and contexts, conventions and constraints, codes and variations, forms and performances, expectations and ruptures, Kaluli abstractions and verbalizations, and my own interpretations and deductions.

The Interpretive Setting

Sound and Sentiment is a deliberately eclectic book. As I worked among the Kaluli, I began to find a pattern that connected myths, birds, weeping, poetics, song, sadness, death, dance, waterfalls, taboos, sorrow, maleness and femaleness, children, food, sharing, obligation, performance, and evocation. As I continued to work through the materials, the pattern kept pointing to linkages between sounds, both human and natural, and sentiments, social ethos and emotion. I thus decided that what should be in the analysis was what shaped the pattern. At moments when this became difficult, I considered writing a book about just birds, or weeping, or poetics, or song. But each time I found myself coming back to the myth that relates them all, "the boy who became a *muni* bird," thus reconfirming that the form of the book should follow the form of the myth. Ultimately the most important issue at the cultural level is this pattern that connects all these elements and not the discrete entities involved or the analytic means necessary for their specific explication.

The thesis of this work is that the Kaluli expressive modalities of weeping, poetics, and song, in their musical and textual structure, are mirror representations of the symbolic circle constructed by the myth, "the boy who became a *muni* bird." The argument is that this myth is a crystallization of relations between Kaluli sentimentality and its expression in weeping, poetics, and song. Furthermore, the myth's central theme of "becoming a bird" stands out as a metaphoric base for Kaluli aesthetics. By following the myth's structure, the book is constituted as something of an exercise in *explication de texte*. My concern, however, is only partially mythologic and folkloric interpretation. The broader aim is to construct a symbolic interpretation that shows how expressive modalities are culturally constituted by performance codes that both actively communicate deeply felt sentiments and reconfirm mythic principles.

The analytic means necessary for this task are diverse, but the intellectual positions I have found most helpful are the structuralism of Claude Lévi-Strauss (1966), the thick description and interpretive ethnography advocated by Clifford Geertz (1973), and the ethnography of communication paradigm proposed by Dell Hymes (1974).

In the analysis of myth and the structure of cultural domains, I follow the tradition promulgated by Lévi-Strauss in order to make a case for symbols being logically connected in a rather formal manner. Yet this is only a partial baseline for building a cultural analysis, because ethnography is much more than the reduction of normative scenarios to logical ones. Elegant structure may be a component of cultural forms, but the armchairism and speculation that sometimes go along with formal analysis have a tendency to trivialize interpretations from direct experience. For this reason a major portion of my study supports structural arguments with detailed descriptions of how symbols activate meaningful activity. In these descriptions, I follow Geertz's notion of ethnography as a kind of detective work. Evidence is accumulated in detail, then the work begins again with the piecing, sorting, editing, and weaving of evidence into interpretation. In a sense, this puts the ethnographer on the same level as the *bricoleur* of Lévi-Strauss's *La Pensée Sauvage:* a combined inventor, scientist, artist, technician, jack-of-all-trades. In ethnography, *brico-lage* is the sorting through of "facts," impressions, remarks, texts, and recodings of many viewpoints in order to assemble the bits and pieces of substance whose collage properly illuminates the cultural construction of actions and events.

These two positions, the structural and hermeneutic, are considered by many to be clearly opposed: In one instance the anthropologist is thought of as decoder and translator and in the other as experiencer and interpreter. It appears to me, however, that it is necessary to integrate the study of how symbols are logically connected with the study of how they are formulated and performed in cultural experience. For such an integration, I turn to the views developed by Dell Hymes on the ethnography of communication.

Hymes proposes an organizing framework comprising four levels of specificity, which while analytically separable, ultimately link together. The first area concerns communicative events and the close description and specification of the participants, modes, channels, codes, settings, message form, attitudes, and content whose simultaneous, ongoing activity characterize the event. The second area extends this to the varieties and forms of co-occurrence among these components. The third area reaches out more directly into the social arena to question how capacities and forms are related to functions, differential competence and performance, and general salience of activities to participants and society. Fourth, and finally, the activity of the system is considered as a whole in terms of its ongoing sustenance, maintenance, and balance, as well as its character in relation to other systems.

This approach to communicative means and social ends offers much as a meeting ground of formal and interpretive methods. For purposes here, it organizes the linguistic and musical detail to scaffold a cultural argument. Therefore, Kaluli communicative resources are addressed, following Hymes's lead, as logical patterns of symbolic material that exist not for themselves but in order to activate and bring forth meaningful social relations through structured expression. From this assumption follows the notion that the explication of a syntactic choice, a phonological alteration, a lexical set, a melodic phrase, or a metric pattern are not activities intended to reify linguistic or musical form, but are instead concerned with demonstrating how communicative capacities are involved in a cultural construction of pattern.

Turning now to the form of the book, chapter 1, "The boy who became a *muni* bird," centers in structuralism and myth analysis, presenting and analyzing the myth whose constituent themes form the topics for the core chapters of the study. The analysis argues that the myth is logically structured by three paradigms: provocation, mediation, and metaphor, which embody social sentiments, birds, and sounds. Becoming a bird mediates expressions of sentiment in sound forms.

The focus of chapter 2, "To you they are birds, to me they are voices in the forest," is on folk ornithology and bird symbolism, considering the Bosavi avifauna and the ways Kaluli understand it through the creation of an intersection of natural historical observation and mythic deduction. Kaluli taxonomize birds both morphologically and by families of sound. The social construction of these classifications shows how the avian world is a metaphoric society, ideal mediators of myths, and ideal makers of sounds that inspire feelings.

The next three chapters build on this foundation to present studies in the musical and linguistic codes of sung-texted-weeping, poetics, and song. "Weeping that moves women to song," chapter 3, is about emotional expression in weeping and the cultural pattern of sounds that embody sadness. Kaluli consider melodic-sung-weeping, performed improvisationally by women at funerals, to be the human sound expression closest to being a bird. The melody of this weeping mirrors the sounds of the boy who became a *muni* bird in the myth. Weeping is thus equated with bird sound and links expressions of grief with the metaphor of turning into a bird.

Chapter 4, "The poetics of loss and abandonment," discusses the language of evocation and Kaluli concepts of poetic persuasion. It deals with expressive constraints in grammar and the linguistic and metalinguistic means that make song texts a code of "bird sound words." Kaluli consider poetic language a special set of conventions suited to the task of making song texts sad and birdlike so that they will have an emotional impact. Analyzing these conventions indicates how Kaluli utilize linguistic creativity for explicitly social ends.

The fifth chapter, "Song that moves men to tears," concerns the terminology and conceptualization of Kaluli song and the shaping of form in performance. Song combines the bird sound melody of weeping and the bird sound words of poetics. It is the complete construction of communication from a bird's point of view, articulating through staging features and visual and choreographic symbols that parallel the same bird trope.

Chapter 6, "In the form of a bird: Kaluli aesthetics," draws together all previous arguments to suggest that "becoming a bird" is the core metaphor of Kaluli aesthetics, mediating social sentiments in sound forms. Weeping moves women to song and song moves men to tears; in both cases performers use sound codes that symbolize bird communication, and aesthetic evaluation compares the performers to certain birds. In the process of summarizing these issues, the chapter additionally reflects on culture theory and aesthetics in anthropological thought.

The Linguistic Setting

Bosavi is a non-Austronesian language with verb final word order, complex morphology, and subject-verb agreement in all tenses save the past and habitual, which have single forms. The majority of isolated examples in the text cite verbs in one of three forms: an imperative, marked by end shape -*ma;* a third-person present, marked by end shape -*ab;* and a habitual marked by end shape -*an.* More involved textual examples explain morphology and markings in the context of the specific terms.

The orthography utilized here modifies the one found in E. Schieffelin (1976) by the deletion of /æ/ and /ɨ/, which I analyze as noncontrastive with /a/ and /i/. I also do not use /r/ but simply /l/ for the flapped and retroflex lateral; hence the reader will find *gisalo* rather than *gisaro,* which appears in his publications. I have not changed the spelling of the word Bosavi (to Bosafi) since it appears as the former in official and government publications and maps.

Orthography

Print	Phonetic Symbol	Notes on Pronunciation
vowels		
/i/	[i]	like English "beet"
/e/	[e]	like English "bait"
/ɛ/	[ɛ]	like English "bet"
/a/	[a]	like English "bother"; in initial position it is short, like English "bat"
/u/	[u]	like English "boot"
/o/	[o]	like English "boat"
/ɔ/	[ɔ]	like English "bought"
plosives		
/b/	[p]	voiceless initially, finally,
	[b]	and usually medially; some speakers voice it medially for emphasis
/t/	[tʰ]	highly variable with [s], but there are some words where all speakers use [tʰ]
/d/	[t]	voiceless initially, voiced
	[d]	or voiceless medially, and unaspirated like English /d/
/k/	[kʰ]	
/g/	[k]	voiced or voiceless medially
	[g]	
fricatives		
/f/	[f]	
/s/	[s]	
/š/	[ʃ]	as in English "shoe" or "bush"
/h/	[h]	
affricate		
/j/	[ǰ]	as in English "judge"

nasals

/m/	[m]	voiced initially and medially; voiceless finally
/n/	[n]	voiced initially and medially; voiceless finally; in final position alternates with /m/ for most speakers

lateral/flap

	[ɾ]	alveolar flapped lateral;
	[ɻ]	preceding back vowels it is also retroflex

nonsyllabic semi vowels

/w/	[w]	like English /w/
/y/	[y]	like English /y/

In addition to dialectical differences in pronunciation, Kaluli vowels vary considerably from speech to song. This is particularly apparent with the pairs *e*/ɛ and *o*/ɔ. Most examples cited in the text derive from performances as recorded on tape and transcribed. Few derive from repeated and careful elicited speech. The transcriptions have not been altered to correct the pronunciations to standard spoken Kaluli.

1

<hr>

The Boy Who Became a Muni Bird

"Once there was a boy and his older sister; they called each other *adɛ.*
One day they went off together to a small stream to catch crayfish. After
a short while the girl caught one; her brother as yet had none. Looking
at the catch, he turned to her, lowered his head, and whined, *'Adɛ, ni galin
andoma' (adɛ,* I have no crayfish). She replied, 'I won't give it to you; it
is for mother.'

Later, on another bank of the stream she again caught one; her
brother was still without. Again he begged, *'Adɛ ni galin andoma.'* Again
she refused, 'I won't give it to you; it is for father.' Sadly, he continued
to hope for a catch of his own. Finally, at another bank, she again caught
a crayfish. He immediately begged for it, whining, *'Adɛ,* I really have
nothing.' She was still unwilling: 'I won't give it to you; it is for older
brother.'

He felt very sad. Just then he caught a tiny shrimp. He grasped it
tightly; when he opened his palm, it was all red. He pulled the meat out
of the shell and placed the shell over his nose. His nose turned a bright
purple red. Then he looked at his hands; they were wings.

When she turned and saw her brother to be a bird, the older sister
was very upset. 'Oh *adɛ,'* she said, 'don't fly away.' He opened his mouth
to reply, but no words came out, just the high falsetto cooing cry of the
muni bird, the Beautiful Fruitdove (*Ptilinopus pulchellus*).

He began to fly off, repeating the *muni* cry, a descending *eeeeeeeeee.*
His sister was in tears at the sight of him; she called out, 'Oh *adɛ,* come
back, take the crayfish, you eat them all, come back and take the crayfish.' Her calling was in vain. The boy was now a *muni* bird and continued to cry and cry. After a while the cry became slower and more
steady:

E   E   E   E

Then it turned to sung crying:

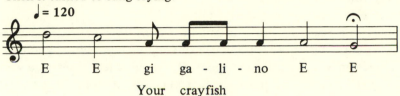

E   E   gi   ga - li - no   E   E

Your   crayfish

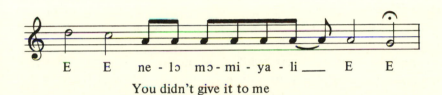

E   E   ne - lɔ   mɔ - mi - ya - li ___   E   E

You didn't give it to me

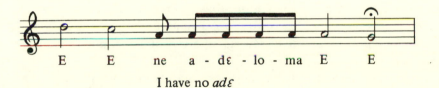

E   E   ne   a - dɛ - lo - ma   E   E

I have no *adɛ*

E   E   ni - i - mo - la - bo   E   E

I'm hungry

1. These are not actual pitches. All transcribed examples in this book have the common reference center ♭ G to avoid ledger lines and accidentals and to facilitate comparison.

I heard this story[2] after I had been in Bosavi a few months and was immediately struck by it as a statement about birds, social values, and soundmaking. It is one of twelve Kaluli stories about birds, and several of the others are also about sounds as well. All of these stories are quite short and are known by the majority of the Bosavi population. None are part of a body of esoteric or ritual lore, and there are no restrictions on who may tell them and when or where they may be told. Though women generally know less of the repertoire than men do, the *muni* story turned out to be one most women knew well.

There is a real casualness about bird and other animal stories in Bosavi. No formal events are regularly staged for their telling, and there are no performance specialists to speak of, though a few older men were known to tell longer and more explicit versions of some of the more vulgar myths, or at least to elaborate quite successfully when telling funnier sections. In general, the short texts are matched by quick and casual renditions, as tellers stick to the point or get to the punchline quickly and directly.

Most often, stories were told to me in the context of a concrete experience or event. Off in the bush to observe the local forest, I frequently asked my companions about a strange sound, a fleeting movement, or some other sensate feature that was new to me. Sometimes the response was short and descriptive; other times I might be answered with a myth, or a portion of one or several, as a way of explaining the queried behavior.

One time I was sitting on my back veranda talking with Kiliyɛ. We were interrupted by one of his daughters who had brought food; since her hands were full, she had left the front gate open, and Kiliyɛ's loyal dogs, who had been whimpering away in front of the house, rushed in behind her. Startled by the intrusion, my cat jumped off the nearby shelf where he had been sleeping and chased the dogs across the room. The event was not atypical. I had the only cat in Bosavi, and it stayed in the house; dogs, on the other hand, were kept by most Kaluli men and were not permitted to come into the house. Kiliyɛ immediately laughed. "You see, there really is an enemy relationship between dogs and animals," he said, quite animated. "What do you mean?" I asked, surprised. "Well,

2. The version of the myth cited here is a composite of five tellings. While all tellings were identical in form, two were a bit more detailed. The translation attempts to preserve the rather quick pace and direct buildup typical of Kaluli narration.

dogs and animals have *giš* (warfare or hostile relations) . . . once, a long time ago . . . ," and he began to tell me a story I had not heard previously. By explaining how dogs and animals came to be enemies, the myth provided a rationale for why dogs are used to hunt animals and equally underscored why Kaluli have such different relations with domestic dogs and domestic pigs. In effect, the telling was brought forth by a behavioral event that was worth commenting upon.

This casualness in telling style and in length and complication of events only applies to myths about animals. This is in marked contrast to another set of myths, a cycle of trickster stories about *Newelesu*. The *Newelesu* stories tend to be told by men at night in the longhouse. A really animated raconteur can produce long and engaging performances employing improvisation, special voices, and other sound effects to enhance and develop the core theme.

I often found myself confronting the strangeness of these Kaluli myths by thinking about analogues in American popular culture and natural history or the "just so" stories familiar to me. When I pondered the *muni* story and the association of birds with sadness, a number of things came to mind, like the common names "mourning dove" for the Western wild dove (*Zenaidura macroura*) or "mourning warbler" for an often-heard little bird of my native Philadelphia (*Oporonis philadelphia*). Presumably both were named by an attribution of plaintiveness to their descending or falsettolike melodies, but my associations with them went no further.

More pointed comparisons developed when I thought of literary and musical imagery, such as the common use of the mournful sounds of the whippoorwill (a noctural nightjar, *Caprimulgus vociferus*) in poetry and songs about sadness and love. In several popular songs emanating from Tin Pan Alley, the whippoorwill is prominent in the text. One I thought about often was "The Birth of the Blues": "From a whippoorwill, out on a hill, they took a new note; pushed it through a horn, 'til it was worn, into a blue note! And then they nursed it, rehearsed it, and gave out the news, that the Southland, gave birth to the blues."[3]

By associating a bird of the night with minor or descending pitches, sad sounds, blacks, the South, and the beginnings of instrumental blues,

---

3. "Birth of the Blues," lyrics by B. G. DeSylva and Lew Brown, music by Ray Henderson. © 1926 (Renewed) WARNER BROS. INC. All rights reserved. Used by permission.

the text presents a sort of symbolic compression not uncommon in folklore and music. By analogy I felt that the symbolic compression in Kaluli
myths like "the boy who became a *muni* bird" held an important key to
the social life of sounds in Kaluli expression.

The first work, then, was to unravel the myth from the point of view
of its component ethnographic themes. There are seven of these: male,
female, and the *adε* relationship; food, hunger, and reciprocity; sorrow,
loss, and abandonment; birds; weeping; poetics; and song. Initial comments on the importance of each of these in Kaluli ethnography will
outline how sound modes become expressive embodiments of basic
Kaluli concepts of sentiment and appeal.

Male, Female, and the Adε Relationship

Sex roles are clearly demarcated in Kaluli society. Men and women have
visibly separate daily social routines. However, the Bosavi pattern is
different from the Highlands of Papua New Guinea, where ethnographers
have reported that the separate realities of men and women are marked
by antagonism and outright hostility (Brown and Buchbinder 1976). For
the Kaluli, the trend is more toward balance and complementarity in
typical interactions, which follows the generally egalitarian nature of
Kaluli society (E. Schieffelin 1976:73–93).

After marriage a couple settles into the husband's longhouse community and soon thereafter has children. Children are spaced at two- to
three-year intervals, following the traditional two-year post partum sex
taboo. Children of the union call each other by sibling terms, *ao* for
brother, *ado* for sister.

With the appearance of the first child, a mother's role becomes that
of primary caregiver; she will keep the child with her at all times. In part
this is due to a woman's structural position in her husband's village,
where she has no sister(s) to help with childcare. When a woman bears
subsequent children, the pattern changes, and the older siblings help
watch, feed, and care for a younger child while the mother takes care of
the infant. From ages two to seven, brothers and sisters spend a great deal
of time together in all activities; they have not yet formed independent
relationships with outside agemates of the same sex.

Sex-role socialization begins from the child's first days. The mother
is the primary source of interaction with the child; she emphasizes the
child's sex by the way she talks to the child, whether alone or in a group
with others.

Mothers tell sons that they will grow strong; as boys grow older, their mothers assist them in games and routines involving assertion and aggression. Boys learn to be both demanding and persistent at an early age; they are socialized to beg, cajole, and have tantrums until they get what they want or feel is due them. From the time of early youth, they develop the social skills necessary to create and sustain attention around their acts and desires.

Young girls, by contrast, are moved out of the "helpless child" framework as soon as possible. Mothers encourage them to aid in daily chores as soon as they are able to do so. They learn quickly about gathering firewood, weeding gardens, fetching water, and other activities that help or serve others. Little girls find out about nurturing as soon as their mothers have another child. An older sister becomes accustomed to placing the needs and desires of others before her own wants, especially when the other is a baby.

While the notions of *ao* 'brother' and *ado* 'sister' exist by virtue of the Kaluli notion of "shared substance," the concept of *adɛ* and the relationship it implies are socially constructed by sex-role socialization and Kaluli assumptions about appropriate behavior between older sisters and younger brothers. Unlike *ao* and *ado*, *adɛ* is a reciprocal term, and it is not elicitable as a kin term (hence its absence in E. Schieffelin's discussion [ibid.:52–58] of kinship terminology). Rather, its meaning derives from social expectations taught as part of sex and gender role socialization (B. Schieffelin 1979).

Returning now to "the boy who became a *muni* bird," it is clear that in the opening scenario, there is a rupture of the social order deriving from a direct breach of expected *adɛ* behavior. The boy begs his sister for food, using a specific verbal formula and intonation aimed at making the sister feel sorry for him. She refuses by placing thoughts of others before him. In the three successive appeals, she worsens the denial by repeated refusal, finally making the situation as abnormal as possible by stating that it is an older brother who is to receive the crayfish. In effect this sequence of events runs contrary to all norms of Kaluli etiquette and social practice.

The modality of the appeal, the whining and begging of "I have no crayfish," is a basic sociolinguistic routine in Bosavi. To say plaintively "I have no *X*" is a named strategy of talk (*gesema* 'make one feel sorrow or pity') that abbreviates discussion and immediately accomplishes the speaker's objective, namely, to put the touch on the addressee for goods and/or services. It usually creates instant closure of talk.

A group of Kaluli children posing in the courtyard on their return home from an afternoon of play, which has included body painting with white clay. In the center Mobia holds her younger brother Abi in a protective grasp that typifies their *adε* relationship.

For the Kaluli, saying "I have no *X*" implies three things quite directly:

1) You obviously have something that I don't have.
2) I want some of it and believe that I have rights to it.
3) You should not only give some to me, but feel sorry for me because I have none.

Interactions of this form are a daily feature of Kaluli social intercourse and are not limited to any age segment of the society. Moreover, they are particularly typical of *adε* interactions. A basic part of a boy's socialization is the acquisition of these communicative skills, combining verbal, intonational, and gestural channels simultaneously, for demanding attention from his *adε*.

In the story, the *adε* concept is the vehicle for an event sequence that defines betrayal and rupture of the social order. Here culturally focused and basic interactional routines are not brought to their appropriate outcome. By denying food to her *adε,* the sister breaks the most basic of Kaluli standards for being social. Denying a child anything is rather un-Kaluli behavior, but denial set in the context of an older sister placing the needs and desires of others before those of a younger brother make the act particularly disruptive.

This leads to the next major theme in the story, reciprocity and exchange, and their relationship to food as a medium of affection and obligation.

Food, Hunger, and Reciprocity

The fact that food is the medium of appeal and denial in the story makes the rupture as total and pathetic as it can be within the canons of expected Kaluli behavior and sociality. To deny food to a child is unthinkable. The giving of food to children is a highly focused form of interaction that starts at birth.

In *The Sorrow of the Lonely and the Burning of the Dancers,* a chapter is devoted to the topic of food; there E. Schieffelin emphasizes that food is the major vehicle in expressing, developing, and validating social relationships in Bosavi (1976:46). This giving and sharing "communicates sentiment; it conveys affection, familiarity, and good will" (ibid.:47–48). Moreover, food "represents the general mode of establishing relationships among all people, friends, and kinsmen" (ibid.:63); through such acts, relationships become "socially real" (ibid.).

An important example of the pervasiveness of food sharing in Bosavi is the institution of *wi εlεdo.* When two people share the same food, particularly meat, and when the situation surrounding the getting, cooking, or sharing is socially significant, the two can thereafter call each other reciprocally by the name of the food instead of using their common names. Thus, two people who share crayfish (*galin*) will address each other as *ni galin* 'my crayfish'. The institution stands for the special nonkin-derived manner of expressing affection and comradery on a daily social level. The reciprocal naming comes to stand for bonding through shared experience, mediated by food. (The institution of *wi εlεdo* is discussed in ibid.:56–58.)

It should be pointed out that food sharing is more a cultural assumption underlying everyday life than a formally arranged event. While gardens, forests, streams, and sago palms are plentiful and yield enough to keep Kaluli well fed, at times people can get caught short. When this happens the slack is taken up through assistance from kinsmen and friends alike.

Food sharing embodies a deeper reality, one even more basic than assisting someone who may be experiencing a bad crop in the gardens or making ample prestations at formal social events. I frequently observed situations where men were socializing and food was delivered to one member of the group. Immediately the recipient would begin to divide and distribute the food among his fellows. Sometimes one party would put up a slight refusal with either gestural and/or verbal "go ahead, I've already eaten." Such responses would then be met with a more insistent "really . . . go ahead," usually gestural but perhaps verbally marked by "you . . . ." In the midst of this, or perhaps later, food would be delivered to another in the group. The same routine would follow.

What happens in these situations is that each person eats as much or more than he was personally given. In the end it is not the balance of quantity that matters, but rather the immediate reaction to receiving food, namely, to share it with one's fellows. Whether or not a man has calculated that eventually he will eat as much or more than what he himself has cooked or been given, it is the automatic response of sharing whatever one has that is basic to normal Kaluli sociality.

Cast in this light, the begging of food by the younger brother is even more poignant. Previously it was noted that the adɛ relationship is not a kin category but is built up from shared behavioral expectations of obligation, affection, nurturing, and caretaking, and that the passage of goods is very much from the older sister to the younger brother. A clear instance of this is the pattern of the younger brother feeling owed something and begging what the sister has. Of course, the sister has been taught to respond immediately to this kind of appeal. In the story, then, denial of adɛ relationship expectations, particularly with regard to food, symbolizes rupture of the canons of Kaluli sociality.

Summarizing his remarks about food giving and sharing among the Kaluli, E. Schieffelin (ibid.:71) writes: ". . . in effect, food is not only good to eat, but as Lévi-Strauss has remarked, good to think. It doesn't only mediate social relationships; it comes to stand for them as well. To be hungry therefore, implies more than merely a condition of physical need. It also implies isolation from companionship." In the muni bird story, hunger is equated with the loss of what the boy feels owed, first rights to his sister's food. Hunger and loss are thus at the center of a basic Kaluli symbolic equation; they stand for isolation and abandonment.

Sorrow, Loss, and Abandonment

A consistent theme in *The Sorrow of the Lonely and the Burning of the Dancers* is the importance Kaluli attach to fellowship, comradery, and companionship. "Nothing warms the Kaluli heart like a house full of friendly people. Noise and movement mean the presence of others, assistance, support, familiar faces . . ." (ibid.:152). And ". . . Kaluli social events are characterized by a high level of exuberance, crowding and noise. Presences, interactions and feelings are rendered explicit, projected into the open" (ibid.:154).

The absence of a friend or kinsmen at a gathering can set off a great burst of nostalgia and sentimentality. At one such occasion I observed, the absence was first bemoaned by a man, after which many of his fellows immediately chimed in *"heyo,"* an emotional expression of distress indicating "what a shame," as well as "I feel sorry for you." Such consensus on making the sorrow and nostalgia of absence felt is important to Kaluli because their deepest fears are those of loneliness. The imagined possibility of loneliness, no companionship, no assistance, no one to share food with, is perhaps the most awesome human state, the one Kaluli are likely to think about at their lowest, most depressed moments. The state of loneliness and isolation is quite literally conceptualized as the state of nonassistance, the condition of being without relationships.

E. Schieffelin emphasizes the basic Kaluli urge to be and share with others: "Most of the important things in a man's life—his wife (through bridewealth), his safety (through hospitality), his gardens (through labor assistance), and even his protein intake (through meat prestations)—he owes in large part to others. As human relationships are actualized and mediated through gifts of food and material wealth, so these things come to stand for what is deeply felt in human relationships" (ibid.:150). It thus makes sense that Kaluli equate breakdowns in reciprocity, assistance, sharing, hospitality, and comradery with vulnerability, loss, abandonment, isolation, loneliness, and ultimately, death.

In the additive process, this is precisely the state of the boy in the *muni* bird story when the consistent denial of food by his *adε* signals that he quite literally has no *adε*. Her lack of assistance, denial of obligation, and unwillingness to fulfill a role snaps the thread of the social bond. For the boy, hunger becomes isolation; denial of the expected role becomes abandonment. The anxiety that results is both frightening and sad; instantly the boy is diminished to a nonhuman state.

Birds

Speaking of the way Kaluli imagine or anticipate isolation, E. Schieffelin notes that the absence of human relationships is equated with the presence of death (ibid.:151). This attitude is precisely mirrored in the story when the boy passes from a human state to that of a *muni* bird, because Kaluli believe that birds are *ane mama* 'spirit reflections' of their dead.

Kaluli are avid ornithologists. Their knowledge of the habitat, ecology, and migratory patterns of Bosavi avifauna is extensive. They are particularly adept at identifying and locating birds by sound. Even though Kaluli ornithology organizes families of birds on the morphological principle of shared beak and feet characteristics, more natural and spontaneous comments categorize birds in families based on sound properties: those that sing, those that weep, those that whistle, those that speak the Bosavi language, those that say their names, those that "only sound," and those that make a lot of noise. Great attention is paid to ascertaining just which birds make which sounds, and Kaluli clearly differentiate contact, alarm, and social calls for each of their designated taxa. Their knowledge of calls extends well into issues that occupy ornithologists, such as the duet and antiphonal singing of the Brown Oriole (*Oriolus szalayi*) and the New Guinea Friarbird (*Philemon novaeguineae*).

The important points about birds, however, lie neither in the detail of Kaluli ethnoscientific taxonomy nor in the accuracy of the identifications vis-à-vis Western ornithology. The important fact is that bird sounds are simultaneously heard as indicators of the avifauna and as "talk" from the dead, *ɔbɛ mise* 'in the form of birds'. The most impressive part of Bosavi ornithology is the degree to which Kaluli people construct culturally metaphoric ideals from natural historical observations that are accurate in their zoological minutiae.

E. Schieffelin remembers hearing the call of the *kalo* bird, the Pink-spotted Fruitdove, *Ptilinopus perlatus,* when he was out hunting (ibid.:96). His companion remarked that it was the cry of a young child, hungry and calling for its mother. I, too, experienced spontaneous comments of this variety when off in the bush or just sitting on the porch with friends, observing the late afternoon congregating of birds at the village edge.

The key to this kind of perception is found in the Kaluli notion that two coextensive realities, one visible, one a reflection, make up the world. In the unseen world, men and women are reflected respectively as wild pigs and cassowaries living on the slopes of Mt. Bosavi. If something befalls a person's wild pig or cassowary aspect, a resultant state affects the actual person. Upon death, a person's wild pig or cassowary *mama* 'reflection' disappears from the mountain *mama* world. An *ane mama*, literally 'gone reflection', that is, a spirit reflection, appears in the visible world in the form of some animal; very frequently the form is that of a bird. Thus, to each other birds appear as people, and to the Kaluli their calls are vocal communications from *ane mama.*

In this context, birds become a metaphoric human society, and their sounds come to stand for particular forms of sentiment and ethos. The important detail in the context of the *muni* bird story concerns the sound quality of the fruitdoves. This group of birds (genus *Ptilinopus,* with six different species represented in Bosavi: *P. pulchellus, P. iozonus, P. perlatus, P. ornatus, P. superbus, P. nanus*) is most important in terms of Kaluli notions about the sounds of sadness, weeping, and song. Because of their high, human falsettolike, and melodically descending sounds, the fruitdoves are likened to children by Kaluli. The whining, begging, and other whimpering nonverbal vocalizations of children are, like the calls of the fruitdoves, interpreted as appeals for food, attention, and care. The image of a hungry child crying for its mother is a common Kaluli response to fruitdove calls.

A central bird in this complex is *muni,* the Beautiful Fruitdove, *Ptilinopus pulchellus* (see figure 1). This bird is among the smallest of the fruitdoves. Two different calls are apparent: one is very high, fast, and repetitive, dipping up and down slightly in pitch; and another has slower, distinct descending pitches. These mirror the sequence of crying in the story of "the boy who became a *muni* bird"; first the faster hysterical wail, then the more melodic weeping. When questioned in an ornithological context about the *muni* call, Kaluli men tended to make a naturalistic imitation of the first type of call but always gave a symbolic rendering of the second, using either a three- or four-pitch descending melodic contour:

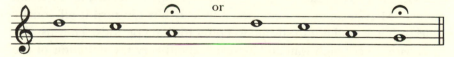

These pitches stand for sadness and weeping and are the ones found in the myth. The *muni* bird stands out as the most metaphorically childlike and pathetic of the fruitdove group. In the story, the adoption of the *muni* voice by the boy is both a symbolic expression of death and a sonic metaphor for the sound of a child abandoned, hungry, and isolated.

Figure 1. *muni*—Beautiful Fruitdove *(Ptilinopus pulchellus)*

Weeping

Two types of weeping occur in the story when the boy turns into a *muni*
bird. The first is a fast, hysterical crying and the second is a more definite
pitched, slower, melodic crying. The social organization for weeping in
Bosavi is rather similar. The contexts include funerals and other occasions of profound sadness over loss and abandonment (examples of the
latter that I witnessed were a house burning down and a family departing
the area for an indefinite period of time) and response to song.

On these occasions the weeping is differently patterned for men and
women. Men become very emotional quickly but can turn it off equally
quickly. They tend not to sustain weeping for long periods. They usually
start with a very high wail and almost instantly cry the imitation of the
muni call, using either three or four pitches. This is done as a repeated
falsetto shriek. Then they may sit quietly, withdrawn and morose, for the
remainder of the event or break out in additional wails of the same type
again, in a chain reaction effect with the others. In addition, men will
sometimes combine weeping with text. The text is placed in between the

first two and second one or two pitches of the cry and tends to remain melodically even with the third pitch. It is here that their style of elaboration stops.

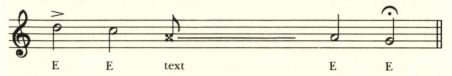

Women, on the other hand, start their weeping in the very fast hysterical manner and maintain a level of great intensity for a sustained time. Then, slowing down and catching their breath, the crying turns melodic, following the same three- or four-pitch contour as noted above. Both of these kinds of weeping are done in a normal vocal register.

Here forms of elaboration begin. One format is weeping as above, with an insertion of slight text in between the first and second two pitches of the melody. Another is the use of text over the entire phase, on all four pitches, but with the main body of the text placed in between the second and third pitches. Finally, the most complete elaboration is a wept song.

In this case lengthy text will be spontaneously improvised with the cried melody, sticking very closely to the same contour. In many instances, particularly at funerals, these forms of women's weeping are found together. First the fast emotional crying, then a settling down to crying with the *muni* call melody, then the addition of slight textual insertions, then full-blown improvised cried song: weeping . . . sung weeping . . . wept song.

The major point about Kaluli weeping in relation to the *muni* bird story is that the three- or four-note melody is used as a sound metaphor for sadness, expressing the sorrow of loss and abandonment. The reduction to a state of loss becomes equivalent to the state of being a bird.

Weeping is primarily a woman's expressive form. Although both men and women use the same melodic cry in the contexts of response to song, response to sorrow over loss and abandonment and death, it is generally women who add text and only women who turn the sung weeping into wept song. Kaluli people acknowledge this fact, indicating that women's cried songs are the most intricate and developed form of weeping. In effect, while sadness moves both men and women to weeping, it is weeping that moves women to song.

The texts of the wept songs are improvised but follow several consistent patterns. In deceased- or departed-person contexts, all texts begin with a singing of the name of the kin relation. Later reflections contain a great number of place names (lands, rivers, gardens, longhouse sites) that add up to a textual map of shared experiences.

In song, text and melodies are composed simultaneously and consciously by the composer. The uniqueness of weeping for women is that it gives way to another type of song—one sung *while* weeping, where the melodic contour is fixed by the three or four notes of the *muni* call symbol, and where the text is spontaneously improvised by the weeping singer as a personal recollection of shared experiences with the deceased or departed.

Poetics

Poetics are integral to song and do not exist as an isolated verbal entity. Besides stories, there are no forms of oral art in Bosavi, such as riddles, rhymes, limericks, or epics that are performed verbally. While the Kaluli concept of metaphor, *bali to* 'turned over words', is diverse and is used in ordinary everyday talk, song poetics are the only modality of Kaluli expression that makes extensive use of linguistic resources whose function is "auto-referential" (Jakobson 1960) and oriented to the communication of the message for its own sake. In song, text is not primarily a proxy for a denoted subject but self-consciously multiplies the intent of the word.

The key to this is in the function of conversational discourse in daily Kaluli interaction, where language is used in a highly assertive, pragmatic manner. Talk gets you what you want, need, or feel owed. Song is different because it is a communication from the point of view of a person in the form of a bird. The text of song, cast in a poetic grammar, is a special modality of appeal, rather than of assertion (see E. Schieffelin 1976: 117–35). Song poetry goes beyond pragmatic referential communication because it is explicitly organized by canons of reflectiveness and self-consciousness that are not found in ordinary talk.

The uniqueness of poetic language is unveiled in the story of "the boy who became a *muni* bird." Once the boy has exhausted the speech codes for begging, he must resort to another communication frame. Conversational talk, what the Kaluli call *to halaido* 'hard words', is useless once the boy has become a bird; now he resorts to talk from a bird's point of view, ɔbɛ gɔnɔ *to* 'bird sound words'. Poetic language is bird language.

Turning to the text, *gi galino* and *nelɔ mɔmiyali* are in fact ordinary

Kaluli expressions. The break is specifically signaled with *ne adɛloma.* The word *adɛloma* 'no *adɛ*' is formed by a regular grammatical rule in Kaluli. The rule takes the word *andoma* 'no', 'empty', or 'without', and makes a suffix of *-doma* or *-loma* that can be tagged to nouns and pronouns. Although the term *adɛloma* is well formed and grammatical in every technical sense, it is completely inappropriate and never uttered in ordinary conversation. *Ne adɛloma* in the story context signals the departure from *to halaido* to *ɔbɛ gɔnɔ to,* the shift from conversational to poetic language.

Ni imolabo is also not found in Kaluli speech, where the verb *mayabo* would be the equivalent expression for 'hungry'. *Imolabo* is not a Kaluli word but comes from the related Sonia language. Kaluli interpret the word to mean "hungry" in a more profound and metaphoric sense, related to isolation; its best gloss would be "empty." Additionally this text is uttered in the story with *ni* instead of *ne* for 'I'. Kaluli say that *ni* and [*nɨ*] are the terms that children use, in contrast to mature *to halaido,* which is *ne.* The implication here is that *ni* adds childlike plaintiveness, begging, and appeal.

The point of the story in relation to language, then, is the definition of poetic convention, the origin of language use specifically marked for reflection and contemplation over loss and abandonment. When questioned as to what these kinds of talk imply, Kaluli said, "to talk like that means that you feel like a bird."

Song

There are six vocal song forms in Bosavi: *gisalo, kɔluba, sabio, iwɔ, heyalo,* and *kelekeliyoba.* [4] Of these the Bosavi people claim to have originated only *gisalo,* which is also the most complex from the standpoint of performance, poetics, composition, and melody. *Kɔluba* and *iwɔ* are said to come from the south side of Mt. Bosavi. *Kelekeliyoba* is the woman's variant of *iwɔ. Sabio* comes from the Fasu and Lake Kutubu areas, east of Bosavi on the other side of the Kikori River, and *heyalo* comes from the Lake Campbell area west of Bosavi.

The Kaluli have borrowed extensively and have become quite creative in song and poetic forms that are not of their own origin. In this they are unique among their neighbors and are known by surrounding

4. For short descriptions of each of the ceremonies see E. Schieffelin 1976:225–29.

groups to be musically and ceremonially prolific. Yet from their own point of view, the singularly Bosavi version of song is to be found solely in *gisalo*. Indeed, the term *gisalo* can stand for the ceremony or song form of that specific name, or it can be used as a generic term for "ceremony" or "song composition"; the other terms must be used specifically.

Another key to the clear distinction of these song forms is in the contexts of their use. *Heyalo, kɔluba, sabio, iwɔ,* and *kelekeliyoba* are sung at ceremonies of these names, or they are sung less formally to accompany work. *Gisalo,* on the other hand, appears both in ceremony and as the song vehicle of spirit medium seances. *Gisalo* is never sung outdoors for work; it is restricted to performance in the darkness.

Independent musicological evidence shows that *gisalo* is, in fact, a distinct song form with regard to tonal organization. *Heyalo* and *kelekeliyoba,* both of which are principally women's compositional forms, generally utilize three pitches. Many of these songs are limited to a range of a fifth, with melodic alternation of major and minor thirds in the melody line. *Gisalo, kɔluba, sabio,* and *iwɔ* are all pentatonic in tonal structure, though each has a different internal organization.

In the *gisalo* structure, the organization is identical to the *muni* bird representation and to the tonal structure of weeping. No other pentatonic mode is organized in this way. These mirror representations are strengthened by another piece of independent data. Observe the tonal centers, indicated by the *fermata* ⌒ . In the other song forms, the tonal center is always the lowest pitch, but the lowest pitch in *gisalo* is a minor third below the tonal center; the songs always end on the second-to-the-lowest pitch.

So, in *gisalo,* as well as in weeping, the melodic organization is identical to the representation of the *muni* bird call. Thus, the sounds in the myth are maintained in expressive modes used by the Kaluli.

For ceremonies, *gisalo* is composed with the deliberate intention of moving others to tears. (The songs are not composed for the seances; spirit mediums claim the songs they sing simply come up through their mouths, and they move listeners to tears equally efficiently.) To accomplish this, *gisalo* songs make full and dramatic use of all poetic resources. Moreover, the melodic resources of the song must match perfectly with the climaxing poetic structure. This is what the Kaluli call *halaido domɛki,* the 'hardening' of a song, that is, the development of an aesthetic tension. Finally, the performance must be moving and evocative.

The dramatic performance in song, dance, costume, and weeping makes the *gisalo* performer ɔbɛ *mise* 'in the form of a bird'. The degree to which the performance was felt to be deeply moving is articulated by which of the four major fruitdoves one mentions when evaluating it. *Muni* is a frequent reference and evokes a powerful image. Sad, like a bird, a man spins weeping and poetry into song. That song moves others to tears and to the evaluation that the performer has "become a bird."

Structural Analysis of
"The Boy Who Became a Muni Bird"

The preceding sketch separated seven topic areas relevant to an understanding of "the boy who became a *muni* bird"; I called these ethnographic themes, namely:

(1) Male, female, and the *adɛ* relationship
(2) Food, hunger, and reciprocity
(3) Loss, abandonment, and sorrow
(4) Birds
(5) Weeping
(6) Poetry
(7) Song

These seven ethnographic themes correspond to seven story episodes whose presentation is linear. As Lévi-Strauss says, stories first present themselves as a syntagmatic chain, composed of metonymic links (Lévi-Strauss 1963). The work of a structural analysis is first to cast the story onto a vertical axis where the episodes can be "added up." This process clears the way for uncovering how a syntagmatic chain is at the surface of paradigmatic association. In other words, a structural analysis shows how metonymy becomes metaphor, how it is that the mixing of contexts in story episodes turns intrinsic relations into symbolic ones.

In order to begin such an analysis, the seven ethnographic themes can be restated as seven additive episodes:

(1) denial of *adɛ* relationship
(2) denial of food
(3) boy left in state of abandonment
(4) boy turns into *muni* bird
(5) *muni* voice = voice of weeping
(6) addition of text = poetics
(7) weeping melodically plus poetics = song

These seven episodes are themselves readily divisible into larger organizing units, which I will term structural sequences. There are three of these:

(A) Provocation sequence
(B) Mediation sequence
(C) Metaphoric sequence

The first, provocation, is created by the addition of the first three episodes:

$$(A) = Provocation = \begin{matrix} \text{(1) denial of } ad\varepsilon \text{ relationship} \\ \text{(2) denial of food} \\ \text{(3) boy left in state of abandonment} \end{matrix}$$

(1) plus (2) adds up to rupture of the social order; by denial of food and *adε* obligations, there is a breakdown whose resultant state is (3). These first three episodes thus add up to a structural sequence that defines the conditions and consequent state of breach of the social order. In Lévi-Strauss's sense of the term, they provide a paradigm; in this case, one of provocation.

The second structural sequence, that of mediation, is a fulcrum between provocation and metaphor. It is contained entirely in one episode:

$$(B) = Mediation = \text{(4) boy turns into } muni \text{ bird}$$

The mediation sequence provides a consequence of provocation that, at the same time, sets up a further consequence by changing contexts.

The third structural sequence, that of metaphorization, is symmetrical to the first, as it is also composed of three episodes:

$$(C) = Metaphorization = \begin{matrix} \text{(5) } muni \text{ voice } = \text{ voice of weeping} \\ \text{(6) addition of text } = \text{ poetics} \\ \text{(7) weeping plus poetry } = \text{ song} \end{matrix}$$

Essentially, the addition of (5) plus (6) creates (7) in much the same way that (1) plus (2) creates (3). The last three episodes thus define the consequence of the themes presented in the provocation sequence.

In terms of the overall organization of the structure, three diagrams show the stages:

I. *Structural addition and separation*

    (A)

(1) denial of *adɛ* relationship
(2) denial of food
(3) boy left in state of abandonment
---- ---- ---- ---- ---- ---- ---- ---- ---- ---- ---- ----
= Provocation

           (B)

        (4) boy turns into *muni* bird
        ---- ---- ---- ---- ---- ---- ---- ---- ---- ---- ---- ----
        = Mediation

                (C)

                (5) *muni* voice = voice of weeping
                (6) addition of text = poetics
                (7) weeping plus poetry = song
                ---- ---- ---- ---- ---- ---- ---- ---- ---- ---- ---- ----
                = Metaphorization

II. *Structural paradigm*

(A) = Provocation

```
┌─────────────────────────────┐
│ Rupture of social order     │
│         =                   │
│ Abandonment                 │
└─────────────────────────────┘
```

        (B) = Mediation

```
│ Boy turns into muni bird │
```

                (C) = Metaphorization

```
┌─────────────────────────────┐
│ Weeping and poetry          │
│         =                   │
│ Song                        │
└─────────────────────────────┘
```

III. *Structural summary*

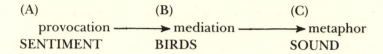

(A)   (B)   (C)

provocation ⟶ mediation ⟶ metaphor
SENTIMENT   BIRDS   SOUND

From here we can trace the path that creates metaphor out of metonym, paradigm from syntagm, what Leach calls the logic by which symbols are connected.

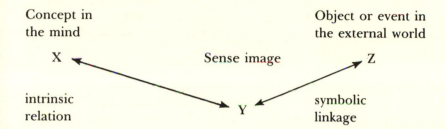

Concept in the mind   Object or event in the external world

X   Sense image   Z

intrinsic relation   Y   symbolic linkage

Leach (1976:19–20) argues that the X-Y relationship is of the sign-index type; in other words, one implies the other; they are contiguous, hence metonymic. On the other hand, the Y-Z relationship involves an arbitrary association derived from the mixing of contexts, hence metaphoric. In light of the Bosavi data and the discussion thus far of the *muni* bird story, the scheme would appear:

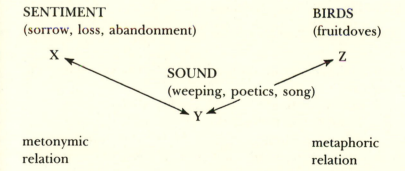

SENTIMENT   BIRDS
(sorrow, loss, abandonment)   (fruitdoves)

X   Z

SOUND
(weeping, poetics, song)

Y

metonymic relation   metaphoric relation

The last diagram shows the point Lévi-Strauss has made about *bricolage.* By taking an intrinsic relationship and recasting it against an entirely different context, myth can accomplish the work of establishing homologies and analogies between the social order and the external world, thus causing nature and culture to mirror each other.

Seen in this light, the story sets up an exercise in generating cultural
metaphors. In sequence A, provocation is defined by stating cultural
equivalences among lack of social relationship, hunger, isolation, and
abandonment. In sequence B, mediation is defined by stating the cultural
equivalence of death, abandonment, and becoming a bird. In the case of
death or loss, one is reduced to the state of a bird. In sequence C,
metaphorization is defined by stating the cultural equivalence between
sound and sentiment, linking the condition of being a bird (dead/aban-
doned) to the sounds of weeping, poetry, and song.

Further, an explicit link is made between the substance of provocation (denial of *adɛ* relationship, denial of food) and the substance of
metaphor (poetic base metaphors in song being *ne adɛloma* 'I have no
adɛ' and *ni imolabo* 'I'm hungry').

Looking at the relationship between the scenarios of provocation,
mediation, and metaphorization, and casting these paradigms against the
expressive domains of birds, sound, and sentiment in Bosavi as sketched
ethnographically, it is possible to illustrate Lévi-Strauss's notion of transformation (T), that is, the process whereby a mythic sequence results in
an expressive sequence that serves to reconfirm the mythic base.

MYTHIC (nature → culture)

    BIRD → WEEPING → SONG

EXPRESSIVE (culture → nature)

    (♀) WEEPING → SONG → BIRD

    (♂) SONG → WEEPING → BIRD

T

Stating the equivalences in the classic structural manner, without the
mediating scenario:

WEEPING : MOVING WOMEN TO SONG ::
SONG : MOVING MEN TO TEARS

To summarize, a structural analysis of the story organizes the episodes into sequences that embody provocation, mediation, and metaphor. Structurally, the argument is that social *sentiment*, mediated by *birds*,
is metaphorically expressed in *sound*. Sonic forms of melody and poetics
are given in the expressive modalities of weeping and song as metaphoric
means for symbolizing and sharing the sorrows of loss and abandonment.
Mythically these forms are reached through the mediation of becoming

a bird. They are then culturally activated by turning weeping into song, and song into weeping, both of which involve the canon of the performer becoming a bird. Thus the mediation position, becoming a bird, has a multivocal status: on the one hand pointing to death and spirit reflection, on the other pointing to aesthetic codes that are cultural means for expressing sadness and grief.

With these themes now established and their connections initially linked, the task is to probe the deeper layers of how these domains are formulated and experienced in the normal course of Kaluli daily life and events. The foundation chapter for this exercise addresses the ways Kaluli think about and experience the Bosavi avifauna. If it is true that Kaluli expressive forms are constituted by analogies with nature, then it follows that the relations among bird perception, classification, symbolism, and inspiration underlie the meaning of bird sound metaphors in the form and performance of weeping, poetics, and song.

2

To You They Are Birds, to Me They Are Voices in the Forest

Once it became evident that a socially situated study of Kaluli sound expressions required an understanding of Bosavi avifauna, I began a formal study of bird perception, classification, and symbolism. My object was to analyze the content and organizing principles of Kaluli folk ornithology. The first step was a survey of the birds in the area and an analysis of their corresponding lexical organization in the Kaluli language,[1] which amounted to a description of the internal workings of Kaluli folk ornithology by comparing Western zoological taxa with Kaluli taxa. My assumption was that the Western system's systematic and heirarchic terms label and specify discontinuities in nature based upon genetic and phylogenetic criteria, while the corresponding Kaluli heirarchical system labels natural discontinuities based on a broader set of criteria. An understanding of that latter set of criteria, it seemed, would get me to the center of how birds were important to the Kaluli.

I soon discovered that collecting and organizing information this way indicated basic weaknesses in my conception of how culture interprets nature. The fault was never better realized than by Jubi, who expressed it in a remark one afternoon. After months of constant work on bird taxonomy and identification, carried out observationally in the forest and more experimentally in the village, we came to an impasse trying to

1. I used Bulmer 1969, Diamond 1972, Rand and Gilliard 1967, and Peckover and Filewood 1976 as field guides to visual and aural identification of Bosavi birds. Two professional ornithologists, Harry Bell and Thane Pratt, each have made systematic observations of the avifauna from the airstrip of the A.P.C.M. station at 850 meters to the caldera of Mt. Bosavi at 2,600 meters. Their reports (Bell 1974; Pratt n.d.) helped establish extended contents of Kaluli taxa and also identified important ecological considerations.

specify the zoological content of closely related Kaluli taxa. With characteristic patience, Jubi was imitating calls, behavior, and nesting. Suddenly
something snapped; I asked a question and Jubi blurted back, "Listen—
to you they are birds, to me they are voices in the forest." I was startled
by this, not because it was so direct (Kaluli tend to be very direct, even
confrontative, in face-to-face interaction) but because it so thoroughly
expressed the necessity of approaching Kaluli natural history as part of
a cultural system.

Jubi's comment was symptomatic of my naïve acceptance of the proc-
lamation that ethnoscience was a way to "meet the natives on their own
terms," a way to grasp the formal language-internal coding of categories
of reality as directly salient and empirically verifiable. It pointed out that
I was equating contextless tests, disembodied words, and taxonomic
nodes with knowledge and reality, as if knowledge was simply a sum of
taxa, a mirror of content. Knowledge is something more: a method for
putting a construction on the perceived, a means for scaffolding belief
systems, a guide to actions and feelings.

"To you they are birds" meant that I was forcing a method of
knowledge construction—isolation and reduction—onto a domain of
experience that Kaluli do not isolate or reduce. "To me they are voices
in the forest" meant that there are many ways to think about birds,
depending on the context in which knowledge is activated and social
needs are served. Birds are "voices" because Kaluli recognize and acknowledge their existence primarily through sound, and because they
are the spirit reflections *(ane mama)* of deceased men and women. Bird
sounds simultaneously have an "outside," from which Kaluli attribute a
bird's identification, and an "inside," from which they interpret the underlying meaning as a spirit communication.

In modifying my approach to understanding Kaluli birds, I decided
to probe the essential unity of natural history and symbolism, to approach
Kaluli feelings about birds as a complex and many-layered cultural config-
uration that intersected with other areas of thought and action. Instead
of trying to separate zoology and myth as distinct and neatly bounded
modes of observation and deduction, I needed to see just how Kaluli
packaged them together in a mutually supportive way, based on certain
fundamental premises about the world, such as the belief that things have
a visible and invisible aspect; that sounds and behaviors have an outside,
an inside, and an underneath; or that human relationships are reflected
in the ecology and natural order of the forest.

From the point of view of methodology, this meant largely rebalancing the empirical questioning and hypothesis-making activities to which I had grown accustomed with a less direct approach that put considerable emphasis on spending leisure time with people in the forest, asking questions in more appropriate contexts, and trying to evaluate the meaning of remarks Kaluli made to each other in situations I neither constrained nor controlled. What emerged was a sense of how bird taxonomy intersects with more fundamental daily realities, and most significantly, with sound as a symbolic system.

Taxonomic Overview of Kaluli Folk Ornithology

Figure 2 illustrates the basic levels of descriptive folk ornithology for the Kaluli.[2] The classificatory scheme is based generally on similarities of beaks and feet. The top node is ɔbɛ 'birds'. The immediate next branch divides *hena sab,* or terrestrial birds, from the *iwalu sab,* or arboreal birds. The next branching figures separate what the Kaluli call *esolo* 'families'. Each of these is named for the largest or most typical member, with two families in the terrestrial group and five in the arboreal group. Only one of these families, *hi,* the arboreal pigeons and doves, is labeled by a name that is generic and not specific to a single member. Each *esolo* then branches into *esolo hɛlu,* or 'small families'. Finally, each of these branches contains a list of member taxa, the ɔbɛ *wi* 'bird names'. Within these lists are additional groups that are not labeled but are nevertheless covertly recognized as sharing certain features.

A brief review of each family will suffice here as an orientation to the major issues in classification of birds as they are perceived by experienced Kaluli hunters and natural historians. It will further be useful as a baseline for comparing taxonomic constructs with broader realities of Kaluli natural history.

Uluwa Esolo

The *uluwa* family is divided into two branches, "flying" and "nonflying" members. This is hardly surprising, since the anomalous feature of the cassowaries *uluwa* and *guŝuwa* is their flightless character (see

2. A taxon-by-taxon comparison of Kaluli and Western ornithological terminology is found in the appendix.

figure 3). Indeed, why should the cassowaries be considered birds at all?

When asked directly whether cassowaries are birds, Kaluli give both positive and negative answers. "Yes" because cassowaries are members of a family that shares characteristics of beaks and feet. As with all bird groups, the family is named for the largest member, which in this case is *uluwa*. On the other hand, negative responses all cite the fact that cassowaries do not fly; in this they are said to be unlike all other birds.

The complex nature of these initial judgments is revealed when one pursues the discussion further. In rebuttal to the negative responses, some Kaluli men point out that like other birds, cassowaries are sexually dimorphic and lay eggs; the immature ones whistle, and the taboos associated with cassowaries are like those associated with other ground birds. Moreover, they note that cassowaries are the spirit reflections of young women, that men wear the silky-textured black feathers for ceremonies in order to make themselves beautiful, just as they wear feathers of other beautiful female birds.

When one looks into the biological facts, these judgments become even more significant. Many Papua New Guineans inaccurately judge the gender of the cassowary because the larger of the two is actually the female, who is also more aggressive and fights to control territory and mates. The females are more brightly decorated, do the courting, are polyandrous, and lay several clutches of eggs. The males incubate and guard the eggs, fiercely attacking intruders. Kaluli men generally judge these zoological facts accurately; the "reversed" pattern of sexual dimorphism poses no problem to them because it is consistent with the feminine symbolic status of the cassowary. Zoology and cultural beliefs here support one another to sustain a mutual set of reasons why the cassowary is a bird (see Bulmer 1967; Majnep and Bulmer 1977:148–57).

The flying branch of the family is headed by *kɔ-guŝuwa,* a large megapode whose name means 'like-*guŝuwa'.* Included in this branch are other megapodes (more commonly known as scrub-turkeys), cormorants, egrets, ducks, sandpipers, rails, and most curiously, *alin,* the Great Goura pigeon (see figure 4). The inclusion of this bird again raises questions about the perceptual and morphological bases of taxonomy and their intersection with cultural principles.

On certain levels Kaluli perceive the Goura to be like birds of the *fɔ* family (ground pigeons) and the *hi* family (arboreal pigeons and doves). Kaluli references to this relation are made in several contexts. In

Figure 2. Overview of Kaluli folk ornithology

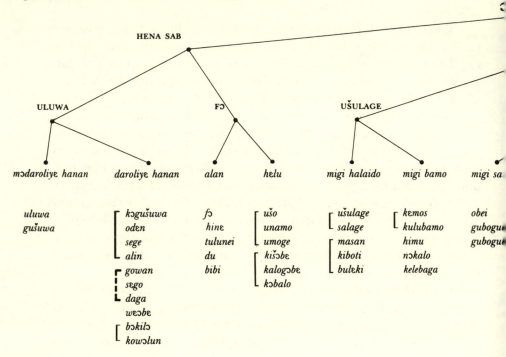

| = covert groupings
| = vague covert groupings

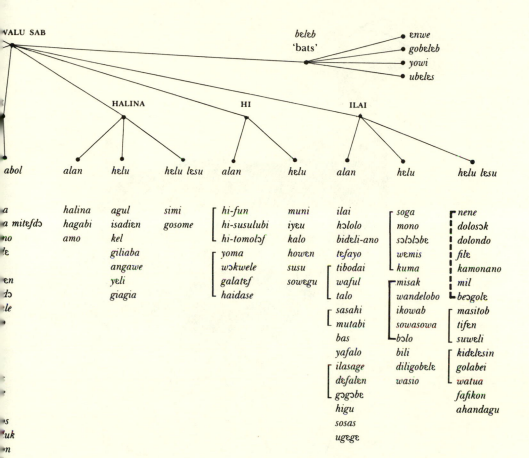

WALU SAB

bɛlɛb
'bats'

ɛnwe
gobɛlɛb
yowi
ubɛlɛs

HALINA   HI   ILAI

abol   alan   hɛlu   hɛlu lɛsu   alan   hɛlu   alan   hɛlu   hɛlu lɛsu

a	halina	agul	simi	hi-fun	muni	ilai	soga	nene
a mitɛfdɔ	hagabi	isadiɛn	gosome	hi-susulubi	iyɛu	hɔlolo	mono	dolosɔk
no	amo	kel		hi-tomolɔf	kalo	bidɛli-ano	sɔlɔlɔbɛ	dolondo
ɛ		giliaba		yoma	howɛn	tɛfayo	wɛmis	filɛ
		angawe		wɔkwele	susu	tibodai	kuma	kamonano
ɛn		yɛli		galatɛf	sowɛgu	waful	misak	mil
dɔ		giagia		haidase		talo	wandelobo	bɛɔgolɛ
le						sasahi	ikowab	masitob
						mutabi	sowasowa	tifɛn
						bas	bɔlo	suwɛli
						yafalo	bili	kidɛlɛsin
s						ilasage	diligobɛlɛ	golabei
						dɛfalɛn	wasıo	watua
						gɔgɔbɛ		faʃikon
s						higu		ahandagu
uk						sosas		
n						ugɛgɛ		
lo								

Figure 3. *gušuwa*—Little Cassowary *(Casuarius bennetti)*

Figure 4. *alin*—Great Goura *(Goura scheepmakeri)*

the story of how birds got ash-colored feathers, *hi-fun,* the largest arboreal pigeon, is referred to as *"alin*'s little brother"; *alin*'s side feathers
are worn in the hair in the same manner as *hi* tail feathers; *alin* meat is
likened to pigeon meat; the call is deep, like pigeon calls; also like pigeons, *alin* has stones in the stomach.

   Yet at the perceptual level, there are also clear differences between
the Goura and other pigeons and similarities between the Goura and the
megapodes. Like the megapodes, the Goura pigeon is a large bird, easily
three times the length of small ground pigeons or fruitdoves and almost
twice that of the large pigeons. It also has an elaborate crest, which no
other pigeons have. Megapodes have tufts on the crown though they are

not nearly as elaborate, but megapodes are unique in their habit of building mounds and leaving eggs under the ground. So aside from the fact that *alin* is the same size as the megapodes, there does not seem to be much perceptual basis for it being thought to be one.

In the end, Kaluli emphasize two elements to explain why *alin* is like the megapodes: *alin* and *odɛn* both are in a story of the creation of the earth; together they stamped on the mushy ground to harden it. They are "brothers" because they are actors in the origin myth of the universe. Moreover, *alin* has the same taboo restrictions as *odɛn* and the other two megapodes. They are taboo to children lest they be retarded and not walk, only crawl. The eggs are particularly taboo lest a child become mushy and not "harden," an important notion about Kaluli growth.

Fɔ Esolo

The division of the *fɔ* family is between *alan* and *hɛlu* 'large' and 'small'. The "large" branch is composed of ground pigeons; these are well known to Kaluli and have distinct calls. The "small" branch contains two covert groups, one of babbler-thrushes, the other of pittas and one babbler-thrush. The babbler-thrushes are linguistically marked by the shared morpheme *u*, but the terms are not binomial, and the three are not referred to as *u*-birds; use of the whole term is obligatory. Kaluli insist that one can tell the difference among the three by the loudness and length of their calls and by their opening and closing staccato whistles.

The two pittas have the final morpheme *ɔbɛ* in their names. In this they are similar to three other birds, but the final morpheme is not indicative of taxonomic status. The question, "What kinds of *ɔbɛ* are there?" would not be answered directly with the names *wɛɔbɛ*, *kiˇɔbɛ*, and so forth, indicating that the construction of these terms is like English "bluebird" or "jay bird."

Turning now to the *iwalu sab,* or arboreal superfamily:

Uˇsulage Esolo

The first branch of the eagle family is *migi halaido,* those with 'hard (or strong) beaks'; this group includes eagles, hawks, and goshawks. The first two taxa share the end shape -*lage;* the etymology of -*lage* has to do with 'one who looks after the others' or 'guardian', important roles attributed to eagles and hawks.

In contrast there is the *migi bamo,* the 'flat and wide beaks' grouping, comprising owls, frogmouths, owletnightjars, and nightjars. In addition to the purely morphological features that group these *migi bamo* birds together, they are related by food taboos as well. Their voices are considered to be suspect, and eating one results in a weak voice and general stupidity.

Obei Esolo

Named for the Kokomo, or Papuan Hornbill (figure 5), this family is composed largely of birds of paradise. It divides into *migi sambo,* those with "long beaks" and *migi abol,* those with "short beaks." Why is the hornbill grouped with the birds of paradise? The answer parallels the discussion of why the Goura Pigeon is considered a megapode. The hornbill has the largest beak of any bird in Bosavi, and when Kaluli think of bird groupings, they immediately tend to think of beaks. The only bird whose beak is nearly similar in size is the Black Sicklebill Bird of Paradise, and this is the bird with whom *obei* is grouped in the "long beaks" branch. The hornbill is sexually dimorphic with immature birds colored like the male; in this it is similar to the birds of paradise. The casque on the hornbill's beak increases in the number of folds as it ages, and this is similar to bird of paradise plumage changes. There are also real differences, however: the hornbill is a large bird, ranging up to thirty-six inches in length, and in bodily appearance, legs, and general plumage resembles no bird of paradise. In the end, the hornbill is most like the birds of paradise because it is the prominent male spirit bird and male symbol, therefore closely parallel to the Raggiana Bird of Paradise, ɔ*lon* (see figure 6), the most prominent female spirit bird and female symbol.

An unusual feature of the classification of birds of paradise is the way in which Kaluli inaccurately assess sexual dimorphism, reversing roles so that the brightly-plumed male birds, well known for loud, grating calls and superb visual displays, are considered to be the females, and the dull-plumed ones are considered the males. The marking is accomplished in a variety of linguistic ways; one is by the addition of the morpheme -*kɛn* to mark the duller-plumed, nonlongtailed member. *Kɛn* is a term for the skirt worn by girls and unmarried women; it contrasts with *jowa,* a term for the cinnamon-colored skirt worn by women after marriage. The bright, fluffy plumage of mature birds of paradise is referred to as their *jowa;* for the nonelaborately plumed ones (biologically the fe-

Figure 5. *obei*—Papuan Hornbill *(Aceros plicatus)*

males, for Kaluli the males or immature females), the plumage is called
kɛn.

The *migi abol* 'short beaked' group contains several birds of paradise
whose names further emphasize the Kaluli theory. For instance, the Mag-
nificent Bird of Paradise is named *ɛfe-ano* and *ɛfe-idɛ.* The clearing it
makes is called an *ɛfe-ba* or *ɛfe-tobɔ.* *Ba* is the term for de-grassed land;
tobɔ derives from the verb 'sweep'. This distinct display ground is a
clearing of a few square meters of the forest floor, with nearly vertical

Figure 6. ɔlon—Raggiana Bird of Paradise *(Paradisaea raggiana)*

bare stems remaining from which the male calls and displays. The Kaluli names come from this activity; *ano* is third-person 'mother', and *idɛ* is third-person 'daughter'; the "mother" sweeps and clears the ground and then calls her "daughter."

Some birds of paradise have lexically unrelated terms for male and female. The male Raggiana Bird of Paradise (Kaluli female) is ɔlon, and the term for the male and immature bird is *amo-kɛn,* again using the *kɛn* to mark distinctness from the fully developed plumage *jowa.* For the

Superb Bird of Paradise, the naming is explicitly related to sound. This is a dark bird, and the male (the Kaluli female) displays by puffing out a luminescent blue breast cape while uttering a loud two-syllable call. The *uwɔ* of the name *uwɔlo* is the onomatopoeic representation of this call. Kaluli men like to compare the call to the sound of women's ceremonial cheering. They imitate the women's strutting breast displays with a loud *u-wɔ!*, claiming that this is intended to seduce the men!

Other birds are clustered here with the birds of paradise because of clear morphological and behavioral similarities. Like birds of paradise, the Frilled Flycatcher, butcherbirds, and grackles all have conspicuous loud calls that are heard from forest edge and middle spaces. They have patterns of coloration similar to the birds of paradise, with fluffy-textured feathers, shiny beaks, or irridescent plumage.

Halina Esolo

As a whole, the *Halina* family corresponds to the parrots. The three Kaluli branches are *alan* 'large', *hɛlu* 'small', and *hɛlu lɛsu* 'tiny'. The "large" branch contains the two cockatoos and the equally large Pesquet's Parrot. The "small" branch contains lories, lorikeets, parrots, and king parrots of seven different genus groupings. The "tiny" members, the pygmy parrots, are the only very small birds in Bosavi not classed in the *ilai* family.

Hi Esolo

The *Hi* family, the arboreal pigeons and doves, is named with the generic *hi* and not *hi-fun,* the name of the largest member. *Hi* is never used with terrestrial pigeons of the *fɔ* family but can be used binomially with large arboreal pigeons. Its use is obligatory in *hi-fun* and optional but usual in *hi-susulubi* and *hi-tomolɔf.* Of these two, *susulubi* stands alone more easily because it is onomatopoeic for the booming call.

The *hɛlu,* or "small" branch, includes six primary and two secondary fruitdoves of the same genus. *Muni* is usually grouped with *iyɛu, kalo,* and *howɛn* on the basis of sound more than size or coloration, while *sowɛgu* and *susu* are grouped together because of their smaller size. The first four birds are most important in terms of the sounds of Kaluli weeping, poetics, and song. They are also the ones whose names are used to evaluate how moving weeping or song is felt to be.

Ilai Esolo

This family is extremely large, and one might reasonably ask whether it is cohesive as a group at all. Kaluli alternated between calling it a family with three branches and calling it three families named for *ilai, soga,* and *nene.* Many birds in this family are alike in crosscutting ways; the fuzziness of boundary conceptualization is thus directly reflected in taxonomy here, in marked contrast to such well-defined and well-contained perceptual groupings as pigeons, parrots, birds of prey, or birds of paradise.

The "large" *(alan* or *ilai)* branch is very diverse. Among its prominent members are the cuckoos, which are often heard but rarely seen. One cuckoo seems specific and the other two quite vague. *Bidɛli-ano* signifies 'mother of the *bidɛli* tree'; this koel is always seen in trees whose leaves are covered with *bidɛli* 'tent caterpillars'. Such trees are called *"bidɛli* trees," and this bird "mothers," or, makes a home, in them. The Kaluli taxon for the Bare-eyed Crow also includes the Channel-billed Cuckoo, which looks incredibly similar.

Sasahi and *mutabi* refer to the color phases of several local and mountain species of cuckooshrikes, which are more commonly called greybirds. *Mutabi* is prominent in the myth of how birds got ash-colored feathers. Etymology gives *mu* as 'ash' (there is no basic color term for grey). Also included in this group are birds of the open country: the swift, the swiftlets, the woodswallow, and the dollarbird.

In comparison with this *ilai* or "large" group, those classed as *soga* or "small" fall together more clearly, distinguished by the similarity of long beaks. The first group is the kingfishers, whose trilled calls are well known to the Kaluli. The general onomatopoeic representation for "trill" is *sɔlɔlɔ,* found in the name of *sɔlɔlɔbɛ,* the Yellow-billed Kingfisher. Also included here are the honeyeaters, which are equally well defined for the Kaluli by a similarity of beaks.

In the next group, the Brown Oriole is considered to be the "female" of a pair whose "male" is the New Guinea Friarbird. Both are called *bɔlo.* These two birds are visually similar, but the criterion for sharing a taxon is aural; the two birds sing together (duet) and sing in synchrony (antiphony). Despite the auditory and visual similarities, the Brown Oriole is smaller than the friarbird and has black and white coloration at the neck, clearly distinguishing it even at a good distance. The Kaluli key on the similarity of calls and have an interesting way of explaining the black and white coloration. They say that the coloring comes from a cross-mating of the Brown Oriole with the Hooded Butcherbird, the explanation being that the Brown Oriole, New Guinea Friarbird, and Hooded Butcherbird are often seen and heard together and are known to nest in the same trees.

Kaluli have generally ribald associations with *bɔlo* and say that the female is promiscuous. The loud pumping call of the butcherbird is interpreted as a seductive *wego we we we!* 'I'm right here' to the female, the oriole, to which the male reply from the friarbird is an insulting *ku genelɔ yabo!* 'red cock is coming'! or *we ku halaidɔ!* 'here's hard cock'! These Kaluli deductions, based on observations that are themselves zoologically accurate, are the source of the taxonomic ambiguity of *bɔlo*. While most Kaluli place *bɔlo* with the honeyeaters, others locate *bɔlo* primarily with the birds of paradise. Given the importance of sexual dimorphism, male and female symbolism, and symbolic associations with noisy and seductive sounds in the birds of paradise, this taxonomic ambiguity is logical.

The final three birds in this group are the bee-eater, berrypicker, and flowerpecker, again placed here due to a perceived similarity of beaks. Though bee-eaters catch and take their prey back to a perch to thrash and swallow it, the Kaluli do not liken them to the kingfishers, who share this habit.

The third and smallest group, *hɛlu lɛsu,* or *nene,* includes many warblers, scrubwrens, flycatchers, fantails, robins, flyrobins, whistlers, and strikethrushes. Most of these birds were rarely seen and a number of them have not yet been identified. At the end of every classification comes the tiny creatures that are vaguely differentiated and little known; the tiny branch of *ilai* family is such a group, with each taxon potentially extending to several birds.

Rank and Taxonomic Structure

To summarize, Kaluli folk ornithology is organized into heirarchic, labeled branches that demarcate levels of inclusion (Werner and Fenton 1970). Kaluli primarily divide the bird world according to an arboreal/terrestrial dichotomy, and then they isolate families, which are named for the largest member, and further subdivide smaller groups, which generally distinguish size of bodies, aspects of beaks, or both. This form of taxonomic organization is different from some classic ethnobiological studies in two ways: the existence of explicit mid-level groups and the existence of labeled branches (Berlin 1976).

The arboreal/terrestrial division shows, above all, how the functional and ecological aspects of Kaluli bird taxonomy are integrated with classifications based on morphological and symbolic discontinuities in nature. When confronted with a picture or a dead specimen, Kaluli men would make movements with their arms, or get on the ground, or imitate rustling or flying sounds in order to indicate the arboreal or terrestrial context in which the bird was usually observed. When I said, "Tell me some names for birds," they would quite often name all of the ground birds they could think of, then pause and name the arboreal ones, always beginning with the Kapul Eagle.

When I asked, "What kinds of birds are there?", Kaluli responses would often be "ɔbɛ esolowo?" 'bird families?', and they would name the different families. Only half of the time would people then reflect back and say the first two families were terrestrial and the others arboreal. While astute assistants made this distinction immediately, some made it after listing the families or while doing so, and others did not do it at all. Thus, the terrestrial/arboreal split is sometimes overt, while the listing of families by name of the key member is always explicit.

The same pattern holds for the organization of family branches. Here sequence in membership listing conformed to the principle of a split, even when the split itself was not explicitly labeled. If, for example, I read back names randomly, respondents would correct me by reorganizing the list in an order more consistent with the branches. Alternately, respondents would name family members and when all the similar ones were named, say "idɛni asi, kɔm" 'sit down together, finished' to indicate that these constituted a group.

Finally, within the organization of the lexemes listed for each family, several other clearly marked groups are covert; they are never labeled but grouped only when people are presented with tests.

In summary, there is a set of focused points within the taxonomy, the beginner[3] and the families, and intermediate sets of fuzzy ones, the superfamilies and the subfamilies. These intermediate sets are abstracted by some Kaluli, so that the lexical contrasts are articulated. They are not

---

3. "Beginner" or "unique beginner" refers to the highest node of a branching taxonomy; in this case, the beginner is ɔbɛ 'birds' (Berlin, Breedlove, and Raven 1968).

articulated by others except when presented with tests to reveal covert
organization.

Birds and Lived Realities

While studying linguistic and zoological issues relevant to Kaluli bird
taxonomy, I worked closely with two people, Kulu and Jubi. I checked for
consistency with another ten and discussed the topic informally with
many other people on a day-to-day basis. The taxonomy presented here,
then, is neither the union nor the intersection of Kaluli collective knowledge, especially because it represents nothing of what Kaluli women
know about birds, which is generally quite limited when compared to the
knowledge of experienced middle-aged male hunters.

Taxonomic knowledge, like all knowledge, is clearly stratified in
Bosavi. It is shaped by a combination of personal experiences, memories,
and cultural constructs. Moreover, it is shaped by certain clear ecological
constraints: dialects from Bosavi areas of lower altitude have more terminology for lower-altitude birds, and people know more about them;
speakers of dialects from areas higher up the mountain have more names
for mountain birds and more knowledge about them. Kaluli speakers
generally applied names of local birds to an appropriate set of mountain
extensions when they did not really know the mountain birds from direct
experience. In some cases, they were aware that two or more species of
the same genus filled different niches, in other cases they were not.
Knowledge of mountain birds was particularly variable; the only ones
generally well known were birds considered mythically or symbolically
important.

In the face of such variation in taxonomic and natural historical
knowledge, can it be claimed that a core set of shared understandings
typify the way Kaluli think about birds? If taxonomic sophistication, interest, and curiosity are not equally shared by different sectors of Kaluli
society, what features of the bird world are more broadly salient?

Seasons, Time, and Space

Kaluli are very much oriented to a cycle of seasons, and E. Schieffelin
(1976:141) points out that the seasonal terms *dona, imɔ,* and *tɛn* are
respectively characterized by the fruiting of *dona* trees (a magnolia, *El-
mirillia papuana*), the falling of leaves around the bases of trees, and the

fruiting of *oga* (marita fruit, *Pandanus* spp.). He notes that in principle the Kaluli are not counting months or moons or noting changes in the weather, but reading the indications of forest vegetation.

Kaluli are quick to remark on the relationship between this cycle and that of the avifauna. The appearance of the Rainbow Bee-eater, *bili,* is a prominent feature of *tɛn,* roughly April to September. At the beginning of *tɛn* in 1977, I heard several youths running across the courtyard yelling, "*Tɛn's* really here; we heard *bili.*" During *tɛn, bili* stays in the gardens and forest openings. The season from October or November to mid-March corresponds to *dona,* and Kaluli know it to be the time that *yoma* 'Mountain Pigeons' come in large groups to feed on *dona* and other tree fruit. Kaluli say *dona* is the season when pigeons and fruitdoves are highly present and vocally conspicuous.

Perhaps more significantly, the daily cycle of events is marked by the presence of birds. Kaluli say, "Only bats work at night; people are like birds; we get up with their calls in the morning and sleep when they do." Women note that the early morning calls of *bɔlo,* the Brown Oriole and New Guinea Friarbird, and *sagelon,* the Hooded Butcherbird, tell children to wake up, while their late afternoon calls tell children to gather with their families. Others told me that the late afternoon appearance in the open courtyard of *bas,* the Black-breasted Woodswallow, and *dɛfalɛn,* the Uniform Swiftlet, with the former calling *bas bas bas* 'brother-in-law' to the swiftlet, means that people should come and sit together and have food. In these instances the presence of birds stands for the passage of time and the cycle of sociality.

Similarly, birds are important in the demarcation of social space. Birds are never hunted on lands directly adjacent to village clearings. The presence of birds and the sounds of their calls in the trees at the very edges of the villages are frequently remarked upon, as these birds are believed to be the spirit reflections of deceased friends and relatives. They are not disturbed, and their calls are listened to attentively.

When indicating space, pointing, or describing places, Kaluli often make references to where birds eat, nest, perch, or move about. On the trails they locate places according to where birds are calling. Auditory, rather than visual, recognition guides hunters; I found men expert in mimicking calls to attract the birds.

In addition to distance, height is also frequently referenced to birds. Kaluli utilize levels of bird nesting and flight patterns to make comparative statements about vegetation and forest life. When recording bird calls in dense forest, I frequently confused auditory depth with height; Kaluli men always corrected me by moving my arm to point the microphone in the right direction, and they were almost always correct.

Adaptation to life in a forest environment develops acute spatial skills for audition, and Kaluli use these to advantage over vision. In my experience, bird calls and bird life constituted the most accessible domain from which many of the experiential aspects of this perceptual system were linguistically marked.

Taboos, Sayings, Spells

Another domain marked by a strong consensus of shared understandings in Bosavi is food taboos, and this is hardly surprising in light of the important role food plays in crystallizing social relations. While noting that food taboos are "miscellaneous and complicated," E. Schieffelin (ibid.:65) shows that occurrences across numerous contexts (supernatural restriction, illness, mourning, pregnancy), at various age levels (infants, youths, marrieds), for men and women, both involuntary and voluntary, involve expanding the notion of food as mediator of relationships to that of food as mediator of social categories. Food must ultimately fulfill social and symbolic as well as nutritional requirements. The underlying pattern of food taboos in Bosavi derives from perceiving the food substance as a representation of nature with potentially harmful properties in a cultural context.

For instance, children do not eat birds whose principal habitat is the ground or they will be retarded (wɛfian) and not walk properly. A similar pattern forms around bird eggs: they are "mushy," and taboo; a child who eats one will not "harden" and grow physically mature. Birds with red feathers are taboo to women lest they have a very bloody menses, and —using an analogy to leaves, which yellow before they drop—birds with yellow feathers are taboo lest one quickly decay.

What a bird looks like may be potentially less harmful than what it sounds like. There is thus a large class of birds that children must avoid or they will not develop proper speech, or, in several related cases, will be phlegmy and hoarse and make only unintelligible noises. The transfer is based on the assigned cultural status of voice quality for birds. For the Kaluli, then, the notion that you are what you eat is both a visual and an auditory construct.

There are verbal correlates to many taboos, formed like the "you're a rat"-type phrase in English. For example, if children ate *ilai* (the Black Jungle Coucal), they would not be able to walk a straight path, because the bird weaves in flight, zigzagging and hopping, rather than flying directly from point to point. One can say *ge ilai ɔngo* 'You're like *ilai*' to one who zigzags when walking. The form *"ge* [bird name] *ɔngo"* is productive with about twenty different bird names, and in many cases the focused quality is the one in the taboo. Prominent in these sayings are phrases for individuals or groups who are noisy, well decorated, angry, or have birdlike qualities of movement.

These sayings are distinct from spells and curses on certain levels, but bird names appear in all with the same intention: to assimilate a natural quality to a cultural object. Thus, the spell required in the making of a drum uses the name of *tibodai,* the Crested Pitohui, commonly called the Papuan Bellbird (see figure 7). Invoking this bird's name in the spell ensures the drum a continuous resonance, like the throbbing, pulsating quality that characterizes the call. And on the other side, a man can curse a woman by invoking the name of a red bird (such as one of the birds of paradise or a red parrot), and she will have a severe menstrual period. Table 2-1 summarizes these basic Kaluli concepts.

Figure 7. *tibodai*—Crested Pitohui *(Pitohui cristatus)*

Food Taboos (*nɔ mal*)

Bird group or members	Focused quality (NATURE)	Focused consequence (CULTURE)
megapodes turkeys ground doves various small ground birds	all are terrestrial some are quite slow and heavy in their movements	taboo to children lest they retard, not mature to walk properly, only crawl
owls hawks goshawks various small birds	have "weak" voices only make noise redundant calls	taboo to children lest they retard, not mature to speak properly, only make noises
red parrots red birds of paradise	have red feathers that are extremely bright in color	women may not eat lest they have very bloody menstrual periods

Spells/Curses ("*ge————ɔngo*" or more specific curses)

Bird group or members	Focused quality (NATURE)	Focused consequence (CULTURE)
Black Sicklebill Bird of Paradise	long tail feathers	said to one who is well decorated with cordyline leaves in rear of belt
Sitella	noisy, flocking	said to children who only play in a group and make noise
red parrots	redness	said to one who is bloody from fight
(negative examples below contrast with benign or positive above; negative sayings involve longer specific formulae)		
bats	scrawny, no voice	curse to make one sick or disabled
red birds	redness	curse to make a woman have a debilitating men- strual period

Table 2-1. Food taboos, spells, and curses

Turned-over Words, Spirits, and Bird Metaphors

Another pervasive Kaluli linguistic convention is called *bali to* or 'turned-over words'. This concept involves several linguistic means and encompasses aspects of analogy, metaphor, euphemism, litotes, irony, and sarcasm. (The concept is discussed in detail in chapter 4 with reference to poetics, and in chapters 3 and 5 with reference to the layers of meaning, connotation, and insinuation in weeping and song texts.) Most generally, *bali to* is a device used to mask meanings, obfuscate items, or create broad inferences.

The simplest way to turn words over so that they have a *hega* or 'underneath' is by lexical substitution. One common paradigm of lexical substitution uses bird names for human referents. On the one hand, these referents assign a cultural analogue to natural properties, and on the other hand, they are directly representative of the way humans appear as spirit reflections. For example, the term *amo,* for the Sulphur-crested Cockatoo, is substituted for "grandmother" or for any older woman, particularly one who has a whiny voice. This derives first from an analogy between the grating voice quality of old women and cockatoos, and second from the belief that after death old women appear in spirit reflection as white cockatoos.

Adult women can be spoken about in *bali to* by referring to ɔlon, the Raggiana Bird of Paradise, or ɔgowa, the King Bird of Paradise. In both cases it is the zoological male of the bird pair that is referred to, because each of these wears a red or cinnamon-colored *jowa* 'skirt' that sways as the bird moves. Younger unmarried women of marrying age are spoken about by substituting the name of *gušuwa,* the Little Cassowary, a bird with stiff plumage like the *kɛn* skirts of unmarried women. When a young man asks another, "Did you dream of hunting a cassowary?", he can be joking about his friend's sexually aroused state or asking more benignly if marriage has been on his companion's mind. In these instances, classes of women are the "underneath" of bird names because of analogies between natural and cultural domains. At the same time, *amo, ɔlon, ɔgowa,* are the principal spirit images of these different groups of women.

Bali to patterns for men in precisely the same way, with *obei,* the Papuan Hornbill standing generically for adult males; when young women blush and note, "That *obei* has a long nose," they are speaking about an attractive man. Perhaps more common in marked situations is the use of the names of *ušulage* (the Kapul Eagle) or *salage* (the Long-tailed Buzzard) for adult males who are aggressive, often angry, or possess a volatile temper. The hostile, fighting, hunting character of these birds of prey makes them ideal models for the spirit reflections of dominant male figures and ideal metaphors for talking about men whose intemperate behaviors stand out in everyday actions.

By identifying resemblances in morphology, behavior, sound, or color as indicating underlying shared features between humans and birds, Kaluli set up the cultural basis for using bird names as lexical substitutes for human actors, as well as provide for the construction of a spirit realm consistent with cultural articulations. The logical basis for this practice is linked to the dominant Kaluli notion of the duality of the world in visible and invisible domains. People who have left the visible, living domain become *ane mama,* spirit reflections. The notion that things are not only what they appear to be but have another side—a reflection —or an underneath is a pervasive Kaluli mode of thought. This mode underlies the construction of bird/human analogies and makes *bali to* possible as a shared symbolic means manifest in lexical substitutions.

Personal Names

The largest source of terms for human names comes from geographic place names in Bosavi. The other major source also comes from the natural world, and bird names are common. Out of 125 Kaluli bird names and 20 secondary or alternate names, I found 84 that are given to humans. In almost half of these instances, the name is identical; in the rest, it is a closely related name that Kaluli identify as being derivative. The gender of the human recipient of the name never violates the patterns of gender attribution for birds as *ane mama.* There is a consistency among the properties attached to a bird that makes it male or female in either context, whether naming or spirit representation.

Myth, Color, Gender, and Beauty

There is a further set of connections here between gender and beauty, beauty and color, and color and myth. Kaluli consider human and bird females to be more attractive than males. Birds identified as being female have the brightest red, white, and black feathers. Men make themselves beautiful by costuming in the feathers of these female birds. The silky black cassowary feathers and the bright, silky red Raggiana Bird of Para-

Gisa, Hedɔ, and old Yafolumi cast a watchful eye as a pig is butchered and the meat distributed for cooking. All three have the traditional heart-shaped bird-face tatoo.

dise feathers, both of which are important for costumes, are linked to these female spirit birds with a myth. The Raggiana is said to have stolen feathers from the cassowary and stained them red by sloppily eating a meal of pandanus on the run. The transformation of black into red is related to that of young, nonmenstruating girls into mature, menstruating women; cassowaries are the youthful female *ane mama* and Raggiana Birds of Paradise the older ones. There is also a maturity analogy, youth to adulthood, in the movement. When viewed from the rear, the swaying motion of the stiff, unmarried women's skirts *(kɛn)* is likened to the movement of a cassowary, while the swinging of full hips in *jowa* skirts is represented by the more seductive movements of Raggiana Birds of Paradise in tree perches. The black and red relationship is further solidified by the fact that *hagabi,* Pesquet's Parrot, has black and red running together on its feathers. Thus,

black : red   ::
gušuwa (cassowary) : *ɔlon* (bird of paradise)   ::
kɛn skirt : *jowa* skirt   ::
nonmenstruating youth : menstruating adult   ::
filling out/swaying : full hips/seductive swing

In costuming, men wear black cassowary feathers in a headdress and red *ɔlon jowa* (Raggiana skirt) above their elbows. In their up-and-down bobbing movements, the sway of these feathers creates a birdlike flap and flow that is said to beautify the dancer, making him like a bird.

The final component of the basic color scheme is white, primarily associated with *amo,* the Sulphur-crested Cockatoo (figure 8), the older female *ane mama.* The natural analogies here are plentiful, providing a rationale for separating white as representing a more mature beauty. With age the hair turns white, and a woman's voice becomes whinier. *Amo* is not only white but has a considerably louder screech then *ɔlon.* Unlike birds of paradise, which display seductively in trees, cockatoos fly in large groups. After menopause, the redness of womanhood is neutralized and the purer white beauty emerges.

Besides the white cockatoo, the one other major source of white feathers in Bosavi is *obei,* the Papuan Hornbill. Kaluli take care of the fact that this most prominent male *ane mama* and symbol has white tail feathers with a myth showing how they were stolen from the cockatoo. Ultimately this myth is about male and female oppositions in Kaluli society.

Figure 8. *amo*—Sulphur-crested Cockatoo *(Cacatua galerita)*

Its resolution is that man *(obei,* the hornbill) is transformed into beau-
tified man by wearing the white feathers of woman *(amo,* the cockatoo).
In analogous manner, men wear the feathers of symbolically female birds
when they dance at ceremonies; by doing so they become more beautiful,
colorful, and seductive.

Bird feather usage in both costume and personal decoration patterns
into three groups. In the first (group A in table 2-2), black and red

	BIRD	ITEM	COLOR	CONTEXT	♀ / ♂
A	gušuwa Little Cassowary	body feathers	black	three types of strung headdress	unmarried adult ♀ spirit
		body feathers	black	worn for ceremonies	
	uluwa Two-wattle Cassowary	side quills of both	black	worn as earrings	
	ɔlon Raggiana Bird of Paradise	jowa 'skirt' under-plumes	red	worn above elbow for ceremonial dancing	adult ♀ spirit
	hagabi Pesquet's Parrot	body & tail feathers	red & black	worn in dance headdress	
B	amo Sulphur-crested Cockatoo	body & tail feathers	white	worn in dance head-dress and on arms and legs for ceremonies;	older ♀ spirit
	obei Papuan Hornbill	tail feathers	white	(main color and item for kɔluba ceremony)	adult ♂ spirit
C	hi- pigeons alin Goura Pigeon wɔkwele Giant Cuckoodove ušulage Harpy Eagle (hawks)	tail feathers (some body) tail feathers	bubɛlo barred with grays and browns	not worn for ceremon-ial perform-ance; worn by men when tra-veling to a cere-mony or occasion of importance	older ♂ spirit
	giliaba Rainbow Lorikeet ɛbɛlɛs Flame Bowerbird amo	small body feathers crest	red and yellow yellow	red, yellow, and some-times white also are attached to tips of headdress	young ♀ spirit

Table 2-2. Bird feather usage

feathers are taken from birds that are all female representations. These are the primary feathers worn by men in ceremonial costumes. In the second (group B), white feathers come from both a female bird (the cockatoo) and a male bird (the hornbill), but this male factor is neutralized by the mythic evidence that the feathers were once stolen from the female. While less significant than red and black, white feathers are also important for men's costumes. Finally, the third group (group C) contains several male and female birds whose feathers are worn for other, less significant public occasions. Men wear the dark-barred feathers of male birds like the eagle, Goura pigeon, cuckoodove, or hawk for activities that primarily involve demonstrations of male energy and strength, such as large communal work events, group celebrations, or speechmaking. The additional female birds here contribute small feathers, sometimes used to tip the more primary ones, sometimes worn more randomly in the hair or beard. The addition of small amounts of bright red, yellow, or white parallels the use of small amounts of red or white parrot down to tip the black feathers in the cassowary headdress. The effect in both cases is to add a touch of beauty to beauty, ensuring the desired effect.

Sound

The ways Kaluli think about birds have thus far been articulated along two axes. The first indicates that a taxonomy of birds in terms of lexical contrasts and zoological observations involves many important aspects of symbolic construction. Why the cassowaries are birds, why the Goura Pigeon is a megapode, why the hornbill is a bird of paradise, why birds of paradise are sexually dimorphic, and why the Brown Oriole and New Guinea Friarbird are considered to be a single bird are examples that show how natural historical observations are shaped by cultural constructs and upheld by symbolic needs. The second axis indicates that processes of metaphoric thought underlie the broader everyday realities of Kaluli interpretation of the presence of birds.

Continuing with the implications of socially shared meanings of birds for Kaluli, one domain makes the links between classification and metaphor even more explicit, and its pervasiveness is overwhelming in the everyday area; this is the domain of sound. Kaluli categorize and think about routine experiences of birds most often and most thoroughly in terms of the sounds they hear in the forest and at the village edges. Recognition of birds by sound is immediate in everyday situations, spontaneously available, and, most importantly, a significant feature of the conversations Kaluli have among themselves.

Evidence for dominance of the routinely shared character of sound over image categories is manifest in a number of different ways. When presented with pictures or specimens out of context, Kaluli tend first to think of and imitate the sound, then to say the name of the bird. In the bush or at the village edge, they point out birds by saying, "Listen, . . . do you hear X?", and then an interpretation is made, such as, "It says its name." When asked direct questions that include the name of a bird, the response "It sounds like X" is universally presented by Kaluli before any sort of "It looks like X" statement. Virtually all Kaluli men can sit down in front of a tape recorder and imitate the sounds of at least one hundred birds, but few can provide visual descriptive information on nearly that many.

When one hears a bird, and they are by far more often heard than seen in Bosavi, one makes a statement that recognizes the bird through focusing the sound, attaching the sound to a taxon (the two are often identical, as many taxa are formed from bird call onomatopoeia), and attaching an appropriate cultural attribution to the sound. This is precisely how sound classes work. As diagrammed in table 2-3, there are seven groups: those that "say their names" *(ene wi salan);* those that "make a lot of noise" *(mada ganafodan);* those that "only sound" *(imilisi ganalan);* those that "speak the Bosavi language" *(Bosavi to salan);* those that "whistle" *(holan);* those that "weep" *(yɛlan);* and those that "sing gisalo song" *(gisalo molan).*

Ene wi salan 'Say Their Names'

The *ene wi salan* birds constitute the largest group, which includes almost half of all the Kaluli bird names. The naming of birds by onomatopoeia or some pattern of mimesis is most likely to be universal. There are several Kaluli interpretations of how birds say their names, for example:

(1) Say the entire name:

Type	Name	Representation
a) 1 syllable	*bas*	*Bas bas bas bas*
b) 2 syllable	*kɔgɔ*	*Kɔgɔ Kɔgɔ Kɔgɔ*
c) reduplicated	*gubogubo*	*Gubogubo Gubogubo*
d) 3 syllable	*iyɛu*	*I-yɛɛɛɛ-uu*

e) 4 syllable	*susulubi*	*Susulubi Susulubi*	
f) extended	*soga*	*So-gaaaa gya gya gya*	

(2) Say part of the name:

a) 1 syllable derived	*wɔkwele*	*Wɔk wu Wɔk wu*	
b) 2 syllable	*tibodai*	*Tibo Tibo Tibo Tibo*	
c) 3 syllable	*sɔlɔlɔbɛ*	*Sɔlɔlɔɔ Sɔlɔlɔɔ*	

All of the *ene wi salan* birds fall into one of these patterns. As elsewhere in Kaluli onomatopoeia, reduplication iconically marks continuousness.

Some of these sound terms can also productively function as verbs and then stand for large classes of sounds. These verbs are formed by adding the onomatopoeic root to ɛlɛma, a contraction of ɛlɛ 'like this' and *sama,* present-singular-imperative 'speak'.

Bird Name	Sound	Verb	Gloss
1. *uwɔlo*	*uwɔ*	*uwɔlɛma*	"cheer" (women only)
2. *sɔlɔlɔbɛ*	*sɔlɔlɔ*	*sɔlɔlɔlɛma*	"trill"
3. *iyɛu*	*yɛ*	*yɛlɛma*	"weep"
4. *hɔlolo*	*hɔ*	*hɔlɛma*	"pant; breathe quickly with almost a whistling sound"

There is no origin myth relating how birds came to say their names as there is with four of the six other sound categories.

Mada Ganafodan 'Make Noise'

In the "noisy" group are several birds whose sounds are always represented with *"Sɛ sɛ sɛ sɛ sɛ sɛ,"* uttered with a nasal quality and with a facial gesture that twinges the upper lip and nose and squints the eyes, signifying disgust. While these birds are not particularly offensive on any other levels, the comment *dagano mɔgago* 'bad voice' quite frequently accompanies imitation of call. The undisputed leader of this group is *sosas.* As might be suspected, there is a saying that goes along with this: when

ƆBƐ

(branching tree from **ƆBƐ** into the following categories)

ENE WI SALAN 'say their names'	MADA GANAFODAN 'make noise'	IMILISI GANALAN 'only sound'	BOSAVI TO SALAN 'speak Bosavi'	HOLAN 'whistle'	YƐLAN 'weep'	GISALO MOLAN 'sing gisalo'
fɔ	sosas	ikowab	bɔlɔ	fɔ̌	amo	sagelon
bibi	kɛmos	salage	wasio	ušo	bidɛli-ano	susulubi
du	obei	masan	tifɛn	unamo		sowɛgu
talo	ɔlon	kiboti	nene	wɔkwɛlɛ	**SA-YƐLAN**	yɛgɛl
odɛn	yɛgɛl	bulɛki	nɔkalo	howɛn	muni	
daga	gowwa	ahandagu	bidɛli-ano	muni	iyɛu	**SA-MOLAN**
hinɛ	cɔcy	bili		iyɛu	kalo	muni
sabin	waidos	kelebaga		galatɛf	howɛn	iyɛu
ušo	halina	alin		ɛfe-ano		kalo
himu	amo	(obei)		ɛfe-idɛ		howɛn
bili	agul	(bɛlɛb)		sagelon		
mil	yɛli			waful		
wasio	giagia			soga		
mono	sege			mono		
soga	ušulage			sowasowa		
bas	kulubamo			bidɛli-ano		
higu	ɛfe-ano			bɔlɔ		
yɛli	wemale			tibodai		
kel	sabin			kalogɔbɛ		

say their second name

bɛɔgolɛ
sɔlɔlɔbɛ
yafalo
kiboti
giagia
susulubi
gubogubo
sowɛgu
wɔkwɛlɛ
agul
yɛli
suwɛbise
hoida
ea
guwɛnge
cmcn
biyobiyo
wɛs

tɛkɛsιyɛ

			HOLAN (con.)
cɛ̌gcʌ	iligo	kǐcɔbɛ	kidɛlɛsιn
ɪɲaʌ	ɛbɛlɛs	dolondo	fafιkon
tɛʌɔɲaʌ	uasele	kɔɔlopɔ	watua
ɔɲcʌn	hagabi	uaʌio	gowalo
iligo	isadιɛn	tιfɛn	kɔbalo
amɔgc	kel	mil	uluʌa (immature only)
ugɛʒɛ	giliaba	ɔɔlɔlɔbɛ	gǔsuʌa (immature only)
sasahi	angaʌe	golabei	
hclolo	kɔg̃ɪsuʌa	bɛɛgolɛ	
fafιkon		nene	
suʌɛli		hclolo	
hagabi		ɔcʌo	
umuge		ʌʌandɛlobo	
salage		ikowab	
kalogɔbɛ		misak	
sowasowa		sowɛgu	
tibodai		susu	
kesιbalɔk		ilai	
dolondo		fιl	
diligobɛlɛ		kamonano	
gɔgɔbɛ		suʌeli	
		masιtob	

Table 2–3. Bird sound categories

children are playing in a group and making a lot of chatter that is disturb-
ing to adults, they may be referred to as *sosas ɔngo* 'like *sosas*', or may be
addressed *Sosas tolɛsabo!* 'Stop talking, *sosas*'. Other sayings for remarking
on noisy people also use bird names; this one is marked for children.

Imilisi Ganalan 'Only Sound'

Birds in the "only sound" group make sounds less with their voices than
with their bodies. The verb for 'sound', *ganalɛma,* is explicitly used here
in contrast to 'speak' *sama* or 'talk' *tolɛma.* Members of this group *towɔ
mɔtolan* 'don't talk words'.

   Bird sounds are assumed to be communicative to other birds. To
each other the birds converse; humans do not understand these "words,"
but spirit mediums do. What humans *do* understand is the words spoken
by a small group of *Bosavi to salan* 'speak Bosavi words' birds. Kaluli do
not consider it peculiar that some birds do not talk, only sound. The fact
that several hawks are included in the group is anthropomorphized by
Kaluli to mean that just as angry people sometimes are simply noisy and
do not say much, hawks, which are associated with male anger, do not
talk, and only hunt. Kaluli imitations of these birds involve wing sounds.

Bosavi to Salan 'Speak Bosavi Language'

Seven birds are considered by all to speak phrases in the Bosavi language.
In some cases, the bird's call is interpreted as a set phrase; in other cases,
the bird is claimed to say several different things. This category originates
in a myth that is specifically about *bɔlo,* the New Guinea Friarbird (figure
9) and the Brown Oriole (figure 10):

   "Once parents sent their two children off to fetch water. The children did not return. More and more the parents called out for them to
come home and bring water. The children remained out of sight, but the
parents heard them calling 'we'll get some.' Finally the parents went in
search of the children. They found them dead, killed by enemy people;
bɔlo had taken their voices *(dagan)."*

   The birds in the *Bosavi to salan* group are said to have a human
dagan and not a bird one. Hence they speak real Bosavi words. Other
birds speak *ɔbɛ gɔnɔ to* 'bird sound words' and are said to converse in
this special talk. But all birds can understand *Bosavi to,* both as spoken
by these six special birds with human voices and as spoken by people.

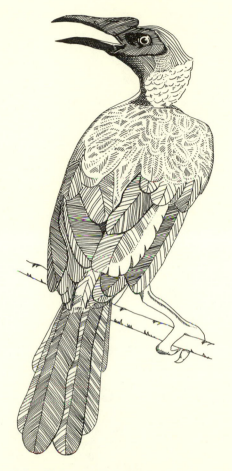

Figure 9. *bɔlo*—Helmeted Friarbird *(Philemon novaeguineae)*

Bɔlo (New Guinea Friarbird and Brown Oriole) is clearly the most prolific bird speaker of *Bosavi to,* and many of its phrases are ribald; they are considered to be *mugu to* 'taboo talk' by the newly developing Christian sector of Bosavi society. Directly related to the story are calls of *dowo, nɔwo,* on long drawn-out pitches that dip down and then up. These words, "father" and "mother," are the sad calls of dead children to their parents. The quick twitching call made with the head turning is said to be *hɛ gɔ fɔn* 'where are my feathers', which refers to the baldness of the bird around the head and neck.

Raucous calls are interpreted as sexual insults about erections and

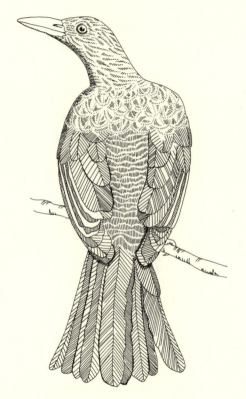

Figure 10. *bɔlo*—Brown Oriole *(Oriolus szalayi)*

are in the form of short statements, such as *ku genelɔ!* 'red cock', *Ku halaidɔ!* 'hard cock'. *Hɔ, hɔ, Gigio ku genelɔ!* is a longer version in which a person (here Gigio) is specified. *Bɔlo*'s special skill is the ability to heckle all men with this call. On the trails Kaluli men blush when they hear *bɔlo*'s insults and shout back, with both laughter and scorn, *wɛfio, kɔm!* 'shut up, retard'! or *towɔ dabɛno mobiakɛ!* 'we're unwilling to listen to your talk'. *Bɔlo*'s longer late afternoon and dinner-time call is stand-ardly *ninɛli monowo id alu nagalakɛ-o hɔɔ!* 'I just ate and my asshole really hurts, ha'!, sometimes given in a cleaned-up version, *ninɛli monowo kufɔ hɔsulowo hɔɔ!* 'I just ate and my belly is really full, ha'!

Wasio, a berrypicker, says *wa wa wasio, ugufɔ oga genelɔ,* which refers to the redness *(ugufɔ, genelɔ)* of ripe *oga* 'pandanus'. People say that this bird tells them when to begin picking pandanus.

Tifɛn, the Black-throated Warbler, says *siyo gogo bayo; gogo* is onomatopoeic for pig burrowing sounds, and the rest of the phrase means, "I'm really staying right here." Kaluli say this bird talks to them when they are looking for lost or stray pigs; this bird is also associated with the spirit of pigs.

Nene, the Chanting Scrubwren (figure 11), has numerous melodious calls of three, four, and five pitches:

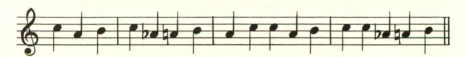

On these pitches the bird says *sei yabɛ* 'a witch is coming', *kalu yabɛ* 'a person is coming', and many other phrases with *yabɛ;* the most common interpretation, however, is *ne mayabɛ* 'I'm hungry'. This is related to the spirit image of *nene,* which is that of a helpless child. The bird's name comes from this, too; children always whine or beg by saying *ne, ne, ne, ne,* indicating 'me, for me, give to me, do for me'. Parents who have lost a child may go off to the bush in the afternoon, leave some food on a branch, and say, "This is for you, *nene.*" Once I was in the bush with a group of Kaluli and heard this bird's distinct calls; one of our party instantly remarked, *heyo, sowa lɛsu yɛlab* 'what a shame, a little child is crying'.

In the evening, the call of *nɔkalo,* the Large-tailed Nightjar, is interpreted as *nu de uu* 'grandmother bring firewood'. In a larger sense, this means "make yourself warm," which is the desired state of affairs once it has become dark.

Bidɛli-ano, the White-crowned Koel, calls out on three descending pitches *nɛ fɛs ɔn* 'my back hurts', and this is supposed to be an indication of the pain it feels from not sitting down, just flying around constantly. To a person whose back hurts because of bending over at work, one says *wafio!, ge bidɛli-ano ɔngo!* 'Wow, you're like *bidɛli-ano'.* Sometimes people say *nɛ fɛs ɔn* while working, in a rhythmic, semispoken, semisung way. This bird also utters a longer version of the same call; Kaluli interpret it

Figure 11. *nene*—Chanting Scrubwren *(Crateroscelis murina)*

as the cried version, which is why *bidɛli-ano* is also classified with birds who weep.

Holan 'Whistle'

While the *Bosavi to salan* birds are said to have a human voice *(dagan)*, those that whistle simply have a human tongue *(ean)*. These birds are all considered to be spirits, and whistling is considered a special kind of spirit bird sound. The verb *holan* has the root *ho,* onomatopoeic for the sound of whistling.

Usually all of the birds that whistle are lumped together. In the context of discussions of birds that weep and sing, some people distinguish two smaller subsets, the first being those that *gese-holan. Gese* comes from the verb *gesema* 'make one feel sorrow or pity'. Nine birds are included here, and of these, four are further specified as being *sa-holan,* the second subset. *Sa* is the generic term for 'waterfall' and is used throughout sound terminology to mean that the sound comes down and inward. *Sa-holan* means 'whistle with words in mind'. The melody of the whistled pitches is symbolically associated with textual conventions.

When one is whistling *sa-holan,* the implication is that he is whistling the melody but thinking the text that goes with it.

The *gese-holan* ('whistle sorrowfully') birds are among the most important images in Kaluli sound symbolism attached to social sentiments of loss and sadness. *Wɔkwele,* the Giant Cuckoodove, and *galatɛf,* the Amboina Cuckoodove, whistle two-pitch calls as they bob up and down by waterfalls, where they nest in rock gorges. Birds whistling at a waterfall is a prominent spirit image. *Bɔlo,* the New Guinea Friarbird and the Brown Oriole, whistles many of the calls that it speaks; it recalls the image of the dead children in the myth when it whistles the call whose "inside" is "father" or "mother." Kaluli hear drumming as the whistling voice of *tibodai,* the Crested Pitohui, calling *tibo tibo.* The sense image becomes *dowo dowo* 'father, father'. Mediated by the drum sound, the bird thus becomes a spirit child calling for its father. When *nene,* the Chanting Scrubwren, whistles, people think of children, as they do when the bird calls *ne mayabɛ* 'I'm hungry'.

When these birds whistle, Kaluli hear what they are "saying." The whistled sounds thus have conventional symbolic equivalents in verbal phrases. This *gese-holan,* or 'whistle sorrowfully', group is thus like the next group of *sa-holan* birds; what they whistle is what Kaluli believe them to have "in mind"; there is a meaning "inside" the sound.

The four birds that *sa-holan* are the fruitdoves *muni, howɛn, kalo,* and *iyɛu.* Kaluli feel a deep association of textual phrases with the melodies of their whistling. In each case the text comes "down inside" the person's head when hearing these birds. Composers cite the inner experience of hearing these birds when a song comes to them; this can be the hearing of actual texts or whistled phrases that stand for them.

Yɛlan 'Weep'

The *yɛlan* group (note the relation of the bird name *iyɛu, yɛ* as onomatopoeia for the sound of crying, and *yɛlɛma* as the verb for "weep") has only two other members besides the four fruitdoves: *bidɛli-ano* and *amo.* In fact these two are not explicitly named as frequently as the others. *Bidɛli-ano* is considered by most to be appropriate here because of its call, which descends in pitch like calls of fruitdoves, and because of the symbolism of looking for a home. The call of *amo* is quite loud, and some Kaluli consider it awful and grating. Many others, however, say that *amo*'s call is *yɛlan* because it is the voice of an old woman. The group most commonly associated with weeping, in fact, is older women, because they are the most proficient performers of sung-texted-weeping.

The most prominent conventional symbols of weeping are *muni* and *iyɛu*. The association with the former is explicitly linked to the story "the boy who became a *muni* bird." *Muni* sound is that of a boy who has turned into a bird, that is, a dead, lost, or abandoned child. *Iyɛu* is the adult version, marked as female because of the prominent association of women with funerary weeping.

Gisalo Molan 'Sing Gisalo Song'

Although many Kaluli say that *susulubi, sagelon, yɛgɛl,* and *sowɛgu* sing *gisalo,* a more specified set usually comes to mind, namely, the fruitdoves *muni, kalo, howɛn,* and *iyɛu,* sometimes noted as the ones that compose *(sa-molan).* These birds "originate" song in the same sense that *muni* originated song in the myth. They give song to the Kaluli, but the Kaluli themselves shape (code and perform) that which they hear. Composers hear these birds' sounds in their heads and flood their inner senses with the call until it unravels into the melody of a song. These birds give them melodic form. The intervals in their calls are the ones used in the melodies of *gisalo.*

Also included in the *sa-molan* group is *wɔkwele,* the Giant Cuckoodove (figure 12). This is the only bird that *gisalan,* dances *gisalo. Wɔkwele* makes a bobbing up and down movement. In the down position it calls *"wɔk"* and then *"wuuuu"* when it bobs up. Kaluli attribute the origin of dancing to this, and all Kaluli dancing is done with a basic up and down movement while proceeding from one end of the longhouse to the other. In ceremonies dancers wear a set of long streamers *(fasela)* in the rear of the dance costume; these shimmy about, creating a *"shhhh"* sound as they move. Kaluli liken this sound to the sound of water and compare the dancer to *wɔkwele;* the bird is usually heard calling near a waterfall, with the call being heard just above the rushing sound of the water.

Conclusion

An understanding of what birds mean for Kaluli involves a balance of the specialized knowledge of the most sophisticated naturalists in Bosavi with the less stratified cultural assumptions that underlie everyday life in the tropical forest. With minor variations, adult males generally agree that

Figure 12. *wɔkwele*—Giant Cuckoodove *(Reinwardtoena reinwardtsi)*

the avifauna of Bosavi is organized by families and by levels of family inclusion. The linguistic evidence for these organizing schemes indicates the importance of a practical and ecological orientation (dividing birds by arboreal and terrestrial habitats) as well as a morphological and behavioral focus (separating families by groupings of beaks and feet).

These schemes are not utilized for purposes of recognition or practical matters by women or youths, and among young men there is also a considerable variance in sophistication. But all these people share something with experienced hunters that is much deeper and more culturally significant, namely, a set of beliefs that organizes the interpretation of everyday living in a world that is full of birds and alive with their sounds. Myths, seasons, colors, gender, taboos, curses, spells, time, space, and naming are systematically patterned; all of these are grounded in the perception of birds, as indicated foremost by the presence of sound.

Take, for example, the ways Kaluli think about two very anomalous creatures, bats and cassowaries. Bats *(bɛlɛb)* are considered by many to be birds because they are arboreal. Kaluli will openly discuss *bɛlɛb* (which include four taxa: two for large flying foxes and fruit bats and two for tube-nosed bats and horseshoe bats) as if they were birds by noting the similarities of food taboos, the use of bat names and bat bones in magic and spells for hunting. But if asked directly "Are bats birds?", the answer is a fairly immediate "no," often followed by "It has no voice." Indeed, *bɛlɛb* sounds are always imitated instrumentally and not vocally, save when the imitation is of eating and sucking sounds. Kaluli, then, do not differentiate bats from birds primarily on the basis of meat, feathers, bodies, or ways they live and eat, that is, observable morphological or behavioral criteria. Associations with the night and with strong magic do not matter so much either. The real defining factor is the voice, or rather, the lack of it.

The contrast with the cassowaries is notable. As with bats, Kaluli give both positive and negative answers when queried about the status of the cassowary; most of them finally conclude that it is a bird because of its similarity to a well-defined group of birds and the logic that the largest member of a group gives its name to the whole group, as *uluwa* does. In both cases Kaluli resort to a fair amount of argument and logic to keep the cassowaries *in* the visual taxonomy and the bats *out* of it. At the same time, simply invoking the facts that immature cassowaries whistle and that bats have no voice settles the matter instantly. The whistled sound is taken to be hard evidence that the cassowary is indeed a bird, while the lack of a voice is taken as equally hard evidence that bats are not birds, because they lack both the natural and the metaphorical means to be true birds, despite their arboreal status.

Sound, then, is not only an alternate method for organizing bird categories but is a dominant cultural means for making sense out of the Kaluli world. Bird sounds are particularly important because they embody so much of the way Kaluli identify with their forest home and so much of their feelings about death and the reflection realm. Actively listening to birds on a day-to-day basis is a way of reckoning time, space, season, and weather. Living with birds is an extension of living by myths, maintaining the coherence of bird and human analogies that make domains like gender, beauty, color, and "turned-over words" logically patterned.

Bird sounds metaphorize Kaluli feelings and sentiments because of their intimate connection with the transition from visible to invisible in death, and invisible back to visible in spirit reflection. The four important fruitdoves, *muni, howɛn, iyɛu,* and *kalo,* are all associated with the saddest sounds of grief and abandonment, deriving from the myth "the boy who became a *muni* bird," as well as from their placement in categories of birds who weep and sing. All have descending calls with falsettolike timbre, given in Kaluli representations as three- and four-note pitch sequences, which include intervals of the descending major second and descending minor third. All are associated with texted or "inner" varieties of whistling, weeping, and song. Kaluli understand their sad sounds as having "inside" words, and when women weep or men compose songs, these same sounds and words come inside their heads. As we will now see, when Kaluli perform weeping or song, they become those very birds, and when others evaluate the moving nature of their performances, they compare the performers to them as well.

3

Weeping That Moves Women to Song

I was in Sululib village for less than one hour when I heard wailing for the first time. We were barely finished with lunch, having walked in that morning from the mission airstrip where I had arrived the previous night. In an instant Buck knew it meant that Sɛnɛso was dead. He and Bambi hurried out of the house and urged me to follow with my recording equipment. In complete disbelief, I fumbled around with keys, grabbed for wires, tapes, recorder, and microphones, and made my way to the longhouse. Somewhat dazed and hesitant, I walked in among the assembling group of mourners.

The house was about sixty feet long, thirty feet wide, and filled with some thirty-five people when I entered. It was dark and had a musty smell, but before I could even look around, my attention was drawn to Sɛnɛso's body, laid out on the floor close to the front entrance. Seated around him were six women, rocking back and forth and wailing loudly. Glancing at the other end of the house, I saw men seated along the hallway, some staring blankly into space, others lapsing back and forth into chain-reaction weeping with the women.

Nobody was really paying any attention to me and my bulky equipment, but I very self-consciously placed myself across the corridor from the women seated around the body. I knew this was the wrong place to make a good recording, but I was much too unnerved to move any closer. I began to listen closely to this language I didn't understand, to these weeping and sobbing sounds that had a distinct melody, to snatches of text from the weepers I knew must be terribly sad. A few moments later, Bambi sat down next to me, now and then whispering what the mourners were saying. My strongest impressions centered on the mixture of weeping sounds, actual wept melodies, phrases and longer texts that were semispoken, semisung while tears were being shed.

Hours later, when the initial hysteria subsided a bit and we were back together, Buck and Bambi told me about Sɛnɛso, his illness, the implications of his death, and the general funerary patterns. When they asked about my first impressions, I recalled that the weeping was rather like the sounds on the tapes from their 1966–68 fieldwork, which included several *gisalo* songs that made men weep. The weeping in both cases was tuneful, involving a melody of three or four descending pitches. Also, the vocal production was similar. The difference, it seemed, was that the funerary weeping was in a lower register and started with the wept melody being repeated over and over, with texts sometimes added. The men's weeping in response to *gisalo* was more often a loud, shrieked wail; though it was often repeated and seemed to be accompanied by tears, few texts or phrases were uttered in it. There were some points during the funerary weeping, however, where women added rather long texts, fitting them into the repeated three- or four- pitch phrase. My conjecture was based on very little exposure, but I felt that where the *gisalo* song provoked tears for men, women's funerary weeping seemed sometimes to provoke wept song. Buck confirmed that the sound of funerary weeping was similar to that of weeping in response to song, and from that moment on my work was cut out.

Why do humans shed tears as an accompaniment to emotional distress? This question has interested social and biological scientists since Darwin's *The Expression of the Emotions in Man and Animals* (1872), but not until 1959 did Ashley Montagu hypothesize that weeping was established as an adaptively valuable trait because the inability to shed tears during crying would leave infants open to increased bacterial assaults.

Beyond the evolutionary issues, the social meanings of weeping remain elusive. Psychoanalysts have stressed the interchangeability of weeping and urination, the dissipation of aggression, the resolution of ambivalent feelings, and transitions in emotional states. In ethnography the classic discussion is certainly Radcliffe-Brown's functional and Van Gennepian analysis of funerary and ceremonial weeping in the Andaman Islands (1964), where it served simultaneously as a rite of aggregation and a marker of interrupted social relations. On a larger scale, a recent cross-cultural and psychological survey (Rosenblatt, Walsh, and Jackson 1976) found that in a world sample, weeping is the most noted behavior of bereaved persons; like psychoanalysts, the authors argued that weeping has a global ritual character, functioning to minimize frustration and normatively control anger and attack.

In ethnomusicology "dirge" seems to be used generically for "mourning" music, but "mourning song," "wailing song," "funerary chant," "wailing," and "lament" are often used with little specificity for context of use or code characteristics that differentiate them from "weeping" and "song" in other senses.

For Papua New Guinea, Chenoweth (1968:417–18) specifies Managalasi "vibrato" voice as "wailing," but it is not clear whether this is an intentional vocal style or a result of physical quivering and emotion. Simon (1978) describes "laments" for the Eipo of West Irian as spontaneous, emotional, and individual, with descending vocal dynamics, yet it is unclear whether the Eipo themselves consider this behavior to be "weeping," "song," or something else. While these reports tend to consider the weeping sound patterns tangential, a more productive approach would consider just how these sounds constitute socially meaningful expressions.

Such an approach characterizes Tiwary's brief description (1975) of "tuneful weeping" as a communicative mode in northern India. Women's "wept statements" are verbal messages in weeping intonation, delivered while shedding tears. The social situations for this are specific, as when a woman marries and leaves her own village for that of her husband. On the appointed day the woman, kin, and friends tunefully weep on each others' shoulders; their wept statements have marked refrains that use appropriate address terms among the weepers.

Tiwary notes that with age one acquires skill in this mode. Tuneful weeping is also heard at visits, meetings after separation, and one particular phase of mourning. In all of these cases, the texts discuss personal relationships between weepers or memories of past times.

Although Tiwary describes the code of this tuneful weeping as an articulation of verbal form and melodic intonation performed while shedding tears, the actual processes of construction, manner of interpretation, and linguistic denomination are not described; these will be the points of departure for a description of Kaluli expressive weeping.

Terminology

One place to enter the social and semantic realms of Kaluli weeping is through the lexicon, where dimensions of contrast explicitly demarcate one general and five specific terms for patterned varieties of weeping sounds. A brief excursion into ethnographic etymology allows us to understand, in a preliminary way, the co-relations between named weeping codes and their appropriate actors and contrasts. Table 3-1 provides an overview.

Yɛlɛma

Yɛ is onomatopoeic for the sound of weeping; the verb is formed by adding this sound word to -*ɛlɛma* (from *ɛlɛ* 'like this' and *sama*, present-singular-imperative 'speak'). *Ɛlɛma* indicates 'say', and many Kaluli verbs are formed by this fusing pattern. Kaluli note a close association between the onomatopoeic *yɛ* in weeping and the bird name *iyɛu* (Ornate Fruit-dove, *Ptilinopus ornatus*). The bird's call is imitated with a long, descending, mournful *yɛ*.

Yɛlɛma is generic and is unmarked for the sound pattern of the weeping, the context in which it is produced, or the ends that will result from it. The term most commonly applies when one weeps from pain resulting from fighting, accident, anger, or fear. I often heard it used in everyday talk to refer to situations in which men had hit their wives, children had hit one another, children had gotten hurt in play, someone was ill or contemplated a disastrous event.

In all instances in which *yɛlɛma* applies generically, the form of weeping can be defined as emotional distress accompanied by tears, rapid breathing, and high or falsetto vocalizations of varying length and intensity. Kaluli take these to be instinctive physical behaviors on the part of the weeper; in this *yɛlɛma* contrasts with five marked terms that denote behavior accorded a more explicit symbolic status due to sound pattern and associated specific intentions.

Gana-yɛlɛma

Gana is generic onomatopoeia for "sound"; *ganalɛma* (= *gana* plus *ɛlɛma*) is the common verb for 'sound'. *Gana-yɛlɛma* indicates a loud, breathy weeping with falsetto voice quality and a descending melodic contour. When fully elaborated to three or four pitches, this contour is identical to the call notes of the *muni* bird (Beautiful Fruitdove, *Ptilinopus pulchellus*).

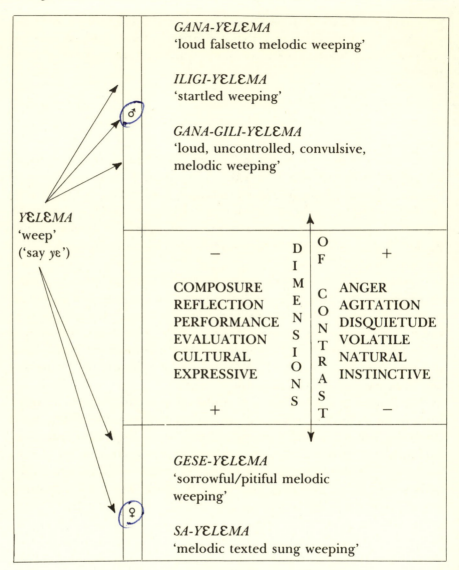

Table 3–1. Weeping terminology and contrasts

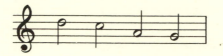

Gana seems to mark the loudness of the wailing as well as the fruitdove quality. This term contrasts with two others that also apply to the onset of weeping in settings of shock and intense emotional distress.

Iligi-yɛlɛma

Iligi is the root of the verb 'be startled' or 'be shocked'. This "shocked-weeping" term has much the same sense as the English phrase, "to get choked up." All of a sudden there is that quick transition—lump in the throat, change of facial expression, tensing of shoulders and body generally—and tears begin to flow. "Startled weeping" does not imply a melodic shape, but rather the shock turning into weeping in which one makes choking and out-of-breath sounds. Kaluli say this is different from the cries of one who has been hurt; *yɛlɛma* always has high vocalizations, though not necessarily ones that are shrill or shrieking.

Gana-gili-yɛlɛma

Gana, as above, is generic onomatopoeia for 'sound', and *gili* is specific onomatopoeia for sounds of rumbling. As a verb, *gililɛma* (*gili* plus *ɛlɛma*) indicates the sound of the earth rumbling or the sound of the house floor shaking under the weight of loud human movement, such as in ceremonies or altercations. Together the two form the verb *gana-gili-lɛma*, which specifies 'thunder' (loud sound plus rumble).

In the domain of weeping, the *gana* and *gili* prefixes convey much the same sense. *Gana-gili-yɛlɛma* is a loud wailing substantially like *gana-yɛlɛma*, except that the weeper's body is shaking and convulsing. The voice quivers more, and the melody contour sounds more shrieked than wept. Kaluli always indicate that this kind of weeping moves others to put their arms around the weeper in order to help him or her regain composure.

Kaluli tend to group these three forms of weeping (*gana-yɛlɛma*, *iligi-yɛlɛma*, and *gana-gili-yɛlɛma*) together because they share basic features that contrast with the two other forms. All three typify male weeping; they are immediate responses that usually are not continuous but turn on and off. Common to all three is a lack of control, a projection of disquietude, a sense of being at the edge of anger and volatile behavior. None is marked by composure, thus contrasting naturally with the two kinds of elaborate, reflective, performed, female weeping containing short or long texts.

Gese-yɛlɛma

Gese is the root of *gesema* 'make one feel sorrow or pity', a verb used in three clear contexts: children, birds, and sound terminology. When children feel denied and turn aside, speaking in a sad, singsong, whining manner, it "makes one feel sorrow or pity." The verb marks both the sad intonation of voice and the evocation of response. When one hears the call of fruitdoves, the high voice and descending intonation is associated with the evocation of sorrow, and the birds are thus said to *gese-ganalab* 'sound evoking sorrow'. Finally, for singing, speaking, whistling, or weeping, *gese* can prefix the usual verb to indicate that the sound has descending intonation and evokes sadness.

Gese-yɛlɛma is a pitiful-sorrowful weeping that is particularly common when women weep to mourn children. Kaluli say the sound is like that of a small fruitdove, that is, like a dead child. The form of the weeping uses the entire *muni* bird call melodic shape but does so in a slurred way, so that the pitches almost run together. It is a whining type of weeping, with both melody and text somewhat indistinctly articulated. In it others say they hear the voice of a dead child or bird and that this is profoundly moving.

This kind of weeping, like the next, is substantially different from the others mentioned because it is considered a controlled performance by the weeper. One therefore comments upon it in an evaluative manner, comparing the weeper's voice to that of an appropriate fruitdove.

Sa-yɛlɛma

Sa-yɛlɛma is the most melodically and textually elaborate form of weeping, and it is also the most moving human sound expression in Bosavi because it is the closest sound to "being a bird." *Sa-yɛlɛma* is a melodic-sung-texted weeping. Following the myth "The boy who became a *muni* bird," it is considered the original sound form expressive of the sad state of loss and abandonment that is beyond the resources of talk. In the myth, the final sung-wept-textual-poetic form is similar to what Bosavi people practice and name *sa-yɛlɛma*.

Sa is the generic term for waterfall; kinds of waterfalls and waterway parts are all prefixed by *sa*. These terms (which are discussed in more detail in chapters 4 and 5 in sections on poetics and music terminology) are polysemous from the semantic field of water to the domain of sound-making. *Sa* is also in the sound semantic field as a prefix for verbs; one can *sa*-weep, -sing, -whistle, -sound. In these cases *sa* indicates a "down and in," "tucking under," "moving inside," motion like that of a water-fall. There is an "inside" to the outer melody, namely, its text. These *sa*-prefixed verbs uniformly indicate a change from pure sound to sound plus text; there are "words in mind," or some kind of aligning "inner" words with "outer" sound. *Sa-yɛlɛma* is a melodic weeping, with the *muni* bird call symbol as its melodic shape; to this is fitted a spontaneous, improvised text, thus elaborating a sung-texted-melodic weeping.

To review: the first contrast is between the generic *yɛlɛma* and the specific prefixed forms, which involves a Kaluli distinction between physical (unmarked) and expressive (marked). On the next level, the five marked forms cluster into two groups: three are considered typically male forms, two are more typically female. The basic dimensions of contrast between these two sets are degree of control, addition of text, and the more specific Kaluli sense of "instinctive" versus "symbolic." In this dimension the first set is unmarked for evaluative commentary, while the second set is marked. Finally, there is a noted relationship between the most general male weeping—*gana-yɛlɛma*—and the most elaborate fe-male weeping—*sa-yɛlɛma*—that relates to the myth "The boy who became a *muni* bird." In both the myth and in Kaluli performance practice, *gana-yɛlɛma* represents the short-out-of-control-hysterical-sad bird voice and *sa-yɛlɛma* the controlled-sorrowful-reflective bird voice. Kaluli use these two poles to caricature male and female expressive weeping.

Settings, Participants, and Styles

There are two settings in which one hears expressive weeping in Bosavi; the first includes ceremonies and seances and the second mourning and funerary events (see table 3-2). Ceremonies and seances feature male weeping in response to performed drumming and song. Ceremonial weeping is generally not extensive and frequently is a prelude to burning, as retribution for the song having moved a listener to tears. The weeping itself sounds out of control, and there is little, if any, text. In seances there

is a greater potential for embedded texts, as one may weep during and
after the song, and there is no burning of the performing spirit medium.
In these two settings the weeping is a response to sorrow provoked by
staged performances.

Contrasting settings are formed around weeping as a response to
loss, provoked by situations of profound anguish. These include funerary
mourning and other occasions of abandonment and fear (a house burning down, people leaving the area, disruption of families, potential loss
or death). While the nature of loss may seem less severe in events other
than actual death, the kind of weeping provoked is potentially the same.
This group of mourning and loss contexts brings forth the most elaborate
forms of weeping, controlled performances with extended texts, produced by women.

To summarize, there is a patterned relationship between the forms
of weeping and the situations in which they occur, marked by a set of
contrasts:

male	:	female
gana-, iligi-, gana-gili-weeping	:	*gese-, sa*-weeping
provoked by song	:	provoked by loss
ceremony/seance	:	mourning/loss
"natural"	:	performance marked
"natural"	:	aesthetically evaluated
angry-volatile	:	reflective-composed
little if any text	:	extended text
mythic/*muni* initial cry	:	mythic/*muni* sung weeping

I will say no more here about weeping in ceremony or seance contexts as these are treated in chapter 5, which discusses the male domain
of song and *gisalo* performance. The remainder of this chapter will con-
centrate on mourning contexts and on the performance styles of
women.

Mourning and the Funerary Setting

In 1968 the Australian colonial government made it law that Papua New
Guineans bury their dead. I, therefore, never saw a traditional Bosavi
funeral and mourning, but E. Schieffelin did. In his ethnography he writes
(1976:158–59):

	Song	*Mourning*
CONTEXT AND SETTINGS	ceremonies and spirit medium seances preplanned and staged at night in the longhouse	funerals and occasions of personal loss occur spontaneously and naturally
ACTORS	staged by and featuring men; women attend as audience and may equally be moved to weep	mostly women but men also participate, although they do not perform elaborate weeping.
CODE FEATURES	 little if any text falsetto shrieking short lack of control	 texted usual vocal register melodic/tuneful elongated controlled
NAMED VARIANTS	*gana-yɛlɛma* *iligi-yɛlɛma* *gana-gili-yɛlɛma*	*gese-yɛlɛma* *sa-yɛlɛma*
MYTHIC REPRESENTATION	initial loud and wailing cry of the boy who became a *muni* bird	controlled and texted cry of the boy who became a *muni* bird

Table 3–2. Expressive weeping

Formerly when a person died, the closest relatives were supposed
to strip the body completely of ornaments and clothes and, covering
the pubic area, suspend the body in cane loops from a pole that was
hung near the front of the longhouse by the women's section. A
smoky fire was lit at the head and the foot, "to keep down the stink,"
and a shallow bark basin was put under the suspended body in case
it dripped. During the following days, friends and relatives from
other house groups would come to mourn and view it. After about
a week, the corpse was carried out of the house and placed in a raised
structure called a *kalu ɔidɔ* a short distance from the house, where
it was left to decompose. When the bones were dry, they were put
in a net bag and hung up under the eaves of the *aa* ['longhouse']
over the front veranda as mementos.

Today the body is not placed in cane loops but laid on the floor of
the longhouse at the front end, near the women's section. In the aftermath of a death, women cluster around the body and weep, and men stay
in the rear portions of the house around their sleeping platforms and
socializing areas. (For diagrams of the Kaluli longhouse, see ibid.:33, 36.)
When visitors from other communities come to mourn, they enter the
house and split up, men going to the men's section and women clustering
with other women in the front hallway around the body.

Since 1971 a Christian sector has been developing in Bosavi. Depending on the extent of Christian influence in a longhouse community
and whether or not the deceased was or aspired to be a Christian, the
body will spend more or less time exposed in the house before burial.[1]
At the funerals I witnessed in 1976 and 1977, the body was in viewing
with traditional mourning weeping for one to one-and-a-half days after
the death, at which point there was a burial.

During this viewing and mourning, men stay in the rear of the house,
usually withdrawn and somber. Occasionally one bursts into loud *gana-
yɛlab* weeping, which may set off a chain reaction. Women who were close
to the deceased sit around the body, weeping quietly or loudly.

Sometimes a single woman will start a *gese-* or *sa-yɛlab,* which may go
on for five or ten minutes. This may set off others, and I have heard as
many as three women simultaneously *sa-yɛlab,* with staggered entrances,
continual overlapping, and completely independent texts. The form is
personal and individual, and the *sa-yɛlab* is equally common as a solo or

1. Christians prefer to get the body into the ground quickly and have generally
adopted the Australian missionary concept (which is not really a Christian concept) that
weeping indicates weakness and undue emotionalism. The Bosavi construction of the ideal
Christian is discussed in E. Schieffelin 1978.

multiple-voice form. Just as the *sa-yɛlab* of different women are independent of each other, they are, as a whole, independent of the men's weeping. Sometimes a *sa-yɛlab* will start off a chain of men to weeping; other
times men will just sit and listen to the women or withdraw. As the women
weep, they rock back and forth slightly, keeping their hands folded or
placed on their thighs. They do not attempt to wipe tears from their eyes
or otherwise restrain the actual flow of tears. Throughout the period that
they weep, others may comfort them and bring them food. The women
closest to the body of the deceased usually have handfuls of long plant
leaves, which they use to fan flies away from the body.

When a death is discovered, local people gather in the longhouse,
and the first hour or so is marked by a great deal of uncontrolled *gana-*,
iligi-, and *gana-gili-yɛlab*. At the same time, people are dispatched to go
off and take the news to other longhouse communities, and within a few
hours, friends and relatives begin to arrive.

The visitors walk slowly through the courtyard and enter the front
of the house. Women choke up immediately upon sight of the body laid
out in the center of their mourning friends and kin. They break out in
gana-, *iligi-*, and then perhaps *gana-gili-yɛlab* and sit down among the other
women. Men enter and quite frequently stop in their tracks, tense up,
bring their forearms across their faces, and make a very loud but short
gana-yɛlab. If closely related to the deceased, this may turn into *gana-gili-
yɛlab*, in which case other men will come from the rear of the house and
help the new mourner gain some composure, after which he will be taken
to the men's section. Sometimes, a man will sit down and weep for a
moment among the women and then stop suddenly, quickly rise, and go
off to join the other men.

Each time a new wave of visiting mourners arrives, there is a new
burst of weeping. The weeping tends to die down after thirty or forty-five
minutes, at which time food is usually brought out and served. By the end
of the arrivals, there may be as many as 125 people in the longhouse day
or night, with the possibility that weeping might begin at any moment.

All forms of weeping are evident in the aftermath of these events. At
the actual burial, and around the longhouse area generally, men may be
prone to burst into a short *gana-yɛlab*. Two weeks after a death, I heard
the deceased's "sister" do a rather long *sa-yɛlab* sitting on her porch with
just her husband nearby. People remarked that sometimes the thought
of a dead person just flashed through their minds and provoked weeping
(*gana-* for the men, *gese-* or *sa-* for the women). In the first few weeks after
a death, this is frequent: the sight of a garden where one once planted

with the deceased, the sight of the children of the deceased, the undertaking of an activity without the deceased, even the sight of the place where the deceased slept in the house may trigger weeping.

As time passes, the *sa-*weeping becomes shorter and less elaborate. As one woman told me, it is when you are with others, sitting around the body, that you think about all of the things you shared with the deceased. Later, it is specific things you are reminded of as you go about daily life without this person. Whereas these reminders may provoke women to short *sa-yɛlab,* the same images provoke men to either *gana-yɛlab,* or may simply bring tears to their eyes. There is always an instant change in the person that produces a quick run of tears and rapid breathing and choking sounds.

The response is precisely the same for other occasions of loss. In September 1976, a house belonging to Gaso and Ofea burned down at Sululib. When they returned to the site and saw the house leveled, they both broke into *gana-* and *iligi-*weeping. At the location, Gaso continued with intermittent bursts of *gana-*weeping, occasionally elaborated by the addition of three- and four-word texts in the middle of the descending melody. Ofea, after gaining some composure, wept a very long *sa-yɛlab,* whose text discussed how nobody liked Gaso, how they should have taken her things out of the house before burning it (implicating arson), how she had doused the embers of the fireboxes before leaving, and how the belongings of her deceased son were in the house when it burned. Gaso's few texts were about losing his wealth and about his deceased son.

In October 1976, it became known that Degelɔ and Osolowa of Sululib and their children would be leaving the area. Degelɔ aspired to be a pastor, and the missionary had placed him in a Bible school in Lae. That night and during the following days, both early at night and in the dawn hours, there was *gana-* and slight text-elaborated *yɛlab* from Kiliyɛ, Osolowa's father, a very traditional elder of Sululib. On the morning of the departure of the family to the Bosavi airstrip, Kiliyɛ's wife Suela (though not Osolowa's real mother) stood at the village edge and as people passed by wept a long *sa-yɛlab* bemoaning the loss to her and to her husband. There was not much other weeping surrounding this occasion because Degelɔ told people that it was un-Christian to weep, and that he did not want to hear it.[2]

2. When a local pastor returned to Bible school, he left early in the morning because he did not want people to see him and weep over his departure.

In January 1977, Buck and I were visiting the longhouse community of Asɔndɔ, west of Sululib. On arrival we were discussing the Highlands plume trader who had just been to Bosavi and hired local men with shotguns as hunters. Birds of paradise, the Goura Pigeon, and Pesquet's Parrot are outlawed to hunters with nontraditional weapons by Papua New Guinea law. It turned out that after leaving Bosavi, the plume trader had been met by police and severely fined; at the same time, word came back to Bosavi that a plane was coming in for Daibo, a man from Olabia longhouse, to take him to a government post for questioning. Daibo had been the main hunter employed by the plume trader. All of this was greatly interesting to Sogobaye, an Asɔndɔ man with a shotgun and a hunter of prowess. In addition to his own fears about potential trouble with the law, Daibo was the brother of Famu, one of Sogobaye's wives.

That night we heard a woman burst into *sa-yɛlab* in the longhouse. It was Famu, and the text of her weeping concerned the possibility that Daibo would be taken and never come back, that he would be placed in jail and starve, and that she might never see him again. The weeping continued for about five minutes and then stopped abruptly.

In these three instances the *sa-yɛlab* weeping was patterned as in mourning, providing a format for stylized expression of fears of actual or potential loss and abandonment, both personal and material. The less prominent male variant in these settings was *gana*-weeping with occasional addition of short, repetitious texts. The women did *sa-yɛlab*, with lengthy elaborated texts commenting on the nature of the loss, as well as past shared experiences. In these last examples, only the immediately affected persons wept; at funerals there are always at least five or six women who perform extended *sa-yɛlab*. In all cases, it is older persons who do the most elaborate *sa*-weeping; younger women weep with shorter texts that are highly repetitive.

Form and Performance Codes

Musically, the tonal system of all *sa-yɛlab* includes four pitches in the relation of D-C-A-G;[3] the total range is a fifth, and the intervals employed are major second and minor third. The tonal center is the lowest pitch.

3. These are not actual pitches. All transcriptions have been transposed to treble clef with tonal center of G in order to facilitate comparison and easy reading.

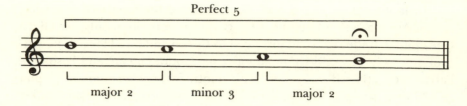

Melodic contours are always descending; there is little or no ascent at all in this mode.

Sa-yɛlab are basically monophonic and solo; however, two, three, or four separate *sa-yɛlab* may occur simultaneously, producing a dense polyphony that sounds like same or similar melodies begun at staggered times (canonic counterpoint) or one larger piece performed by segmented and conjoined parts (hocket). Since each *sa-yɛlab* is improvised, the sense in which the form is iterative, with a repeated formula throughout, is limited. Some *sa-yɛlab* are short and simple, however, producing the effect of iterative form or litany. The resultant polyphonies of several simultaneous *sa-yɛlab* always sound more dense and complex than the parts, because the weepers usually do not start on the same pitch.

The manner of singing is breathy. Though set within a normal vocal register, the choking sounds and slight vibrato add to the generally open timbre. Despite the breathiness, shaky quality, and rapidity of textual delivery, the verbal message seems clear to the audience. Also the pitches are generally clear and distinct, save in long portions of rapid text where they flatten and dearticulate melodically.

Overall, the form is syllabic, with distinct syllable enunciations on pulses, and parlando-rubato, with the text leading the tempo. While there is much variation because of the spontaneous and improvised character of the performances, it would not be fair to say *sa-yɛlab* are free rhythm, chant, or recitative, as the overall pacing tends to be even from start to finish.

Kaluli themselves have a clearly articulated notion of pacing, which is a good starting place for a description of the temporal aspects of *sa-yɛlab*. For the pacing of both song and *sa-yɛlab*, Kaluli use the terms *hɛsa* 'gentle', 'even', 'smooth', and *dinafa* 'careful'. The notion of a controlled and even performance is important in *sa-yɛlab*.

I performed the following simple experiment to test the sense in which *hɛsa* and *dinafa* had standard timing equivalents. I asked ten Kaluli, five men and five women, to sing imitations of the *sa-yɛlab* birds, the fruitdoves. All spontaneously chose the melodic phrase below and paced delivery so that it took between seven and eight seconds to sing.

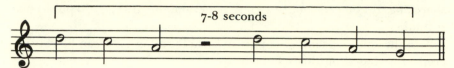

They all said that this was *hɛsa.* I then asked them to imitate *sa-yɛlab* phrases with a text including only kin terms, reciprocal food terms *(wi ɛlɛdo),* or personal names, that is, to imitate the most simple forms of *sa-yɛlab.* All used the same melody and constructed the phrases by subdividing pitch values into groups of two, three, or four. But the overall sung phrase also lasted seven to eight seconds. Hence, it was clear that there was a timing notion that subdivided the time values for a phrase so that the overall length would always be the same, no matter how much textual information was fit inside. For example, every ♩ could be evenly divided for words or phrases of two, three, or four syllables (a), or divided with unequal time values for two, three, or four syllables (b).

This and other experimental and observational material give the sense that the Kaluli concept of *hɛsa* denotes pacing correlated with a culturally shared metronome of about 120 pulses per minute, that is, two pulses per second.

In the simplest sense, the phrase form for all *sa-yɛlab* can be considered to be based on this schematic:

The initial pitch has stress; there is a breath at the rest; the next pitch also receives stress; and the final pitch is drawn out as the weeper runs out of breath.

The expansion of this contour by subdividing pitch values is the major process involved in creating sung-texted weeping. This takes two forms, the first of which is common to both men (in response to *gisalo* song or mourning) and women (who are generally younger and less experienced at *sa*-weeping). A text is inserted in the middle of the phrase. This is precisely the form found in the *muni* bird myth. The texts are short, usually two or three words—personal names, kin terms, reciprocal food terms *(wi ɛlɛdo),* or place names *(hen wi).*

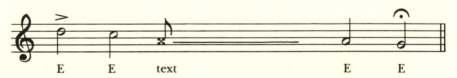

The second form is the basis for *sa-yɛlab* in the elaborated manner, with considerable text. Each pulse expands to two, three, or four syllables, thus covering all the possibilities of text employing personal names, kin terms, and *wi ɛlɛdo.* Only these three kinds of words are used in the initial expansion of the wept melody into a sung-texted-weeping. A table of common permutations follows.

The texts have terms of kin, like *dowo, nɔwo, nosɔk,* 'father', 'mother', 'cross-cousin', and so forth, optionally preceded by *ni* 'my'; these all pattern out to two, three, or four syllables, as does the less common use of personal name terms and *wi ɛlɛdo.* To give a single

example from an actual texted weeping, A3 plus B2 plus C4 plus D2 would create:

In this example, the kin term *nosɔk* 'cross-cousin' is transformed phonologically to *nosɔ* and *nosɔgo*.

These are the basic phrase forms in *sa-yɛlab*. The texts are limited to certain kinds of words, and the melodies only expand by multiplying values for their pitches.

With this definition of the base form and its most simple elaboration, the next question is how a phrase is further expanded so that more elaborate text can be used. This expansion is accomplished by conjoining and embedding. In the text to be analyzed shortly, there are thirty-four phrases in six minutes forty-five seconds. Each one has up to three or four embedded subportions, generally found in the place marked C on the permutation chart; these are conjoined one after the other, in forms like

$$[\ A + B\ ] + \begin{bmatrix} C^1 \\ to \\ C^x \end{bmatrix} + [\ D\ ] \qquad \text{or} \qquad [\ A + B\ ] + \begin{bmatrix} C^1 + D^1 \\ to \\ C^x + D^x \end{bmatrix}$$

Figure 13. Phrase elaboration in *sa-yɛlab*

such that either the C portion or the C plus D portion repeat with variations. Most phrases run from eight to eighteen seconds; other formulaic phrases, such as reductions that use only A and B, also appear occasionally, which accounts for the few occurrences of four- and five-second phrases.

Several relevant linguistic features characterize the language used in *sa-yɛlab*. In Kaluli there are two word orders: agent-object-verb (AOV) and object-agent-verb (OAV). OAV focuses the agent, which takes an obligatory case marker postpositioned on the noun. AOV does not emphasize the agent and does not require an ergative case marker (B. Schieffelin 1981). AOV is found in narrative, descriptive speech, while OAV is found in speech where there is a need to emphasize the agent; as might be suspected, this is frequently found in family speech.

In *sa-*weeping only OAV is found, which emphasizes the way the texts focus the personal experience and point of view of the weeper. This emphasis focusing is also marked by emphatic pronouns like *nain* 'just us two', or *ninɛli* 'I by myself', as well as by double pronouns like *ne ninɛli* 'I, really, just I'. *Giyɔ* 'as for you', and *niyɔ* 'as for me', are sometimes left dislocated for further emphasis.

Another difference between *sa-yɛlab* and conversational speech is in the use of aspect. In ordinary talk, speakers use tense in order to focus immediate foregrounded information. In *sa-yɛlab,* where the personal eulogy recounts past experiences, there is more reporting and backgrounded information, hence, a greater usage of durative aspect markers, like habitual pasts.

Formulaic phrases also differentiate *sa-yɛlab* from speech. These are all of the same form, and they are unique only in that they include no verb.

$$\begin{bmatrix} \text{personal name} \\ \text{kin term} \\ wi\ \varepsilon l\varepsilon do \end{bmatrix} + \begin{matrix} nani \\ \text{'us two'} \end{matrix} + \begin{matrix} hen\ wi \\ \text{place name} \\ \text{(land, garden, river)} \end{matrix}$$

At the funeral for her husband, Sɛnɛso, Madua frequently *sa*-wept, *Sɛnɛso-wo, nani Diligasa-yo.* Diligasa is the name of a sago area near Sululib village; it was the last place that Madua had beat sago with Sɛnɛso present. The phrase means 'Sɛnɛso, you and I were together at Diligasa'.

Sa-yɛlab texts frequently use a question form with the end marking *-ili;* for example, *Ge oba ane-ili?* The *-ili* does more than make the phrase a rhetorical question; it adds the sense of "I'm wondering." In *sa-yɛlab* the weeper is addressing a dead person and asking "I'm wondering where you've gone?", "I'm wondering if you've gone to X?" In practice one would not "wonder" to the addressee in any other speech situation. *-Ili* is never found this way in daily speech; one wonders about something or someone to another party and not to the thing or one being wondered about. In *sa-yɛlab* this form is grammatical and appropriate because the dead person is there in physical substance but elsewhere in spirit, in the form of a bird.

Wept texts, nevertheless, are framed in linguistic codes generally similar to everyday talk, what the Kaluli call *to halaido* 'hard words'. In this feature they are distinct from the special poetic codes that characterize the language of song. *Sa-yɛlab* texts use the same expressives as ordinary discourse, no more contractions, and follow the same convention of using OAV word order to focus the agent. The lines are often enhanced by pronominal usages and by the emphatic particle *-kɛ* postpositioned on verbs. The choked-up and breathy manner of singing while weeping creates some shrinkage of the vowel space, but Kaluli do not attach aesthetic intent or interpretation to vowel lowering or breathiness of delivery. Rapidity of speech in *sa-yɛlab* also tends to centralize vowels, but does so no more than fast conversational speech. To summarize, then, despite certain special linguistic features of the *sa-yɛlab* texts, it is the substance of the speech and the evenness of performance in an overall sense that Kaluli find moving, rather than special linguistic resources or the sound shape of the wept-sung-text.

Turning to the substance of the texts, the first phrases heard after one has discovered a death are all short and reflect astonishment: "Wake up," "Don't trick us," "You never slept like this before," "Go sleep on your own bed." At the same time, other short forms conjoining a personal name with a *wi ɛlɛdo,* a reciprocal food term used as a term of affection, are common; Madua continually wept *Sɛnɛso-wo ni ogayo* 'Sɛnɛso, my pandanus', for her husband. Also one might weep phrases of the "you and I were together at X" formula here.

Sa-yɛlab recount personal and specific aspects of the relation between weeper and deceased; they do not, as in Western eulogy, list virtues and social achievements but focus on how much the weeper shared with the deceased in life. The performance of *sa-yɛlab,* then, communicates the weeper's sadness over the loss of the deceased and invites others to feel sorry for her loss.

Other initial texts have more complex forms: "You were just eating," "You're not an old man," "Wake up, don't trick us this way," "Don't sleep like this, get up and go to your own bed" are all fairly common. These generally go with the rhetorical "wondering" question: "I'm wondering if we will be together again," "I'm wondering if you have gone to X's place," or "I'm wondering if you're tricking me." With close kin or relatives, there is even a more pointed set: "How will I weed the gardens alone?", "What will happen to the children?", "How can I raise a family without you?"

The most elaborated texts, however, are more suggestive and go beyond formulaic phrases, expressions of shock, and rhetorical questions. These texts are *bali to* 'turned-over words' and have a *hega* 'underneath', or underlying meaning. The phrases wept in *bali to* generally speculate about the cause of death and the responsible witch, because all death in Bosavi is believed to be the result of witchcraft (see E. Schieffelin 1976:101–2 for details of the Kaluli concepts of *sei* 'witch' and *sei* attack).

At the mourning for Sɛnɛso, Madua wept about how *yan* fish bones had gotten caught in Sɛnɛso's throat. This is a *bali to* image for a *sei* attack. Later Madua wept, "You are a *mahi,*" the *hega* being that like a *mahi* 'bandicoot', a *sei* had trapped and killed Sɛnɛso. Others wept, "You didn't have a good knee"; this was less a comment about Sɛnɛso's lameness than a suggestion that a *sei* first took his knee, then his life.

At the funeral for Bibiali at Asɔndɔ, several texts mentioned the fact that Bibiali's son Beli often had arguments with him; phrases like "If you had a son. . . ." and "Your son is a *bol* tree" are used in *bali to* to mean that lack of solidarity and family strength are debilitating and make one more vulnerable to *sei* attack. Common *bali to* imagery likens useless or angry people to *bol* trees, which stand alone at the village edge. Similarly, at Sɛnɛso's funeral, several weepers mentioned that all the trees in a line were cut down: "Will they grow again?" Sɛnɛso was the last of three brothers to die; one brother left a very young son when he died, and Sɛnɛso had no sons, which only left Hasili, the son of the third brother as the remaining adult male in the line.

I will conclude with a few notes about the performance context and its effect on the form of *sa-yɛlab*. As a general rule, women are more quiet than talkative when sitting around the body of the deceased. When they do talk, it is not about the same things that they *sa*-weep, nor are their texts first formed or uttered verbally and then sung-wept. There is no "warm-up" of this sort. *Sa-yɛlab* turns on and off, and the weepers consider it spontaneous and improvised; thus they make no attempt to "take turns," structure performance, or constrain or encourage simultaneous performances.

A Case Study of Sa-yɛlab

On November 12, 1976, I was awakened by sounds of *gana-yɛlab* coming from Baseo's house, situated at the edge of Sululib. Gulambo and his wife, Gania, were weeping. They had been staying with Baseo and his family for about one month, because their own house had burned down; Gulambo was in the process of building a new small house close-by. The cause of the weeping was the death of Gulambo's *babo* 'mother's brother',[4] Bibiali, at Asɔndɔ, the new longhouse site of people from clan Wabisi who had formerly lived at Tabili. Bibiali was somewhat of a loner and had been at Sululib visiting Gulambo during the previous week. He spent a good deal of his time away from the longhouse, either visiting with Gulambo at Sululib or visiting Olabia (the ground name of a long-house of clan Didesa); both of these places were within a few hours walk of Asɔndɔ. When he was on his home lands, he frequently stayed away from the communal longhouse, living in a small garden house he had built near the waterfall of the Salo creek.

Before I had even found out this much information about Bibiali, Gulambo and Gania and a small group were getting ready to go to Asɔndɔ for the mourning and burial. I went with them, and we arrived after a two-and-a-half-hour trek at noon. Mourners were coming from Olabia as well, and by afternoon there were 125 people in the longhouse. Between noon and 3:00 P.M. I recorded three long *sa-yɛlab*, one with three

---

4. Gulambo's mother, from clan Wabisi, called Bibiali *ao* 'brother', hence Bibiali was 'mother's brother' *(babo)* to Gulambo. A man's *babo* is an important figure in his life.

simultaneous parts, another with two simultaneous parts, and a third that
was solo. I have chosen this solo *sa-yɛlab,* performed by Hane *sulɔ* (elder
Hane), for discussion here. A musical and linguistic transcription of the
entire *sa-yɛlab* follows, after which there is a textual translation and map
of the place names cited in the text.

Transcription: Sa-yɛlɔ by Hane sulɔ for Bibiali of Asɔndɔ
The original pitches are

For clarity and comparison the transcription is raised an augmented fifth
(eight semitones). For each of the thirty-four sections, a total time in
seconds is given below the phrase number. Time in seconds for each
phrase is given at the beginning of the phrase.
Phrase divisions are marked by ⦙.
Breath divisions are marked by '.
♩ marks semispoken, semisung pitches that are often rapid and melodically dearticulated plus or minus a semitone.
– linking syllables indicates a single or complex lexeme that would normally be written (except in a morpheme-by-morpheme gloss) as one word.
The approximate metronome marking is 120 pulses per minute (♩ = 120,
M.M.)

(1) Cross-cousin,

Cross-cousin, you and I were together at Sɔdim, cross-cousin,

Cross-cousin, you and I left Sɔdim and came here to stay, cross-cousin.

(2) Cross-cousin, cross-cousin,

Cross-cousin, you and I were together at Hansowei, cross-cousin,

Cross-cousin, "Always look up to the top branches of an *odag* tree," you say it like that to me, cross-cousin.

(3) Cross-cousin, cross-cousin, cross-cousin,

Cross-cousin, Beli was always angry with you cross-cousin,
Cross-cousin, Beli really won't feel sorrow, cross-cousin.
(4) Cross-cousin, cross-cousin, cross-cousin,
   Cross-cousin, I hadn't been to your place at Abokini,
   Cross-cousin, "While you were coming then I came too," that's
   what you always said.
(5) Cross-cousin,
   Cross-cousin, I hadn't been to your place at Walabe, cross-
   cousin,
   Cross-cousin, "I'll follow your tracks," that's what you always
   said,
   Cross-cousin, I never thought I'd see this happen.
(6) Cross-cousin,
   Cross-cousin, you and I were together at Misini,
   cross-cousin,
   Cross-cousin, you and I were together at Ukani, cross-cousin.
(7) Cross-cousin,
   Cross-cousin, Siyowa will be startled this afternoon, cross-
   cousin, cross-cousin,
   Cross-cousin, having come by Misini, he will soon come, cross-
   cousin, cross-cousin.
(8) Cross-cousin,
   Cross-cousin, you and I were together at the bank of Sago
   creek,
   Cross-cousin, we were together by the dead trunk of a *wɛ* tree
   there, cross-cousin, cross-cousin.
(9) Cross-cousin,
   cross-cousin, I'm wondering if you've gone to Olabia, cross-
   cousin,
   Cross-cousin, I'm wondering if you've gone to Duda's father's
   place, cross-cousin,
   Cross-cousin, I'm wondering if you've gone to Gania's husband's place, cross-cousin, cross-cousin.
(10) Cross-cousin,
   Cross-cousin, you and I were together at Yɔlisono,
   Cross-cousin, you and I were together at the Salo waterfall,
   cross-cousin.
(11) Cross-cousin,
   Cross-cousin,

Cross-cousin,
Cross-cousin.
(12) Cross-cousin,
Cross-cousin, you and I were together at the source of the Abo
creek; go sleep beneath the bush pandanus leaves;
Cross-cousin, the bush pandanus leaves at Abolib,
Cross-cousin, go sleep beneath the bush pandanus leaves
at Ukani, cross-cousin.
(13) Cross-cousin,
Cross-cousin, you and I were together at the bank of Sao creek,
Cross-cousin, "Always look up to the top branches of a *wab*
tree; I'm going that way"—you say it to me like that,
Cross-cousin, "While you look through an opening into the
women's section"—you say it to me like that—"tears will
secretly flow there"—you say it to me like that.
(14) Cross-cousin, cross-cousin, cross-cousin,
Cross-cousin, you and I were together at Suliyamo, cross-
cousin,
Cross-cousin, you and I were together at the Ya waterfall, cross-
cousin, cross-cousin.
(15) Cross-cousin, cross-cousin, cross-cousin,
Cross-cousin, you never spoke angrily, cross-cousin,
Cross-cousin, you always did things yourself, cross-cousin,
cross-cousin.
(16) Cross-cousin,
Cross-cousin, having left, I'm wondering if you've gone to
Gulambo's place,
Cross-cousin, go cross the Kalasɔk creek, cross-cousin,
Cross-cousin, having left, go along Misini, cross-cousin,
Cross-cousin, having left, I'm wondering if you've gone to your
son's place, cross-cousin, cross-cousin.
(17) Cross-cousin,
Cross-cousin, you and I were together at the Salo waterfall,
Cross-cousin, you and I were together at Yɛbisa, cross-cousin.
(18) Cross-cousin,
Cross-cousin, you and I were together at Yɔlisono, cross-
cousin,
Cross-cousin, "Always look over there toward Yɔlisono," you
say like that to me, cross-cousin, cross-cousin.

(19) Cross-cousin, cross-cousin, cross-cousin,

Cross-cousin, "You haven't been to my place by Abo creek,"
you told me,

Cross-cousin, I haven't seen your place at Dɔke, cross-cousin,
cross-cousin.

(20) Cross-cousin, cross-cousin,

Cross-cousin, I'm wondering if you're going down to the roots
of a *bol* tree, cross-cousin,

Cross-cousin, I'm wondering if we'll go to Abolib together,
cross-cousin,

Cross-cousin, I'm wondering if we'll go to Ukani together,
cross-cousin, cross-cousin.

(21) Cross-cousin, cross-cousin,

Cross-cousin, "You will always weep at Hansowei," you say like
that to me,

Cross-cousin, "You will always weep while looking up to
Mulusi," you say like that to me,

Cross-cousin, you hadn't been coming to Asɔndɔ, cross-cousin,
cross-cousin.

(22) Cross-cousin,

Cross-cousin, you and I were together at Yɛbisa,

Cross-cousin, you and I were together at Walilo, cross-cousin,

Cross-cousin, "Always look over there toward Walilo," you
say like that to me, cross-cousin,

Cross-cousin, you hadn't been staying at a high place before,
cross-cousin, cross-cousin.

(23) Cross-cousin,

Cross-cousin, you really never slept like this before, sleeping in
front of people's eyes, cross-cousin,

Cross-cousin, go sleep on the end bed, cross-cousin,

Cross-cousin, your brother sleeps on the top bed,

Cross-cousin, while Diwa sleeps on the top bed, you go sleep
on your son's bed.

(24) Cross-cousin, cross-cousin, cross-cousin, cross-cousin,

Cross-cousin, I never beat sago at your place at Walabe, cross-
cousin.

(25) Cross-cousin, cross-cousin, cross-cousin,

Cross-cousin, "You will always weep while looking up to Hansowei," you say like that to me,

Cross-cousin, "You will always weep while looking up to
Sɔdim," you say like that to me.

(26) Cross-cousin,

Cross-cousin, if we hadn't left our place and come here this
wouldn't have happened.

(27) Cross-cousin, cross-cousin, cross-cousin,

Cross-cousin, you and I were together at Ifɛ, cross-cousin,
cross-cousin,

Cross-cousin, you and I were together at Wasilibi, you and
I were together at Muluma, cross-cousin, cross-
cousin.

(28) Cross-cousin,

Cross-cousin, you and I were together at Salo waterfall cross-
cousin,

Cross-cousin, I'm wondering if you have secretly gone to sleep
at Salo waterfall, cross-cousin,

Cross-cousin, go secretly sleep at Kišalaba, cross-cousin.

(29) Cross-cousin, cross-cousin,

Cross-cousin, you and I were together at Abolib,

Cross-cousin, you and I were together at Abolib,

Cross-cousin, go sleep under the bush pandanus leaves,

Cross-cousin, the bush pandanus leaves at Abolib, cross-
cousin, cross-cousin.

(30) Cross-cousin, cross-cousin,

Cross-cousin, you and I were together at Misi waterfall, cross-
cousin,

Cross-cousin, we were together at your place at Ukani, cross-
cousin.

(31) Cross-cousin,

Cross-cousin, Siyowa is really going to get a surprise when he
comes this afternoon,

Cross-cousin, Siyowa is on his way and coming this afternoon,
cross-cousin.

(32) Cross-cousin, I'm wondering if you've gone to my namesake's
father's place,

Cross-cousin, I'm wondering if you've gone to Olabia, cross-
cousin,

Cross-cousin, having left and obviously gone to Olabia you will
cross Bowɛl creek.

(33) Cross-cousin,

Cross-cousin, I'm wondering if you've gone to Gania's husband's place, cross-cousin, cross-cousin.

(34) Cross-cousin,

Cross-cousin, from now on you will stay secretly disappeared,

Cross-cousin, from now on you will stay secretly disappeared, cross-cousin,

Cross-cousin, you will clearly go off to sleep at your garden
house, cross-cousin,

Cross-cousin, from now on you will stay secretly disappeared, cross-cousin, cross-cousin.

Explication de Texte

Hane *sulɔ's sa-yɛlab* for Bibiali is a map of shared experiences articulating
feelings and concerns that run deep in Kaluli cultural style. The reader
should pass back and forth between these words, the full text, and map
of place names cited (figure 14) in order to understand how this map
develops and sustains the "hardness" *(halaido)* for which Kaluli often
praised it.

The *sa-yɛlab* opens (1) with an image of Sɔdim, the place name of
the Tabili longhouse (the previous home of Hane and Bibiali), and notes
that they left Sɔdim together to come to their present home at Asɔndɔ.
While this may seem to be a calm beginning, it in fact presupposes a
theme of conflict appearing throughout the text. The move from Tabili
to Asɔndɔ was engineered by the Christian segment of the community,
who wanted to have a common church with the people of Sisono. Many
Tabili elders, like Hane and Bibiali, resisted this move and strenuously
insisted that Tabili was their real home, a home to which they were tied
by tradition. Asɔndɔ would be a new kind of community, in fact, an
unprecedented amalgamation of two longhouse communities at one
common ridge, linked in the center by a church. This new form of social
organization was both emotionally and socially disruptive to the more
traditional Tabili people. The effect of the move on Bibiali was significant; he thereafter spent little time at Asɔndɔ, living largely at his garden
house or visiting the nearby Sululib or Olabia longhouses. Hane, then,
is opening this *sa-yɛlab* with a *bali to* image: we lived at Sɔdim, we left
Sɔdim and came here, and . . . (here Kaluli fill in the punch line) . . . you
no longer had a home and that is why you died.

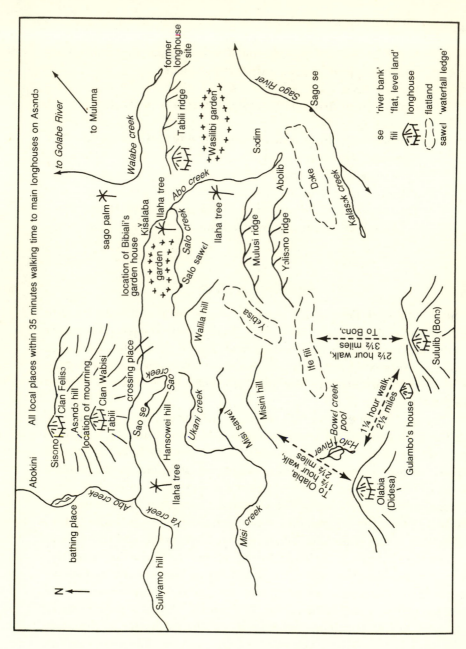

Figure 14. Place names in Hane sub's sa-yɛlab for Bibiali

The text continues with place names, citing them and addressing Bibiali as a bird who now resides at them. In (2) Hane notes that she and Bibiali were together at Hansowei hill, and in the next line she talks about an *odag* tree. This phrase contains the first of several uses of the most unusual linguistic feature of *sa-yɛlab,* a quote directive, where the weeper literally commands words into the deceased's mouth. The term ɛlɛmo contracts ɛlɛ 'like that' and *sama* 'say' (imperative). Mothers often use this term when teaching children to speak; they command them to speak back what has just been said (B. Schieffelin 1979). In *sa-yɛlab* the use also indicates a command to repeat what has been said. But in weeping there is a rich and unusual pragmatic feature that does not appear in mothers' speech to children. The addressee is dead, so what is being addressed is a spirit manifestation. Hence the content of the directed speech must be in the form of an appropriate utterance *to* a living person *from* one who is now a bird. Hane *sulɔ* commands Bibiali to say back to her, "Always look up to the top branches of an *odag* tree," because she assumes that as a spirit, Bibiali is now ɔbɛ *mise* 'in the form of a bird'. The prominent resting place of spirit birds is an *odag* tree, a large buttressed fig. Hane *sulɔ* is thus telling Bibiali to tell her that from now on he will only appear to her as a bird in a fig tree. The phrase "always look up" is cast in a future imperative, with a continual aspect marker and an emphatic; this linguistic form serves to emphasize the message that "from now on and always in the future" Bibiali will appear as a bird.

The next phrase (3) begins another theme that reappears throughout the text, citing how Beli, one of Bibiali's sons, will not feel sorrow because he was always angry with his father. Beli aspired to be a Christian and had no patience with tradition; his lack of solidarity with his father is taken by Hane as a key to the kind of debilitation that creates abandonment, and ultimately death.

Following this rather strong opening, with angry accusations toward the Christians of Asɔndɔ and toward Beli, the next several phrases contain the more typical *sa-yɛlab* imagery. Place names are combined with a remark of disbelief that Bibiali died before Hane visited him there (4,5), and paired formulaic phrases (6) note places where she and Bibiali had been together previously.

In (7) Hane returns to the theme of family, now discussing Siyowa, another of Bibiali's sons, who went to the government school at Wayu, five hours walk from Asɔndɔ. Hane refers to his long walk home, along Misini, just outside of Asɔndɔ, to receive the startling news. The image

is powerful because of the way it contrasts with the previous one about
Beli; though less angry, it is still intemperate, as Siyowa was always at
school, only seeing his father on the weekends. The implication again is
that Bibiali really had no family.

In the next phrases Hane returns to alternating reminiscences of
places she and Bibiali experienced together (8,10) and questions directed to Bibiali (9); she "wonders" if he has gone off as a bird to
Olabia, Bobani's place (cited indirectly as Duda's father's place), or to
Gulambo's place (cited indirectly as Gania's husband's place). The force
of these lines derives from the fact that Hane is maintaining two themes
at the same time: one is the places she and Bibiali shared in life; the
other is places Bibiali went because he had no home at Asɔndɔ. After
lines noting that Asɔndɔ was not Bibiali's real home, and that he had no
sons, the rhetorical "I'm wondering" form, used to ask whether he had
gone to Olabia or Sululib, a few hours walk from Asɔndɔ, is particularly
loaded.

This pattern continues in the following phrases in which the formulaic "you and I were together at [previous lands]" is combined with
direct commands to leave Asɔndɔ and reside elsewhere (12), and quote
directives telling him to tell her that he is going to the tree tops (13). The
final portion of (13) is even more complex, containing a line marked
midway and finally by ɛlɛmo. "While you look through an opening into
the women's section" makes reference to the fact that Bibiali was physically lying next to the women's section of the longhouse, facing the wall
bounding the cooking and socializing area, where other women were
weeping and cooking. The second part tells him to tell her that "tears will
always secretly flow there." At face value this is a comment on the way
Bibiali's face was blankly pointing in the direction of the women's section,
as if looking through a hole in the bamboo thatch. But more significantly
it is a *bali to* statement, meaning that the women must weep in secret lest
they be derided for being non-Christian. If Christians did not think it was
wrong to weep publicly, there would be no reason for Hane to tell Bibiali
to speak such words.

In the next phrases Hane again alternates consecutive formulaic
phrases (the waterfall of the Ya creek is at the foot of Suliyamo hill [14]),
simple statements of virtues (the most often noted features of Bibiali's
behavior were those of being soft-spoken and a loner [15]), and a very
densely texted phrase with complex pragmatics (16). Hane says "Having

left, I'm wondering if you've gone to Gulambo's place." The grammaticality and pragmatics of this utterance rest on the assumption that Bibiali has gone from body to spirit in the form of a bird; Hane wonders to Bibiali's body if his spirit has gone to Gulambo's house at Sululib. The next line, "go cross the Kalasɔk creek," maintains the assumption by telling the spirit-as-a-bird to cross a creek that is on the path to Gulambo's house; the third line continues this imperative form, citing a major landform outside the village. In the fourth and final line, "Having left, I'm wondering if you've gone to your son's place," the message is not only recapitulated but "hardened" substantially by the substitution of "son" for the name of Gulambo. This line says explicitly what has been insinuated at several points. The *hega,* or 'underneath', to this *bali to* is that Bibiali had no real sons; Gulambo, technically Bibiali's *babo,* was for Hane the only person who was really his "son" in the social sense. Kaluli interpreted this line as a message to Bibiali's spirit to get out of Asɔndɔ because he had no sons there.

Following several more place name sequences (17) mixed with quote directives (18), there are references to places Hane and Bibiali did not experience together (19), images that in fact are more pathetic because they evoke for Kaluli listeners the sense of social disruption brought about by death. There is a new kind of shift in the message content, structured by the now familiar rhetorical "I'm wondering" form. Phrase (20) is filled with *bali to;* in several previous phrases Hane suggested that Bibiali left in the form of a bird and went *iduna,* to the treetops. Here she rhetorically questions whether he is going down to the roots of a tree and then questions whether they will later go off together to the places they frequented in the past. Kaluli interpreted this to mean "Will we all go to the treetops like birds when we die and be together later at the places we lived in the past, or will we stand alone, at the roots of *bol* trees, isolated from each other?" In other words, will Bosavi tradition or Christian fragmentation prevail in the future?

In the next section there are several examples of quote directives (21, 22, 25) framed around a sequence of place names where Tabili spirit birds perch in their travels around the longhouse and gardens. As with previous phrases, these images play off of two senses of "home": that Asɔndɔ was not Bibiali's home; and that a bird's home is the trees, mountains, creeks, and sago places where Bibiali and Hane had been in the past. Mixed into these remarks are a set of lines that typify the direct

astonishment and disbelief that is often reflected in *sa-yɛlab,* as Hane tells
Bibiali (23) that he never slept this way before and commands him to go
sleep on his own bed.

Phrase (26) is constructed around a hypothetical verb phrase
kibobowo, which chains together "If we hadn't left our (real) place" . . .
"this (death) would not have happened." Kaluli interpreted the *bali to* as
a statement of Hane *sulɔ*'s anger that Christian pastors persuaded clan
Felisɔ of Sisono and clan Wabisi of Tabili to relocate in order to build
a large dual church. Hane is suggesting that such *ba madali* 'for no reason'
actions, like other parts of Christian ideology, tore apart Bibiali's family,
leaving him with no sons and no home.

Having suggested that this move was so debilitating, the next phrase
(27) derives its force from juxtaposing verbless formulaic phrases that
cite past longhouse sites where clan Wabisi resided, and where Bibiali
and Hane were together. Kaluli listeners took note of the effect, citing the
way these phrases interacted textually as being similar to the "hardening"
structure of song.

In the next series of phrases, Hane alternates naming places where
she and Bibiali had been with commands to him to go again to those
places to reside, as a bird (28, 29, 30). The "underneath" message here
is that Asɔndɔ is not really Bibiali's home, not the place where he can
really sleep. The places named get farther and farther away with each
phrase, paralleling several other sections of the text; this device was
remarked upon by Kaluli as another form of "hardening," similar to the
phrase cohesion found in songs.

Phrase (31) is almost identical to (7), returning to the theme of
Bibiali's sons. Kaluli interpreted the *bali to* here to mean that when Siyowa
came home from school on weekends, he did not think of the change as
a time to be with his father; this time he would have something really
startling to deal with.

In the next-to-final phrases (32, 33), Hane returns to the dominant
theme of the *sa-yɛlab,* that Bibiali's spirit should leave Asɔndɔ because it
was not his "home." First Hane tells him indirectly to go to Olabia,
referring to the home of her namesake, Hane *lɛsu* (little Hane), the
daughter of Waibo and Handa of clan Didesa. The creek mentioned is
Bowɛl, one of the four that must be crossed to enter Olabia from the area
immediately outside of the longhouse. In (33) the same point is taken
further, to Gulambo's place at Sululib. There is a thematic continuity here
that chains from phrases (6), (9), and (16). "Hardening" (*halaido*

domɛki) the weeping plays on the Kaluli song structure notion of *tok,* or path, a map that runs throughout the imagery and builds to a climax. Here the tension peaks in references to the paths away from Asɔndɔ, to Sululib and Olabia, places that were once nostalgically and sentimentally "home" for Bibiali and Hane, but that, with the demise of traditional social organization at the hands of new Bosavi Christians, could no longer be so.

The closure of this *sa-yɛlab* is brought about by a repeated line that refers to Bibiali's aloneness and commands that he remain "secretly disappeared" as a bird in the treetops.

In summary, this text exemplifies the language codes of *sa-yɛlab* through: (1) rhetorical question uses of *-ili* to mark "wondering"; (2) quote directives putting words into the mouth of the deceased, marked by phrase-final *ɛlɛmo;* (3) aspectual markings for continuous past, durative future, evidence, and emphasis, all focused around the past experiences and future isolation of weeper and deceased; (4) OAV word order to emphasize the personal "I" agent; (5) verbless formulaic phrases marked by *nani* and place names to indicate a map of shared lands in the experience of weeper and deceased; (6) prominence of the relationship term *nosɔk* opening and closing each phrase, thus stressing the kin relation of cross-cousin and the naming convention that goes with it; and (7) "hardening" structure *(halaido domɛki)* to sequence place names farther and farther away, abbreviate information, and otherwise develop a song-like textual cohesion.

At the pragmatic and semantic levels, the linguistic code maintains the assumption that Bibiali was physically next to Hane in body but residing elsewhere in spirit, *ɔbɛ mise* 'in the form of a bird'. The socially focused content of the *sa-yɛlab* messages revolves around the terms of Hane's relationship to Bibiali in life and *ɔbɛ mise,* around the anti-Christian *bali to,* including statements of traditional familial values, and around the importance of lands and homes as mediators of identity.

The major musical features of this piece exemplify the sonic codes of *sa-yɛlab* through: (1) singing while weeping throughout; (2) use of four pitches ranging a perfect fifth and divided as intervals of major second and minor third; (3) descending and terraced melodic shapes with very few examples of ascent; (4) consistency of melody and tempo, giving the sense of a controlled performance; (5) prominence of the phrase as the basic musical and textual unit; (6) formation of phrases by subdivision, embedding, conjoining, and expansion of simple pitch and pulse values;

(7) syllabic structure, parlando rubato, with densely texted semispoken, semisung lines; (8) breathy but nonfalsetto vocal quality, slightly shaky; and (9) variable phrase lengths from four to eighteen seconds but with a norm of eight to twelve seconds. At the pragmatic and semantic levels the musical code maintains the sonic structure of the *muni* bird call symbol, elaborated melodically into controlled phrases with pitch and temporal consistency, redundancy, and pattern. It is weeping that turns into a performed wept-song.

Conclusion

In the months following the mourning for Bibiali, people from Sululib and Asɔndɔ who stopped by my house to listen to tapes or just to be social often requested playback of Hane *sulɔ*'s *sa-yɛlab,* which baffled me at first. While it was clear that Kaluli found such expression to be moving, I couldn't understand why it would be treated as such an obviously aesthetic object, equal in significance to song. As time went on though, I found that *sa-yɛlab* generally were among the most often requested materials that I had recorded. Was it not painful and upsetting to relisten to this expression of grief and despair?

Part of the answer fell into place when Ulahi and I made an initial transcription of Hane *sulɔ*'s *sa-yɛlab* text. She remarked spontaneously that the text was like song because the images chained together and had a logical building pattern; as she put it, the words became "harder" as the phrases went on. When I reworked the transcription with Kulu, my regular linguistic assistant, it became clear that the linguistic features of aspect and emphasis focusing contributed much to making the text forceful. Kulu would not go so far as to say the text was angry, but he indicated that the text had a lot of hidden meanings and "turned-over words" that had an essentially angry underside. Shortly thereafter, Gulambo listened to the tapes and began to fill in specific details about Bibiali's relationship to Hane and all the others cited in the text, as well as his relationship to the places that are named. When we made an initial map of the place names cited in the text, both the variety and the developmental style led Gulambo and Kulu to remark that these were almost like the maps of place names that chain from phrase to phrase in song. On a trip to Asɔndɔ, I reviewed the place names with two prominent local men, Mei and Sogobaye, and again, their comments suggested that the *sa-yɛlab* was extremely provocative because of the use of *bali to* and the sequencing of place names. In effect, responses to this *sa-yɛlab* indicated that Kaluli found its construction controlled, deliberate, crafted, and almost composed like song. Yet its delivery was spontaneous and improvised in immediate response to grief. It was this sense of an ability to articulate deeply felt sentiments within the constraints of an improvised form that Kaluli found so forceful and often led them to request its playback.

My understanding of this *sa-yɛlab,* built upon these formal and informal discussions, elicitations, playbacks, transcriptions, and mapping, took place over some seven months. The phrase I heard most often when people spoke of Hane *sulɔ*'s performance was *dagano mada iyɛu ɔngo* 'of a voice really like an *iyɛu* bird' (Ornate Fruitdove, *Ptilinopus ornatus*). People remarked sadly that Bibiali *ɔbɛ mise hɛnɛsɛge* 'having gone as a bird' would always hear Hane *sulɔ*'s weeping; he would listen from the treetops.

To compare a woman's *sa-yɛlab* with the sound of an *iyɛu* bird is perhaps the strongest positive aesthetic comment that can be made of this mode. *Iyɛu* birds weep with a long *I-Yɛɛɛɛ-UUUUU,* a sound that Kaluli find very moving. Less evocative *sa-yɛlab* would only stimulate analogy to *kalo,* while men's *gana-yɛlab* might call to mind *muni,* or, if very melodic and slightly texted, the sounds of *howɛn* and *kalo,* more melodius fruitdoves with longer descending calls.

Sa-yɛlab weeping is the Kaluli expressive modality closest to "being a bird." The *muni* bird wept over the sadness of abandonment by his *adɛ,* and Kaluli funerary weeping embodies the same profound sentiments, mediated by the bird's mythic call. Weeping is the sound form most directly associated with becoming a bird, which is to say, the sound form most closely associated with death and with loss. While seemingly more complex, song is less direct and never a truly improvised and spontaneous embodiment of sadness.

In sum, Kaluli *sa-yɛlab* is constructed as a modality of melodic weeping with a specific pitch code that turns it into melodic-sung-texted-weeping in contexts of death and loss. Kaluli terminology most forcefully marks this style as a patterned variety of weeping, not song. However, in very elaborate *sa-yɛlab* performances, like Hane *sulɔ*'s, the addition of *bali to,* climaxing sequences, *halaido domɛki,* and other manipulations of form for evocative purposes turns the "sung-weeping" into more of a "wept-song." Moving from spontaneous and improvised to compositionally crafted weeping creates an aesthetic tension demanding the response that, like the deceased, the weeper, too, has become a bird.

4

The Poetics of Loss and Abandonment

The spirit of Kaluli ethno-exegesis demands that at this point, which is both the fulcrum of the myth and of the analysis, I briefly review how the stage has been set for a discussion of poetic ideals and composition. Chapter 1 argued that the myth "the boy who became a *muni* bird" provided a structural model for Kaluli sentiments of sadness, as mediated by bird sound and expressed in codes of weeping and song. Birds are ideal Kaluli mediators because they embody death and the existence of spirits as well as sonic expressions of sadness. The *muni* call symbol animates the sounds of weeping and song, and the words of the boy-turned-bird animate the linguistic organization of "bird sound words," the poetic code to be considered here.

Chapter 2, in an ethnobiological context, argued that Kaluli find birds and bird sounds important because of their conception of natural history; the avian world is both a "metaphoric society" (Lévi-Strauss 1966) and source of "natural symbols" (Douglas 1973). Talk from a bird's point of view, talk about birds, and bird sound onomatopoeia are all prominent in the song language to be discussed here.

Chapter 3 discussed *sa-yɛlab* weeping and argued that its melodic form was related to the *muni* call symbol and its linguistic form to conversational talk. Speech forms that moved away from this conversational model were noted as being intentional attempts at provocation. It is this song talk, intentionally constructed for aesthetic ends, that is analyzed here.

This chapter, then, concerns Kaluli poetic concepts in terms of their metalinguistic denomination, formal devices, and aesthetic intentions. Kaluli poetic ideals are in some ways similar to what literary analysts have discussed as the "pregnancy" of words (Empson 1930), "plurisignation" (Wheelwright 1968), or "literariness" (Mukařovský 1964; Jakobson

1968). These terms refer to linguistic usage that amplifies, multiplies, or intensifies the relationship of the word to its referent.

Kaluli make a marked distinction between 'hard words' *(to halaido)* and 'bird sound words' *(ɔbɛ gɔnɔ to)*. "Hard words" are assertive and direct language forms used in face-to-face talk that is supposed to be interactive, engaging, mutual, and productive in terms of getting speakers what they want or need. The ability to speak this way in everyday situations is considered a primary indicator of social competence. On the other hand, "bird sound words" are reflective and sentimental, ideally causing a listener to empathize with a speaker's message without responding to it verbally.

While these two major metalinguistic constructs imply some specific linguistic means and ways of speaking, it is not the case that one is simply referential and the other simply expressive. "Bird sound words" are not just a special set of surface alterations of "hard words"; neither the Kaluli metalinguistic denominations nor the manner of use indicates that one can be approached as "ordinary" language and the other as "literary" language. Certain message forms and content can appear in either, and the different ways messages are interpreted depend on judgments about intention, deriving from contextual constraints as well as from placement in an ongoing textual chain. When Kaluli compose and perform songs, they assume that their audiences will be prepared to listen to them in a reflective and nostalgic way. They consciously utilize this assumption to construct texts that will make their audiences attend to and think about imagery in an amplified manner.

If Kaluli poetic constructs are not made understandable by resorting to a distinction between ordinary and nonordinary language, or referential and expressive functions, what is required to analyze how "bird sound words" are meaningful in their performed setting? Kaluli poetic communication must be approached as a simultaneous articulation of formal properties of language, cultural knowledge (general, personal, specific, contextual) of participants, and audience expectation. Only in this way is it clear why speakers make intentional code choices in order to evoke a shared response. This interaction of form, content, and performance is what ties crafting strategies together with listening strategies, allowing the composer's intention to be interpreted most directly by those with the most personal, specific, and contextual knowledge of the textual path, and yet more broadly by those whose general and contextual knowledge strongly intersect with the textual themes.

There is more to poetic communication, however. Kaluli do not want their listeners to interpret poetic lines only in terms of what they know; they try to reorganize their experiences and customary perceptions of relationships, mostly by the ways in which they structure and chain textual imagery. The notion is similar to Bird's description of the West African Mande, whose performances are so dependent upon aesthetic tension, "the device by which the master jostles the expectancies of his audience, forcing them to participate in his act of creation" (Bird 1976: 91). Jostling expectancies, getting under the surface, reframing usual thought patterns, and evoking a dramatic response are all at the heart of Kaluli poetics, because composers force their audiences to participate in their creations by making them weep. They accomplish this at several levels: staging, costuming, singing, dancing, and performance demeanor are each co-essential to the evocation of sadness and weeping in *gisalo.* But of all the factors involved, Kaluli most often say that it is the *sa-gisalo,* the "words inside *gisalo,*" that do the main work of making listeners sentimental and nostalgic to the point of being moved to tears.

The "words inside *gisalo*" are moving in this way because they are an impregnated language, one that Kaluli say has "insides" and "underneaths." The effect produced when these "insides" and "underneaths" fully register with the listener is what Kaluli call the *halaido domɛki,* the 'hardening', the climaxing, or culmination of the aesthetic tension of song.

The texts themselves are about sadness and sorrow, portrayed in core images of loneliness, loss, abandonment, death, and isolation. Although the texts include some words and phrases that are identical to codes of daily speech, the pragmatics and inferential possibilities are distinct. The technique of song language is different because it relies upon mystification, obfuscatory codes, and multiply interpretable images that are simultaneously explicit and nebulous constructs. Poetic grammar uses only special verb inflections that reference all time to a nebulous and fuzzy present and all space to a short continuum of vaguely near or distant actions. Dependent upon the personal and shared knowledge of audience members, the song comes to mean in more or less pointed ways, singling out one, two, or a number of audience members who may be provoked to tears.

These techniques are what make song language *bali to* 'turned-over words', when all themes have an "underneath" or *hega,* and the manner of speaking used is *sa-salan* 'inside speaking'. These major organizing features are fleshed out by *gɔnɔ to* 'sound words' or onomatopoeia, which casts song in a unique descriptive sensorium. Cohesion of the "underneath" and "inside" themes and the reliance on sensory imagery is accomplished by the *tok,* a map or path of lands, waters, trees, and places that winds throughout the text.

This chapter begins with these major Kaluli organizing devices—*sa-salan, bali to, gɔnɔ to,* and *tok*—and proceeds to the images that connect the *muni* myth with song texts, *adɛ* and hunger, and the verb morphology that creates poetic time and space. The argument throughout is that Kaluli conceive and interpret poetic grammar as a means of symbolic persuasion relating the craft of "hardening" song to the aesthetic ends of moving a man to tears.

Sa-salan

The first Kaluli metalinguistic-poetic concept is *sa-salan* 'inner speaking' or 'meaning inside speaking'. *Sa* is found in two semantic fields: waterfalls and sound. Used alone, it means 'waterfall', and as a prefix to other water terms indicates parts of waterfalls. As a prefix to verbs of soundmaking, it indicates the addition of text "inside" the sound. For instance: *holab* 'one whistles', *sa-holab* 'one whistles with words in mind'; *yɛlab* 'one weeps', *sa-yɛlab* 'one weeps with text'. Thus *salab* (here in the habitual *salan*) 'one speaks', *sa-salab* 'one speaks with an inner meaning'. *Salan* is the present habitual of the imperative *sama* 'speak'. This term contrasts with *tolɛma* 'say words' (*to* 'words'; and *ɛlɛma* 'say like that'). The difference is that between *parole* and *langue;* the former concerns speech, the latter, language (Feld and B. Schieffelin 1982).

Metalinguistic terms like *to halaido* 'hard words', *bali to* 'turned-over words', *mugu to* 'taboo words', and *malolo to* 'narrated words' (stories) all refer to the form of the language. *Wonole-salan* 'speak in a secretive manner', *tɛde-salan* 'speak in a deep voice', *gese-salan* 'speak plaintively', *hala-salan* 'speak with mispronunciations or grammatical errors' refer to the manner in which the speaking is performed. In everyday speech contexts, the form of the first is encountered largely as a noun (*to* 'words') and the latter always as a verb. When the former is used verbally, it is best glossed 'language', for example, *mugu tolab* 'talking taboo language', *bali tolab* 'speaking turned-over language'. The sense is that "taboo" or "turned over" is the systematic form of the language. With *salan,* the sense is always that the adverb describes the style or manner of the speech. *Bosavi to* means 'Bosavi language'; thus one *Bosavi to salan* 'speaks

the Bosavi language', or *Bosavi to asulan* 'understands the Bosavi language'. The only context in which *to* is not directly modified but appears
as the head noun is *to halaido* 'hard words', or, less literally, 'grammati-
cally well-formed language'. *Halaido* 'hard' is pervasive for growth, matu-
ration, strength; *to halaido* is direct adult language.

Sa-salan does not specify formal linguistic features but indicates the
intention to speak with an inside, to mean more than what is explicitly
said. For instance, consider the sentence:

1) *Dowo, ge oba hanaya?*
   'Father, where are you going?'

By varying the intonation, the implication could be benign, a request for
information, challenging, annoyed, or any number of moods. When we
shift from speech to song, these implications shift radically. The audience
knows immediately that the message is really that a father has left someone behind, and the person asking the question is in the resultant state
of abandonment. The singer is not requesting anything or registering an
emotional response to the leaving as much as making a statement to the
audience to "feel sympathy for my obvious loss."

Clearly, Kaluli find the image of someone being left behind by a
"father" to be pathetic, and they would assume death to be the major
context in which this might happen. As soon as Kaluli think about death,
they think about the deceased leaving *ɔbɛ mise* 'in the form of a bird'. The
line is thus impregnated with "Will I hear you in the treetops?", "Will
I see you in the trees above your lands?", and similar questions. What is
"inside" the spoken line is not so much the obviousness of the death, but
the subsequent thoughts associated with abandonment.

"Father, where are you going?", then, makes the audience feel sorrow for its own loss of the deceased as well as for the loss felt by the
singer, whose song demands confirmation. The audience, by weeping,
responds that it feels the inner thoughts underlying what has been said.

Next, consider some examples in which the linguistic structure is of
a form not potentially found in conversational discourse.

2) *sa-ga-lɛma tindabe*
   Hɔfo-wa sa-ga-lɛma tindabe
   gogo-wa sa-ga-lɛma tindabe

Hɔfo is the name of a creek; *gogo* is a tree type; *tindab* is the onomatopoeic
verb for falling water (*tin* being the sound of many simultaneous drops).

Sa-ga is a waterfall outlet to a separate stream; *lɛma* marks the down branch. A translation, then, is:

> Water flows down *tin,* breaking off from the fall,
> At Hɔfo creek it flows down *tin,* breaking off from the fall,
> At the *gogo* tree there, it flows down *tin,* breaking off from the waterfall.

The second and third lines give the new information of a creek and tree name, making the sensation of place far more specific, while the core image continues to repeat, citing the waterfall breaking into a new waterway and the sound of the water flowing down.

The form combines the expectation of more concrete information with the repetition of given information. In speech one could simply say "At the *gogo* tree by the Hɔfo creek, the water goes *tin* as it breaks from the waterfall into a stream." The poetic force lies in the simultaneous character of becoming more specific and more redundant, while the speech force, by contrast, lies in the economy of description. What, then, is on the "inside" of the poetic version?

Kaluli say that the *sa-salan* here is not about description but about journeying. The images build and repeat as they do because someone is taking you somewhere in song. The listener imagines the experience of trees, waters, waterfalls, branching, and water sounds either from the point of view of familiarity with the places, or the novelty of going there. All songs are sung from the point of view of movement through lands. The composer's craft is not to tell people about places but to suspend them into those places. Singing a place name is not a descriptive act but rather one that "impregnates" identity into place, tree, water, and sound names, because Kaluli are known by the lands on which they live, the places they cultivate and frequent. Your life, as Kaluli sometimes philosophically pointed out to me, is a map of where you have experienced living, socializing, journeying. Moving about, traveling, walking, and visiting, all are daily aspects of Kaluli experience, and Kaluli people believe that once they turn into birds, their lives will remain the same in that way.

Progressions of place names immediately call to mind "Whose place is that?"; "What have I done there?"; "What did X and Y do there?"; "Is X there ɔbɛ *mise?*"; "That's on the path to X, just after you pass Y"; and so forth. There are also more specific sets of knowledge that come into play. One, for instance, would only use the word *tindab* to mark a large

amount of water. The assumption most Kaluli would make is that there
has just been a large rainfall or that the particular waterfall is very large.
Hɔfo happens to be a very large creek, and there are numerous *gogo* trees
(small palms common near creeks) at its banks. Depending on how familiar one is with the area where the Hɔfo is situated, this set of images will
provoke specific associations of experiences.

Obviously, everyone does not receive the same "inside" associations; with place names, the range of associations always includes both
specific and general experiences. Even so, everyone feels a deeper meaning than what is implied by the actual referents of the combined words.
When place names are sung in sequence, they invite *sa-salan* interpretation by activating assumptions about spirit (*ane kalu* 'gone men') residence. Kaluli know that a sure way to bring a man to tears is to sing the
places where he once lived, gardened, and, especially, shared experiences
with a recently deceased person. Thus the composer's craft involves
extensive knowledge of residence and personal family histories of other
individuals. Audiences expect a song to make them journey, suspend
their present location, or ponder where various *ɔbɛ mise* friends and
relatives might be. *Sa-salan* provides one means to effect the journey and
the suspension of the literal.

Another area where linguistic form always leads to "inner" text
interpretation is bird call symbolism.

3) *Seyago,*
   gɔlɔlɔ, gɔlɔlɔ, gɔlɔlɔ
   Kidɛn-sa seyago,
   gɔlɔlɔ, gɔlɔlɔ, gɔlɔlɔ

   'A *seyak* bird calls *gɔlɔlɔ, gɔlɔlɔ, gɔlɔlɔ,*
   By the waterfall of Kidɛn creek, a *seyak* bird keeps calling,
   gɔlɔlɔ, gɔlɔlɔ, gɔlɔlɔ. . . .'

Seyago (seyak, seyaka, sagelon) is the Hooded Butcherbird, a conspicuous bird often heard at village edges or secondary forest bordering open
spaces. That it lives close to them and is vocally prominent is the principal
reason for Kaluli to consider the bird a spirit visitor. Men are said often
to go *ɔbɛ mise* as this bird. *Gɔlɔlɔ* is the onomatopoeic representation
specific to *seyak* used when indicating an *ane kalu* 'gone man' *ɔbɛ mise* 'in
the form of a bird'.

These lines are the opening phrase of a *gisalo* song sung at Sululib.
Kidɛn-sa is a waterfall of the Kidɛn creek just at the outskirts of Sululib.

The initial passage signaled to the audience that the song would be from the point of view of a spirit in the form of a *seyak* bird, and that the spirit was either a Sululib man or a visitor staying around Sululib, as Kidɛn is located on a major path. Inside the words, then, is the notion that this song is really being sung from the treetops by the voice of a friend or relative of the Sululib audience members.

Text can also be amplified or impregnated when words are left out of phrases or syntax undergoes modification. Like Kaluli speech, song lines have verbs in final position, but there are situations in song where verbs are completely omitted. For example:

4) *Aigo sa-wɛl-o, nelɔ*
   sɛni-fowɔ, nelɔ
   Aigo sa-wɛl-o, nelɔ

   'At the top of Aigo waterfall, "for me,"
   At the fruited *sɛni* sago there, "for me,"
   At the top of Aigo waterfall, "for me." '

Aigo is a creek name, *sa-wɛl* the top ledge of the waterfall there; *sɛni* is a kind of sago palm, and the suffix *fowɔ* means 'fruited', implying ripeness and availability as immediate food, but sago is inedible once a palm fruits. *Nelɔ* indicates 'I', 'for me', 'give to me', 'what about me', or 'I want' and is a begging form found commonly in children's speech. It is also found in the *muni* story in the speech of the younger brother to his sister. It implies withoutness, plaintiveness, and a demand for the listener to feel sorry for the speaker as well as to do something on his behalf. What is "inside" the speaking is not so much an implied verb to complete the phrase. Several verbs of calling out, coming, going, staying, or yearning would be contextually appropriate, and these are the usual verbs employed to indicate plaintive condition. The audience clearly will be thinking about these, but what is inside the words is the childlike quality of the choice of words and the implication that the singer has been reduced to the sad state of an abandoned child. This device clearly serves to focus the manner of speaking, namely, begging to abbreviate discussion and force an immediate response.

The context that hosts the most abbreviation, ellipsis, and syntactic deviation is the final portion of the *gisalo* song form, the *sa-sundab*. *Sundab* means 'one adds up', 'counts together', or 'knots'; *sa-sundab* is the last set of phrases that "tie up" and "pull together" the imagery of a song. There are two to six sets of paired lines, with a rhyme scheme of final *-o* on the last word of the first line and final *-e* on the last word of the second line. For example:

> 5) *Mo gulu besebo*
> *Wa-mo gulu besebe*

Mo is a Sonia word equivalent to Kaluli *hɔn* 'water'; *gulu* is onomatopoeic for the sound of a small waterfall. *Besebo* and *besebe* (imperative *besema*) mean 'one beats (sago)' with aspect of a close-by and beginning of action marked. Wa is the name of a waterfall.

> "A small waterfall runs *gulu* near a place where
> someone has begun to beat sago";
> "the Wa waterfall runs *gulu* where
> someone has begun to beat sago."

In the first line there is the tension of the most general name for a waterway and a very specific onomatopoeic water sound representation. The second line shifts this to a specific named waterfall and the now redundant sound it makes. In both lines the specificity of the waterfall and sound are played against the very abstract usage of "someone has begun to beat (sago) there." What is inside the words in these situations is the "connecting" of images. There is no linguistic indication of locative connection; the words as they stand are a list of images rather than a grammatical sentence. So, there is an image about a person and a sago place that does not specifically mention any person or name any kind of sago or sago place. While it is natural to have small waterfalls making soft *gulu* sounds near swampy sago areas, the image here is not specific but abstract, like a riddle "What do X,Y, and Z have in common?"

The song has proceeded, the images have built up, "hardened," and climaxed; here, at the end, the singer summarizes not by explicating or giving a précis, but by singing a list of core symbols. The audience finds the connection "inside" the list, just as it has found and inferred meaning from "inside" phrases, lines, and images.

Bali To

Bali to means 'turned-over words'. *Bali* derives from the verb *balima* 'turn over'. When words are "turned over" they show not one but two, and perhaps more, sides to themselves. Specifically, once they are "turned over," they have a *hega*, an 'underneath'. The *hega* is the underlying meaning, a meaning that is not evident from immediate impression. *Hega hɛ?* 'Where's the underneath'? signifies "What does it mean?" in the sense of "I know what you're saying, but what's really on your mind?", or, "I know what you're saying, but what are you driving at?" This is stronger and more pointed than *mowɔ hɛ?* or *mowɔ oba?,* which signify "Why?", "For what reason?", or "What do you mean?" One askes *hega hɛ?* having assumed that something has been concealed or obfuscated. *Hega hɛ?* can be a request for information, but it can also be a challenge, rather like "So what's *that* supposed to mean?"

While Kaluli talk in any context can be turned over, there is a greater expectation for *bali to* when something important is at stake, such as in arguments or protest. In family situations, one commonly finds the most benign kind of *bali to,* lexical substitution for hidden meanings or concealed items or thoughts. In these situations *bali to* can include irony, sarcasm, paradox, and euphemism. There is also the tendency in argument or heated discussion to avoid directness; litotes usages of "I won't mention the fact that . . ." and similar straw man or set-up speech is common. Kaluli has a negative verb *mobeab* 'one is unwilling', which is used *bali to* as a double negative. Thus one might say *ne mɔ-mobeab kɔsiga* . . . , meaning "I'm not unwilling, but . . .", in order to indicate clear unwillingness.

In song, where all text is *bali to,* the device is somewhat different. There is but one object or persuasive action at stake: the intention to make others sentimental, nostalgic, sad, and, ultimately, to move them to tears. To accomplish this, the technique of *bali to* centers in the tension of communication that grows simultaneously more obfuscatory and more explicit. Lexical substitution, metaphor, and fuzziness are found in the *bali to* of song; paradoxical, sarcastic, and ironic constructs are not.

When directly questioned, Kaluli men said that many aspects of song poetics were "kinds" of *bali to.* In concrete settings, however, when they listened to a song, or were in the process of composing one and explaining its imagery, the explication of *bali to* focused on a more specific set of linguistic devices: the use of Sonia, question and answer pair lines, first-person frames, if/then hypothetical sequences, metaphor, and pleas for help.

The first major device is the use of Sonia. Writings in ethnography of speaking (Fox 1974; Fitzgerald 1975) and register usage (Ferguson 1973) have pointed out the importance of borrowing from related languages or dialects as a common feature of ritual languages and religious registers. The focused effect is mystification, marking the form as esoteric or archaic. In addition, the device serves to force a stratification of interpretive knowledge, since familiarity with the borrowed forms is not the same for all users and listeners.

Usage of Sonia in Bosavi song follows this pattern precisely. The borrowing takes place on all linguistic levels in the core vocabulary of song, including land and water names, tree names, types of sago palms, kinship terms, verbs of sunlight qualities, cloud formations, and other sensate descriptives. There are two alternate patterns to Sonia use. The first is to cast entire lines or series of lines in Sonia. More frequent is a mixture of Sonia and Kaluli in lines, sets of lines, or an entire song. Most Kaluli whom I consulted said that the use of Sonia was "hardest" and had the most textual impact on the listener if an image was sung first in Sonia and then in Kaluli. This follows the general song axiom to always be abstract before being explicit.

Looking at one area of core vocabulary, my corpus of songs includes fifty-four different names for kinds of sago and seventy-four names for different types of trees in map *(tok)* images. Each of the names appears in the corpus both in Sonia and Kaluli (except in a few instances in which the sago or tree type is found only in one area and no equivalent lexeme exists). In some cases the names are as phonologically similar as (6) *safe/safo,* so that even a Kaluli speaker unfamiliar with Sonia would know the referent. In other cases, the terms are as different as (7) *yɛlɛ/osa.* Hence the listener must either know the Kaluli equivalent for the Sonia or wait until the same name is sung in Kaluli in a sequence following the Sonia usage. Similar patterns are manifest for bird names and types of waterways. Sago palm names and tree names are, however, quite different from bird and waterway terms in one basic respect. One can sing a Sonia bird or waterway name and then sing the onomatopoeic representation of the sound. While the listener may not know the Sonia lexical item, he will be able to identify the bird or type of waterway by the standard onomatopoeia.

Some Kaluli/Sonia alternations have little performance impact because the Sonia is so frequently used in song that it has become conventional. A good example of this is the pair *ilaha* and *odag,* respectively Kaluli and Sonia for a large buttressed fig tree. This often-sung tree name is considered a spirit home, a prominent place where many of the most important spirit birds are heard. Even Kaluli women and youths will volunteer that *ilaha* = *odag,* although they generally know few or no other equivalences.

The second major linguistic device concerns question and answer pairs and the point of view expressed in first-person forms. Consider the following lines:

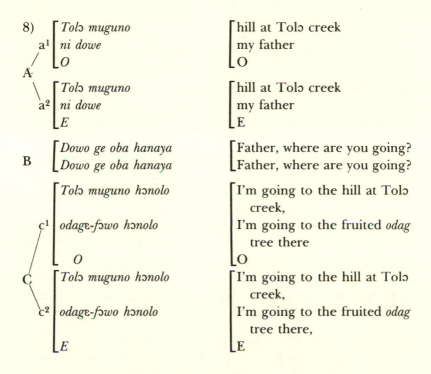

8)			
a¹	Tolɔ muguno	hill at Tolɔ creek
	ni dowe	my father
	O	O

A

a²	Tolɔ muguno	hill at Tolɔ creek
	ni dowe	my father
	E	E

B	Dowo ge oba hanaya	Father, where are you going?
	Dowo ge oba hanaya	Father, where are you going?

c¹	Tolɔ muguno hɔnolo	I'm going to the hill at Tolɔ creek,
	odagɛ-fɔwo hɔnolo	I'm going to the fruited *odag* tree there
	O	O

C

c²	Tolɔ muguno hɔnolo	I'm going to the hill at Tolɔ creek,
	odagɛ-fɔwo hɔnolo	I'm going to the fruited *odag* tree there,
	E	E

Kaluli always assume that a song is constructed in the first person as a personal statement referring to the thoughts and feelings of the singer or of a spirit. The exceptions follow the pattern shown above. Here the singer laments the loss of his father by suggesting that he has gone to the hill at Tolɔ creek (A). The singer assumes that if he names the hill above Tolɔ creek, listeners will know that this local hill is the site of an *odag* tree. It is "inside the words" that the father, as a bird, is in the *odag* tree. From this impregnated phrase, the singer shifts to rhetorical questioning of the father (B). I previously discussed this phrase (1) and pointed out that what is inside the words here is the singer's wish to have the audience feel sorrow for his loss. Then in (C), the singer shifts from his own first-person stating and questioning and supplies the response of the father.

The line is in the first-person present ("I'm going to. . . ."), but it is now the spirit who is speaking and not the singer.

What is going on here is that the composer has crafted three pairs that climax *(halaido domɛki)* by stating, asking, and responding. For the responding, "quoting" an inferred appropriate response, the singer is using first person but not marking "that's what he's saying." Kaluli interpret this to mean that the singer knows exactly where the father is going and is putting the right words in the father's mouth as a response to his own rhetorical question. What is the *hega?* The underneath is that not only does the singer know that his father is going *ɔbɛ mise* to the *odag* tree at *Tolɔ mugun,* but that he feels the presence of the father saying those words.

Whereas the use of Sonia as *bali to* is fairly straightforward (what is underneath the Sonia words is Kaluli meaning), the use of question and answer frames is more subtle, crafted as a *halaido domɛki* device that emerges over sets of phrases. Here one both turns over the words by shifting the point of view, and provides the underneath as well by letting the subject of the words momentarily speak for himself.

The next device is very provocative. The term *kibabe* is found frequently in song; it marks a hypothetical condition or situation and is used as a subordinate verb in the formula "X *kibabe* Y (negative) main verb." The meaning is "if X were the case, then Y would (not) be the case." In song the negative usually appears, and the implied meaning is "X is self-contradictory." For example, where X is a kinship term:

9) *ne ao kibabe* 'If I had a brother'
   (The second part, predictably, follows the "set up" with a verb
      that implies some pathetic state)
   ne mɔ-imolobabe 'I wouldn't be left hungry'
   ne mɔ-fofɔndolobabe 'I wouldn't be orphaned'

Saying "if I had a brother" and meaning "I obviously have no brother, otherwise I would not be in this situation" is one of the most powerful strategies in song. Kaluli always get the *hega* that the singer is completely isolated.

There are also creative and metaphoric usages of *kibabe.* "If an *odag* tree were my home, I could stay here." Without ever saying "man is a bird" or "a tree is a home," both of these metaphors simultaneously register. The difference, then, between formulaic use of *kibabe* and more creative use is in the potential for metaphor.

All Kaluli song metaphors have to do with birds, trees, lands, and waters, but they never appear in the overt form "X is a Y." Songs use lines like "X is calling out to you" or "X, do you hear it?" or "Is X saying something to me?" The implied metaphor is that X is a person. To metaphorize that a bird is a person is the most conventional of these. Singers often initially signal that a song is being sung by a bird by using a bird name and/or bird onomatopoeia.

To metaphorize that a kind of tree, land, or waterway is a person is to say that one is embodied in the places that one lives; you are what you call "home." *Ɛbɛlo dowo kibabe,* . . . 'If an *ɛbɛl* tree was my father . . .', *Ne mɔ-imolobabe* 'I wouldn't starve'. *Ɛbɛl* trees are always found in clusters with very large ones towering over short ones, hence, the appropriateness of the father-child image.

Similarly, when one uses lines like "Sululib, do you hear it?", the metaphor turns on the fact that Sululib is not just the ground name of the longhouse of clan Bonɔ, but also denotes Bonɔ people, life at Bonɔ places, and being with Bonɔ relatives and friends; in short, all aspects of identity that are Bonɔ. The ground name of a longhouse creates an entirely different image, for example, than the name of an old garden place covered by weeds or a creek that has no fish. Metaphor makes a person into the quality of the place. It is a kind of *bali to* because it 'turns over' two semantic fields and gives them a common "underneath."

The final *bali to* device that Kaluli distinguished was the use of plaintive calls or pleas for help. These appear throughout *gisalo* texts and bring the listener back to the themes of aloneness and isolation from the singer's point of view. The simplest form here is the use of a kinship term sung for the duration of a whole line, sometimes with the possessing *ni*. More frequently, a verb requesting attention is added. For instance,

10) *(Ni) dowo, ne bɔbɛ-meno*
    (Ni) dowo, ne ɔsumɛ-meno

    '(My) father, come and see me'
    '(My) father, come and help me'

Another form alternates the kinship term with an expressive, either *wɔ* or *siye,* which marks disappointment and feeling sorrow. For example:

11) *Siye, ne ɔsumɛ-mene*
    Wɔ dowo, ne ɔsumɛ-mene,
    Siye, ne ɔsumɛ-mene.

The other verbs used often in these formulae mark calling out, particularly for one to respond or follow. These phrases beg for help, attention, and recognition.

This device of the plea or plaintive phrases is clearly used both for textual cohesion and for climaxing, and is also essential to the construction of "hard" or moving songs. It promotes cohesion because it repeats through the middle or end of texts, communicating "in case you've momentarily gotten wrapped up in the specifics and forgotten what this song is about, the real message is isolation." It promotes climax because it brackets phrases in which tension has built up through the major *halaido domɛki* strategy of simultaneously becoming more specific and more obfuscatory.

Plea phrases go a step further than other forms of *bali to,* in that they are always sung with a specific plaintive intonation called *gese-molab.* Thus the linguistic code formally co-occurs with a manner of vocal production. Most Kaluli said that the *hega* was not just that the singer was alone or abandoned, but that the singer was crying out like a helpless child whining with the *geseab* vocal delivery. The *gese-molab* delivery makes the lines childlike and thus more pathetic.

Throughout this discussion of *bali to* devices, I have pointed out how linguistic codes are used to mark a tension between literal and connotative, obvious and ambiguous, and explicit and obfuscated. This, in great part, is the source of aesthetic tension in song. It is marked by the Kaluli notion that there is something "inside" and "underneath" both the manner of speaking and the words themselves. Similar ends are achieved through two devices that can be considered to be kinds of *bali to,* but that are in themselves major poetic concepts in Kaluli song. These are *gɔnɔ to* 'sound words', the vowel symbol system; and *tok* 'path', the construction of an unfolding map that gives each song its characteristic uniqueness.

Gɔnɔ To

Aspects of language in which arbitrariness is replaced by an iconic relation between sound and meaning have generally been referred to as "phonetic symbolism" (Sapir 1929). The standard position is that such iconicity derives from the sensations of the tongue in articulation. Linguists (Jakobson and Waugh 1979) have shown iconics to have many functions in language generally and in speech play specifically. Noting that iconicity is responsible for rather large word classes in some Southeast Asian languages, Diffloth (1976) points out that this phenomenon is not confined only to sound terms, although poetic onomatopoeia seems to be the area in which it is most discussed.

In poetic onomatopoeia, sounds describe things or acts by imitation. The Kaluli term *gɔnɔ to* 'sound words', is best translated this way. But *gɔnɔ to* is something more because the iconicity is truly paradigmatic in Kaluli, and novel words are created by using vowels to signify location, motion, or space. Each vowel thus involves both onomatopoeia and synesthesia. The principle of *gɔnɔ to* is best translated by phonesthesia, and the particles themselves called phonesthemes (Bolinger 1950).

It should first be noted that each Kaluli vowel can stand alone, yet none of these words has meaning related to the phonesthesia:

i 'tree', 'wood'
e 'plant', 'seedling'
ɛ 'yes'
a 'house'
u 'rock'
o 'forearm'
ɔ 'knot'

There are additional unrelated vowel uses in grammatical particles. Kaluli iconicity is based upon contrasts in the vowel space articulated as height, in *i* and *ɛ*, and *u* and *ɔ*, and depth, in *e* and *o*. The vowel that is unused in *gɔnɔ to* is *a*, and this is not surprising given its asymmetrical position.

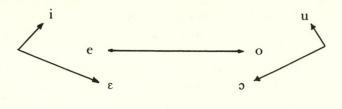

The front vowels "hum" when high *(i)* and "buzz" when low *(ɛ)*. The back vowels "swoop down" when high *(u)* and "swing out" when low *(ɔ)*. The mid vowels "crackle" when fronted *(e)* and "pop" when backed *(o)*. Examples in each of the sets for a variety of contexts will indicate how these conventional sound/meaning pairs operate in Kaluli song poetics.

In the first set, *i* and *ɛ* both mark sounds that are continuous; they indicate sound that is "around," and "in the air." The difference lies in texture, *i* marking "hum" sounds and *ɛ* marking "buzz" sounds. Additionally, *i* sounds are ambiguous and unobservable in terms of their source, whereas *ɛ* sounds have observable sources whose direction is evident. The contrast between *i* and *ɛ* is best characterized by comparing the generic verb forms. *Ii-ɛlab* 'it says *ii*', is generic for bush sounds whose direction or source is ambiguous. Tree or bush rumbling noises, humming sounds of the forest coming to life in the early morning, or background presences of trees moving in wind can be labeled by *ii-ɛlab*. *Ɛɛ-ɛlab* 'it says *ɛɛ*' demarcates a wide range of sounds with a continuous buzzing quality, including sounds of flies, bees, cicadas, and numerous other insects. The source of the sound is visually evident, and the quality of the sound is a "buzz" background.

For some specific examples: *gi* is the call of coucals; *ti* the sounds of rain sprinkling, spraying through the entire forest, or dripping after a rainfall; *di* the continual rubbing of leaves in trees and groves. All of these are continuous, all around, and without a specifically observable source. *Gili,* indicating rumbling, thunderous noises, is the only example of loud sounds in the group.

Dɛ is used for the puckering and sucking sounds of bats eating, *sɛ* (or *sɛgɛ*) the sounds of shellfish claws snapping, the seed pod rattle *sologa,* or the chattering of noisy birds. *Hɛ* is used for wheezing sounds people make when they are ill, *sɛlɛ* for sharpening axes on stone, *ɛlɛlɛ* for swarms of insects, and *dɛgɛ* for dried leaves dropping from breadfruit trees at the end of season. In one newly created usage, our small Honda generator was named *bɛdɛ-bɛdɛ* for its sound. In these *ɛ* examples the timbre or sonority is more precisely sharp or buzzing than is the humming of *i,* and the location of the source is clear.

When used in combination, both qualities are marked. *Gi-gɛ* is the sound of trees turning with the change of season. There is both the perceptual obviousness of source plus the fact that the sound is all around; the forest hums and buzzes as some leaves fall dramatically with crisp sounds and others drop softly but continuously.

The most productive set is produced by the back vowels *u* and *ɔ*. Both of these signal patterns of directionality in the movement of sound from its source; *u* for sounds that originate above and dissipate to below, and *ɔ* for sounds that radiate over horizontal distance or concentrically out from the source. *Uu-ɛlab* is the whooping of men, the sounds of airplanes, and the booming sound of the Harpy Eagle, *ŭsulage*. *Ɔɔ-ɛlab* is the sound of the Raggiana Bird of Paradise, *ɔlon,* and vibrating sounds that carry over long distances. The former marks thumping and rumbling of above to below, the latter a radiating out from the source.

Gu is used for thunder, for waterfall sounds *(sa-gu, gulu, gululu),* and for dancing, in which the up-and-down movement and costume sound is likened to a waterfall. Trees bending and falling through the air or wind are *gudɛ,* or when they crack under pressure from winds, *gudu*. *Hɔn-fu* is the spray of falling water, *hɔn-bu* the rolling of fast white water over rocks in large waterfall-gorges, *hɔn-ku* or *kubu* the splashing sounds of large waterfalls dropping off into small water pools, and *hɔn-du* or *dugu* the sounds of water pouring into or out of bamboo tubes.

On the other hand, *gɔgɔ* is the sound of the earth rumbling, or the house floor rumbling when people dance or drum. *Kɔgɔ* is the name of a grackle and the sound of its everpresent quacking, *gɔlɔ* is the sound produced from banging two objects together. *Sɔlɔ* is the sound of insects and birds at daybreak, and the bird *sɔlɔlɔbɛ* is a trilling kingfisher. The howl of dogs is *gɔmu; hɔ* is breath, and *hɔ-ɛlab* is the verb for panting. In all of these there is a vibrating or resonating quality that surrounds by moving out in waves from the source.

Mixing the "surrounding" with the "coming down," *hɔ-gu* is the term for the sound of wind. *Gu-gɔ,* is the common term for the sound of felling trees, with *gu* the falling down through air, and *gɔ* the vibration and resonance created out and around when they hit the ground. Perhaps the most fascinating combination is *gugu-gɔgɔ,* which means "bush echo," marking both the continuousness of downward dissipating sound and the continuousness of concentrically radiating sound. It is hard to share the semantic feel of this with one who has not heard the natural echo of dense tropical forest. The greatest perceptual adaptation I had to make to forest sound was the differentiation of height and depth; *gugu-gɔgɔ* specifies the melange as the ambiguous location of echos.

O and *e* both mark sounds that stay at the source of their making. Both are observable; the *e* sounds are at the ground, and the *o* sounds move with the source. The *o* sounds have more durative aspect, while the *e* sounds are sharp and crisp. Starting with the main verbs, *oo-ɛlab* 'it says *oo'* is used for *giwɔn,* flying beetles that sound continuously throughout flight, or white water that is rushing in large streams over rocks and making sound at every place it hits the rocks. *Ee-ɛlab* is generic for the crunching sounds of the bush underfoot as one walks on forest paths.

Examples of *o* sounds are found for bird flight, *bobo* for wing-beating sounds; water examples include *hɔn-fo* for fast water continually sounding as it hits rocks and *hɔn-go* for the swirling sound of water pools. *Gololo* is 'belch', and *boto* is used for pop sounds in cooking; *idɔ boto,* literally 'shit pop', is a fart. *Godo* is perhaps the most common in this series for bush sounds; it is the sound of an axe cutting into a tree. Working at clearing the bush for a garden, men cut trees and rhythmically say *godo-godo-gugɔ-gugɔ* 'sounds of many axes cutting many trees and many trees falling and thumping the ground and resonating across the land'.

Frequent agents for *e* sounds are the bush and musical instruments. *Gele* and *kele* are used for the crunch and crackle underfoot of people walking through the bush or pigs stamping around in sago areas. *Gede* is the sound of the *sob,* the mussel-shell rattle that taps the floor during *gisalo* singing and dancing. In these cases the sounds are distinct at the source; the *o* cases, on the other hand, have a duller timbre and generally involve more motion.

In summary, then, each of six vowels iconically relates a semantic aspect of sound quality. Each can be used generically in the form of "lengthened vowel plus ɛ*lab"* for the class of sounds as a whole. With an initial consonant, each can be used singly or reduplicated or used with ɛ*lab.* There is also a pattern of combining the vowel with different consonants. Moreover, it is possible to create mixings of different groups either simply *(hɔ-gu, gugɔ)* or complexly *(godo-gugɔ).* Innovative usages, such as *fɛsɛ-fɛsɛ* for a pressure cooker, *tekɛ-tekɛ* for a typewriter, or *dolo-gili* ("whistle sound" of bird plus "continuous direction ambiguous sky hum") for a jet airplane, indicate that simple and concatenated forms can be newly created from the principles governing the categories.

In song these phonesthemes are mostly used for birds, water, and bush. The bird sounds are often different from standard onomatopoeic interpretations of bird calls because in song they are marking the fact that the bird is really a *kalu ɔbɛ mise* 'man in the form of a bird'. Water sounds are by far the largest group of *gɔnɔ to* used in song, and along with bush sounds, generally function as modifiers for place names.

In conversational speech there are three natural patterns for using *gɔnɔ to:* the sound word stands alone as an utterance; the sound word precedes a sentence; or the sound word is uttered and then followed by one of the following:

-ɛ*lan*	'it says like that'
-ɛlɛ *salan*	'it says like that' (uncontracted form)
-ɛlɛ *ganalan*	'it sounds like that'

These are formulaic and always given with the present habitual verb inflection, even when one is discussing past or future events. In talk syntax, then, *gɔnɔ to* appears initially or stands alone.

The reverse is true of song. Reduplicated and repeated forms of *gɔnɔ to* can appear alone as single lines, but otherwise they are always line final. The pattern is either:

(a) $\begin{bmatrix} \text{land name} \\ \text{water name} \\ \text{tree name} \\ \text{bird name} \end{bmatrix}$ +   *gɔnɔ to* reduplicated sound word (optionally repeated and optionally multiple or complex)

(b) $\begin{bmatrix} \text{land name plus land type} \\ \text{water name plus water type} \\ \text{tree name plus modifier} \end{bmatrix}$ +   *gɔnɔ to* (as above)

As in other poetic devices a basic element of compositional craft and control is the ability to simultaneously make explicit and ambiguous images. Examples generated by (a) are:

12) *Seyago, gɔlɔlɔ, gɔlɔlɔ, gɔlɔlɔ*

13) *Bo-wɛ, godo godo*
    tɛlɛs-ɛ godo godo

In (12) *seyago* is the Hooded Butcherbird, whose call symbol is *gɔlɔlɔ*. In (13) Bo is a land name, *tɛlɛs* a kind of tree, and *godo godo* is the sound of many axes cutting many trees. In (12) the *gɔnɔ to* refers to sound being made *by* the preceding element: "a *seyak* bird (calls) *gɔlɔlɔ.*" In (13) it refers to human action taking place *at* and *to* the preceding element: "At Bo (many axes cut many trees) *godo godo.*"

Similarly, examples generated by (b) follow the same pattern:

14) *Amo sagu, gululu*   15) *odag huyayɔ, bobo bobo*

Amo is a creek name, and *sagu* is generic for waterfall sound; *gululu* is a specific flowing sound; the sound is made *by* and *at* the preceding element. "At Amo creek the waterfall (sounds) *gulu gulu.*" In (15) *odag* is a tree name, *huyayɔ* means 'standing alone', and the reduplicated *bobo* represents wing-beating sounds, often conventionally associated with the loud wingbeats of *obei,* the Papuan Hornbill. Here the sound is taking place *around* the preceding element: "at a lone *odag* tree, *bobo bobo* (sound the wingbeats of a flock of hornbills)."

There are clear differences between *gɔnɔ to* and other word classes. *Gɔnɔ to* can stand alone as a complete utterance, but it cannot be negated. It is clearly not a trivial word class, because it has pattern and a high degree of use, and the elements can be decomposed to generate creative words. The major difference between phonesthesia in conversation and in song poetics is syntactic. In speech syntax a sentence follows the *gɔnɔ to* and contexts it. In song the *gɔnɔ to* is line final, in verbal position. As such it functions as an image verb, marking that the preceding element "is sounding X" or that some unstated source "is sounding X" at the preceding element.

Gɔnɔ to thus fits the general pattern of poetic devices; it adds explicating information at the same time that it adds ambiguating information; the image phonestheme provides an enlarged or impregnated sensation. The range of interpretation can be either very specific or very broad, depending on the knowledge of the listener; when the listener knows the places referred to intimately, a very explicit and potent image is registered. If the listener knows the place referred to but vaguely, a very wide range of images and possibilities may emerge. Listeners, then, are getting many different kinds of images from *gɔnɔ to,* just as they are from *bali to* and *sa-salan.* In all of these devices, the poetic intention involves the axiom that evocative imagery is produced when there is a simultaneity of just enough new information and just enough potential for multiple interpretation.

Tok

Tok means 'path', 'road', or 'gate', but as it is used in song, the sense is more that of "map." The device refers to the way that a song, from start to finish, projects not merely a description of places, but a journey. The song is successful when listeners are totally suspended into a journeying mood, experiencing the passage of song and poetic time as the passage of a journey. Many Kaluli men were able to explicate and describe this state of suspension concretely. They said there would be no song without a *tok* because there would be no "hardening." It is this "hardening" that is involved in getting the audience into a receptive mood.

The attentiveness demanded in looking for an "inside" and an "underneath" in the tension between nebulous images and definite ones is what moves Kaluli to the edges of their seats. Provocation, in effect, cannot take place without *tok,* because it is the song's path that envelops the attentiveness of the listeners. Pathetic images and pleas of aloneness make the listeners sad, but what ultimately moves them to tears is the projection of that sadness onto a map suggesting personal experiences. *Tok,* then, is the creation of a poetic map where images of named places focus land as a mediator of identity and self.[1]

Song composition is not the only situation when Kaluli daydream about journeying to places. While sitting by a creek, staring off into space from the longhouse porch, or relaxing on a trail in the bush, Kaluli often think about their lands. E. Schieffelin heard men say nostalgically, "Ah, my Bosavi" when staring off at the mountain (1976:148). When I was with Kaluli in the bush, accounts of lands, particularly garden sites, places where sago had been or was being made, places where longhouses had existed, and creeks were often noted sentimentally.

Places are not abstract locations for Kaluli. Every site is associated with certain specific aspects of life and social activity. E. Schieffelin's remark, "Kaluli identify themselves with place names because they see themselves reflected in their lands" (ibid.:45) is formally coded in song poetics by the device of *tok.* Constructing a song as a path, or *tok,* sets the listeners on a journey during which they simultaneously experience a progression of lands and places and a progression of deeply felt sentiments associated with them.

The importance of *tok* imagery in poetics is perhaps the foremost strategy for Kaluli composers. In many interviews I asked, "How do you make the audience weep?" Kaluli often responded, "You have to sing a *tok* that has their *hen wi* ('place names'); it is hearing their *hen wi* that makes them weep." In a sense, then, the *tok* is the skeletal aspect of song poetry. All other devices serve to reference pathetic and evocative imagery to the progression of the path.

1. On the importance of place names and geography as poetic inspiration, see Clarke 1975.

For the Kaluli, the metaphor "song is a map" is equivalent to the philosophical outlook that "life is a map." There are no explicit lines stating "life is a *tok*," "a tree is a home," "a garden is food," "a bird is a man" because these are assumed by Kaluli listeners and composers. Use of the *tok* in song maintains, sometimes subtly, sometimes directly, the consistency of these metaphors by juxtaposing land, tree, water, bird, and sensate images with first-person plaintive demands for attention or response. As in speech, lines like "I'm hungry," "Come and see me," "I'm alone," and rhetorical questions of the "I'm wondering . . ." form are never neutral statements: they mean "feel sorry for me and do something about it."

Tok is the locus of symbolic persuasion in song because it provides the most concrete images for listeners who know the sequence of lands and the most provocative images that the composer can craft toward the goal of making the listeners weep. At the same time, the *tok* suspends the listener into a journeying, dreamlike mood, which can be mysterious and nebulous for a great part of the song.

Control of the *tok* sequence is dependent upon the manipulation of form by the composer. In no case will a song really move listeners to tears if the *tok* is not crafted so that it climaxes, with all of the images falling into proper perspective like a puzzle, in the final portion of the song.

There are many styles and forms of making a *tok* in song. These styles are not linear progressions, because the point of the *tok* is to create a riddle of "what do X, Y, Z, have in common?" and then to build up this riddle, line by line, until the common denominator is obvious. The most common styles of *tok* construction are:

1) place names very close together
2) place names very far apart
3) place names that travel from one longhouse site to another
4) no place names; only tree names used to stand for the places
5) place names that surround a longhouse site but do not mention the name of the longhouse land
6) a path that has no place names but follows the course of creeks
7) place names that refer only to sago swamps and name only sago palms
8) hill names only, with co-occurring lines that mention a (spirit) tree found on the hill
9) place names of garden sites only
10) no place names used, only waterway and co-occurring tree names

In addition, these styles can:

a) start at the closest place to where the song is being sung and lead away from it, with places becoming farther and farther distant
b) start at a far place and gradually end up where the song is being sung
c) not reference the *tok* to the place being sung, as in (a) or (b), but move back and forth ambiguously, mystifying the audience about where the *tok* is going

In addition to these diverse resources, the singer can use other stylistic devices to build tension about the *tok*. One device is to sing the first half of the song with generic waterway names and tree names and no specific place names; the second half of the song then lists the specific sets of places that match the first half. Another strategy is to sing the opening part of the song *wɔnole salab* 'secretly speaking' so that the place names are mumbled and unclear. Another device is to sing the first portion of the song with names of very large rivers and creeks; while locating specific places, this leaves some ambiguity because these large waterways touch so many lands that the singer could have numerous places in mind.

The first portion of the song always uses the *tok* to ambiguate. This both draws the attention of the audience ("what lands will he sing?") and sets the mood for the entire *tok* and song. In all cases, Kaluli said that a sure bad start in song was to give too much explicit *tok* imagery. They clearly related the climaxing concept of *halaido domɛki* 'hardening' to a sustained, sequential building of the *tok*.

The actual words in the *tok* include generic and specific names for lands, waters, trees, and sago creeks and palms. All generic terms can be sung in either Sonia or Kaluli, and all of the water, tree, and sago generic or specific names can also be suffixed with a lexicon of descriptives. These adjectives indicate whether the tree stands alone, is fruited, decaying, leafless, small, large, and so forth.

In the first portion of a song, *tok* imagery tends to be embedded in three-line formulae and is not fronted.

(16) *Dowo, dinafa dowɛbi*
      Sululib bol-o
      dinafa dowɛbi

'Father, look out, take care from now on,
while staying at the *bol* tree at Sululib,
look out, and go carefully.'

(17) *Sago, ne domɛni*
milila-mɔwɔ, ne domɛni
sago, ne domɛni

'Cross-cousin I will stay (far away),
at the trunk of a *milila* tree, that's where I'll stay,
cross-cousin, that's where I'll stay.'

In (16) and (17) the *tok* is not the center of the message. These lines come
from the beginning of songs. In (16) the person being called "father" is
staying in the *bol* tree at Sululib, but the focus of the message is in the
repeated lines. The same holds in (17); the singer has used *milila* because
it is a palm tree not found in Bosavi except on the mountain itself or in
far away areas. *Milila* is thus a symbol for the outside world, and the
repeated message is that someone is going to stay there. In these examples, *tok* imagery is not used with any climaxing or focusing syntax or
repetition.

Compare now the patterns in syntax and repetition found in line
formulae in middle and final sections of song, where the imagery has
developed. Example (18) is from the same song as (17); it was sung about
three minutes later, and at the point when it was sung, the weeping
began.

(18) *Sago, ne Musubi misɛni*
Musubi milila-ya misɛni
Musubi misɛni.

'Cross-cousin, I will live at Port Moresby,
Port Moresby, at the *milila* tree, I will live there,
at Port Moresby, I will live'.

The composer has accomplished much by switching the verb from "stay"
to "live"; consultants said that this "hardened" the phrase. But notice
Musubi (Pt. Moresby) in each line. In the first it is focused by appearing
just before the verb, in the second it is focused by appearing line initial,
and in the third both of these features are combined.

The powerfulness of *Musubi* here is because the song is about two brothers who left Bosavi and never returned. *Musubi* is the farthest place in the outside world that any Kaluli have seen. The song built up to a climax using images of the outside world, little by little. Finally when the composer sang the name of *Musubi,* he did so with every emphatic form possible.

Another device in which syntactic form articulates with the building of the climax is a formula for negating, hence mystifying, the *tok.* These are three-line pairs that follow in sequence toward the end of a song, once a general *tok* is fairly well established. The form is used when there are many possibilities for alternate interpretations of the *tok.* For example:

(19) *Kugun-ɔlɔ*
  Gobulu malɔ
  E

  'this valley,
  not the one at Gobulu,
  E'

The composer follows an initially general image with a set of lines to narrow the possibilities. Each set names a generic kind of land or water or tree and then says "but not the one at X," where X is highly specific. In this way, the composer is not giving direct path information as to what place is important but is saying, "If you're thinking of X, you're wrong." After five or six of these, the composer can expect that singing a key place name will bring a member of the audience to tears. This is a deliberate climaxing device.

Finally, consider the following sets of lines:

(20) *Mubi gogo-wo*
  ne bɔbɛ-meno

  'At the *gogo* tree at Mubi,
  come and see me'.

(21) *Tolɔ mugun hɔnolo*
  odagɛ-fɔwɔ hɔnolo
  O

  'I'm going to the hill above Tolɔ creek
  I'm going to the fruited *odag* tree there
  O'.

These are the two most common patterns for place name phrases. In (20) all of the *tok* information is together; (XY) = Y at X, or X's Y. When there are examples like (21) with the verb repeated in the same position (always final) and the *tok* image preceding it, the assumption is always that the line 2 thing exists at the line 1 place. There is no grammatical marking for this in song, although it is necessary in speech.

In conclusion, *tok* usage in *gisalo* is highly flexible, but different sections of the song will host different kinds of syntactic patterns keyed to the climaxing structure. There is no *tok* emphasis in the beginning of the song; in the middle and in the end, the process of getting the right place name in line-initial and/or preverbal position is important to the emphasis the composer wishes to make. *Tok* is a highly manipulable and manipulative feature of Kaluli poetic grammar, the locus of several uses of linguistic resources. It is clearly the element of poetic form upon which all others depend in great part. A song that is otherwise "hard" but poorly organized in the *tok* will not move listeners to tears.

Adɛ and Imolabo: Core Symbols in Text as in Myth

In the *muni* bird story, four lines are attached to the weeping of the boy turned bird:

E E gi galino E E	=	E E your crayfish E E
E E nelɔ mɔmiyali E E	=	E E you didn't give to me E E
E E ne adɛloma E E	=	E E I have no *adɛ* E E
E E ni imolabo E E	=	E E I'm hungry E E

In the first chapter I noted that the first two lines were in fact conversational Kaluli, but the last two were unusual. *Ne adɛloma* 'I have no *adɛ*' is grammatical but never uttered in speech. *Ni imolabo* 'I'm hungry' changes *ne* to *ni* in order to mark childlike plaintiveness, and *imolabo* is Sonia, not Kaluli. These two lines signal the switch from *to halaido* 'hard words' to *ɔbɛ gɔnɔ to* 'bird sound words'. In the *muni* bird story, then, *ne adɛloma* and *ni imolabo* represent a talk of appeal, of begging, of aloneness, of isolation, of childlike bird sound.

The substance of this myth's text is recreated in the substance of *gisalo* songs, in which *adɛ* and *adɛloma* imagery and hunger and *imolabo* imagery are frequent. Indeed, without these two images it would be hard to think of having song poetics at all. They appear in almost all *gisalo* songs and frequently are major climaxing devices, co-occurring with a plaintive voice quality aimed at making listeners feel sorrow and pity.

In everyday speech, *adɛ* is used in begging contexts as a strategy of appeal. It can mark the assumption that the addressee has a role obligation to offer goods, assistance, or help. Invoking *adɛ* rather than the kin term *nado* 'sister' both focuses the utterance as a demand for assistance or goods and presupposes that the speaker feels owed and sad. In children's speech, *adɛ* usage co-occurs with the *geseab* begging intonation. These qualities are amplified and intensified in song, where "I have no *adɛ*" means "I'm alone, abandoned, isolated"; a symbolic equation is made between *adɛ* and family, society, social life, and obligation.

In song, the simplest use of *adɛ* is a yearning *wa adɛyo* before a line, which turns the message into a plea to *adɛ* for help. More common, however, is the use of *adɛ* for address:

(23) *Adɛ, ne bɔbɛ-meno*

'*Adɛ*, come and see me' (usually sung after a place name, implying "come and see me there")

(24) *Adɛ, ne oba hɛnɛno-wili?*

'*Adɛ*, where will I go' (sung before or after a place name)

(25) *Adɛ, ne X hɔnolo*

'*Adɛ*, I'm going to X'

These frames of asking, addressing, and pleading to *adɛ* articulate with the *tok* to indicate that the singer cannot stay at the place where *adɛ* is assumed to be.

The most provocative uses of *adɛ* come in the later parts of songs and take two forms. The first is with the hypothetical *kibabe* formula. *Ne adɛ kibabe* 'if I had an *adɛ*' evocatively sets up the implication, "I could stay here," "I wouldn't have to go," "I wouldn't be hungry," or "I wouldn't be alone." More common is the suffixing of *adɛ* by a negative, either in the final line of a series of references to *adɛ* or used alone in the climax of a song. *Ne adɛloma, ne adɛ-malobo, ne adɛmaka-kɛmi,* and other Sonia and Kaluli forms are employed in many songs to state the "I have no *adɛ*" theme. One explicit formula is the use of *ne adɛloma* lines for climax at the end of a sequence of kin terms. Kaluli find it very moving, despite the conventional symbolism, to hear "I have no *adɛ*" after lines that proclaim "I have no mother, father, sister, or brother." I know of no song texts in which *adɛ* precedes these other terms.

In speech, *adɛ* contrasts with kin terms in that it is never used with proper names, possessive prefixes, or pronouns. The only exception to this convention in song is that *adɛ* can be possessed, for example, in rhetorical uses like "Maybe my *adɛ* will call" or "Is my *adɛ* angry with me?" Even so, no examples of references to someone else's *adɛ* appear. In song, then, as in speech, *adɛ* is reserved for personal begging, plaintiveness, and evocation of sadness; song goes beyond speech uses by framing *adɛ* with *kibabe* or by use of the negative.

I have discussed the use of Sonia as a form of *bali to* that mystifies and intensifies the verbal message. The Kaluli interpretative axiom is "When the words are in Sonia, interpret them as being more pathetic than the Kaluli referential equivalent." Thus, while *imolabo* is the Sonia equivalent of Kaluli *mayabo* 'hungry', Kaluli always indicated that *imolabo* really meant 'empty' or 'starving'. This is quite similar to the way that verbs of "staying alone" are amplified from Kaluli to Sonia, so that they take on the meaning of "isolated" and "orphaned."

In song generally, *ne* and *ni* may freely alternate when used with verbs of pathetic states. In a song-listening frame, Kaluli are prepared to hear all *ne* as *ni* and to attach the extra plaintive-childlike qualities quite unconsciously. *Ni imolabo,* or a variant, appears frequently in *gisalo,* but unlike *adɛ* and *adɛloma,* is potentially found throughout, from the very opening lines to the closing ones. There is no strategic usage of it in specific song parts. It is used frequently with *tok* images to mean "I'm hungry at X"; it is also compounded with other verbs to create images like "sleeping hungry," "staying hungry," "going hungry," "calling hungry." It is often used with final-suffixed emphatics and is common in the second line of the *kibabe* formulae, as for instance, "If X sago was my place, I wouldn't be hungry," or "If I had X, I wouldn't be hungry."

Adɛloma and *imolabo* serve as abbreviations when Kaluli talk about poetic language. I frequently asked men what it was like to get the words to a song in mind. In a great many cases, people used the phrases *ne adɛloma* and *ni imolabo* in conjunction with a few local land and creek names to give a short *gisalo* example. *Adɛloma, imolabo,* and land, water, and tree names are the three most basic images of poetic language for Kaluli. This constitutes good evidence that the *muni* story is a conscious model of expressive form, and that *adɛloma* and *imolabo* are prime symbols of *sa-salan* and *bali to* in Kaluli thought.

Poetic Space and Time: The Verb Paradigm

In terms of the verb morphology specific to *gisalo* songs, most lines have a verb in final position. The root form may be Kaluli or Sonia, but the inflections follow a special system. There are four endings: *-e, -o, -ele, -olo.* (In actual performance *-o* and *-olo* phonologically vary freely with *-ɔ* and *-ɔlɔ*.) In everyday spoken Kaluli, *-e* endings mark past tense, *-o* endings can mark emphasis or familiarity, *-ele* endings mark future questions, and *-olo* is not found at all. For instance,

(26) *Hɔno tindab*
'It's raining'

Hɔno tindabe
'It rained'

Hɔno tindabo
'It's raining'!

Hɔno tindabele?
'Will it rain'?

*Hɔno tindabolo
(I once said this as a response to the question *hɔno tindabele?*; my partner laughed and told me that it was *to halaidoma* 'unhard words', i.e., ungrammatical.)

In song the four endings take on a different set of meanings: *-e* and *-o* are paired as statement and confirmation, and *-ele* and *-olo* are paired as rhetorical question and confirmation. In addition, each set marks an aspect of space and/or time; *-e* and *-o* are given readings of nearby action or action just getting underway, and *-ele* and *-olo* are given readings of more distant action or action that is clearly in process, being already well beyond its onset. With *tindab,* used for rain, large water sprays, or water falling sounds, the song translations would be:

(27) *tindabe*
'water is beginning to drop/spray *"tin"* here and now'

tindabo
'yes, water is beginning to drop/spray *"tin"* here and now'

tindabele
'has water been dropping/spraying *"tin"* there'?

tindabolo
'yes, water has been dropping/spraying *"tin"* there'

Thus, *-e* and *-o* can conventionally be translated with the notions of 'beginning to', 'here' and 'now', and *-ele* and *-olo* with 'has been' and 'there'.

The nature of these endings in no way constrains anything else about the shape of the verb. Usual Kaluli emphatics and evidentials can follow the verb and then be followed by the song aspects. Verbs can be simple or complex, and when they appear in the processual "while" form, marked by *-liki,* they are always marked also with *-e* or *-o,* adding the sense of 'while beginning to . . .' (e.g., speech *hɔidɛliki* 'while in the process of calling out' becomes *hɔidɛlikiyo* or *hɔidɛlikiye*).

The function of these markings is to suspend the time and space of song into a nebulous present, where actions are either beginning or under way and happening either nearby or vaguely distantly. Absent in song are all of the tense and aspectual markers used for specificity of time and the locatives used for specificity of space. The four markings create a tension with the map images because even though the named lands, waters, and trees may be distant from each other, the song journeys to and from them without devices for marking lengthy passage of time or great distance.

Song time and space is like a dream. Kaluli frequently noted that in the darkness of the performance space, with the flickering of torchlight and the mesmerizing rhythm of the dancer bobbing up and down from one end of the longhouse to the other, one lapses into a dreamy sleeplike state, where images become blurry and vague. Once in this state, the language need not be descriptively explicit; one journeys comfortably from place to place, relating to time as only the continuum of beginning and remaining in process and space as only a sense of the immediate and the remote.

One image verbally articulated by several Kaluli similar to "song is a dream" is "song is in your head." Text, like a waterfall *(sa),* is the "inner" part of song that comes into your head and swirls around in the pool of melody. The important thing for performer and audience alike is the inner sensation, in which time and space cease to have the very precise gradations that one experiences when actually journeying. This is consistent with the Kaluli notion that song is not a description of the ways things are, but a suspended state during which one journeys in a sensation world, much like a dream, where space and time do not have precise bounds.

It should be noted, however, that this dreamlike time state does not impoverish song on the descriptive level. Consider, for example, two verbs for the description of sunlight. The first of these (28) indicates walking east or west and marks sunlight on the front/back axis, the second (29) walking north/south, with sunlight on one side or the other.

28) *heselebe*		29) *heselabe*
heselebo	beginning, evenly lit sun	*heselabo*
heselebele	time passage, more sun in	*heselabele*
heselebolo	one direction than another	*heselabolo*

Similar sets exist for sunsets, cloud formations, and other very elaborate images. While such verbs mark highly precise and specific sensations, the time and space frames suspend the listener into a dreamlike, receptive state. This suspended state is coded in the message form, while the message content can be highly specific. As with other features of "bird sound words," verb morphology codes messages that are simultaneously ambiguous and explicit, at the surface level, and underneath, directly referential and impregnated with an inside.

Conclusion

Kaluli poetic ideals and practice utilize linguistic means for social ends by framing messages meant to evoke a deeply emotional response. Listeners interpret poetic lines as having "insides" and "underneaths" because they are not direct and interactive "hard" words but are instead "bird sound words." One does not speak poetically in order to get desired goods, services, actions, or assistance. Rather, "bird sound words" are invoked to alter the framing of interactions, moving them onto a plane where underlying feelings, emotions and thoughts associated with loss come to the listener's mind and result in a feeling of sorrow.

It is hardly surprising that the most prominent poetic images derive from the most poignant social values in Kaluli everyday life. Food as a mediator of relationships, as expressed in themes of hunger and denial, focuses the desired states of giving and sharing and the ruptured states of abandonment or lack of support and family. Social relations as a model of reciprocity and caring, as expressed in themes of lack of kin and family ties, focus the desired states of comradery and cohesion and the ruptured states of fragmentation and isolation. Ecology and environment as a model of balance and a mediator of social identity, as expressed in themes of journeying and bird metaphor, focus the desired states of identification with place and geographical history and the ruptured states of vulnerability and lack of home.

In all cases these content features of poetic imagery resonate with the contextually situated state of mind that listeners bring to song occasions. An aesthetic tension emerges from the ways coding and content articulate to impregnate lines with "insides" and "underneaths" that register with listeners on several levels of knowledge, expectation, and attentiveness. This tension is intimately related to the prescriptive and evaluative notion of *halaido domɛki*, the "hardening" of song, that is so important to the Kaluli sense of drama, buildup, and climax in a song that moves a listener to tears. To flesh out the ways in which musical coding and performance style co-articulate with these poetic ideals and devices, I will turn to the analysis of song structure and the examination of a single song's construction combining "bird sound words" with "bird sound."

5

Song That Moves Men to Tears

It was once a general assumption in ethnomusicology that nonliterate peoples, who did not notate their music, did not have "theories of music." Music theory was accepted as a special accomplishment of the West that allowed "us" to analyze "them." The first book I ever read in ethnomusicology noted: ". . . in primitive music a scale does not exist in the mind of the native musicians, so the musicologist must deduce it from the melodies" (Nettl 1956:45).

I have long felt intellectually uncomfortable with such assumptions, believing, on the contrary, that wherever there is music, there is some kind of theory underlying its production and significance. My conviction was somewhat bolstered by Alan Merriam's important book *The Anthropology of Music* (1964), which advocated an ethnomusicology that integrated studies of musical sound with associated concepts of music and music-making. Yet after reading this program, it was somewhat difficult to assess the statement in his major monograph that "the Flathead (Indians) simply do not verbalize about music" (Merriam 1967:45). Was this statement, like others of its type, a remark about preference, about inability, about a lack of vocabulary, about absence of theory? Was it a remark about difficulties of phrasing questions appropriately, translating them accurately, and reversing the procedure with responses? Was it a remark about listening in on the way people speak or do not speak among themselves, the way they respond to a researcher's questions, or the way they feel about speaking on the topic of music? These are complex issues, and it is clear that the status of language usage in fieldwork praxis is essential to resolving them.

I went to Bosavi with these factors weighing strongly on my mind. Learning to ask questions correctly in Kaluli was, I felt, essential to studying Kaluli linguistic denomination of musical concepts and associated theoretical postulates of the musical system. My contention was that music theory must be approached as a cognitive, conceptual, and social matter and must be dealt with at the ideational level, as well as from transcriptions and deductions from the sounds.

At first I spent long periods of time listening to conversations among various people, often not understanding much of what was said, which seemed indirect. Later I began recording these statements without interrupting them and then worked with an assistant on their transcription and translation. This turned out to be the best way to learn what sorts of questions could be asked and what sort of language was appropriate for asking them. My bias here was the belief that language codes musical concepts into a lexicon whose systematic features embody cognitive arrangements, that is, classifications and categorizations socially learned and shared to differing degrees by different sectors of the community (stratified by factors like age, sex, interest, skill, experience, and social expectation).

As my work progressed, I modified this plan in a basic way by composing songs or singing ones that Kaluli had composed in order to elicit responses from a few men. Often I made calculated mistakes (at other times they were neither calculated nor conscious) in either their construction or performance, and my friends hardly needed to be asked to tell me what was wrong. They commented on mistakes both verbally and by sung correction, and the form of the vocabulary used for responding was most instructive. It seemed that water and waterfall terms were systematically employed as metaphors for sound structure: "Your waterfall ledge is too long before the water drops," "There is not enough flow after the fall," "The water stays in the pool too long," "There is much splashing"; these were typical responses Kaluli made to my melodies, which had unbalanced contours, abruptly ending phrases, overly centered lines, and poorly paced meter.

I found that Kaluli song terminology and conceptualization of musical form relate systematically to the terminology of waterfalls, water sounds, and water motion. Here Kaluli language does more than mediate mental constructs via sounds and words; through polysemy it paradigmatically relates two semantic fields—sound and water—permitting both shared connotative and denotative features of the two domains to be linked in systematic metaphor.[1] Kaluli musical theory, then, verbally surfaces in metaphoric expression. This is hardly surprising, since theories are often expressed as systematic metaphors. Wave, wave equation, wave length, wave band, sine wave, square wave, wave mechanics, and so forth are physical metaphors for forms of oscillation. Similarly, numerous waterway terms in Kaluli are visual metaphors for forms of sound.

The first part of this chapter focuses on Kaluli concepts of musical form and construction, specifically detailing how water, a core natural image in everyday experiences, provides the metaphoric means for thinking about the organization of music. The second part complements this conceptual level by analyzing the form and performance of a single *gisalo* song in musical, poetic, and contextual terms, specifying how its aesthetic intentions articulate to move a man to tears.

Composition, Melody, and Text

The Kaluli notion of composition rests on a distinction between melody and text. *Gisalo* is the term for 'song' or 'melody', and *sa-gisalo* is the term for 'text', that is, 'words inside *gisalo*'. Melody is linked to the call symbol of the *muni* bird. The 'inside' *(sa)*, or text, of *gisalo* uses as a core device the talk of the myth; the talk of the boy once he has turned into a bird, ɔbɛ gɔnɔ *to* 'bird sound words'. Thus *gisalo* "melody" or "song" in the sense of *sound* is conceptualized as a melodic pattern derived from birds, while *sa-gisalo* is the *text*, conceptualized as a talk pattern borrowed from birds. Song composition involves the use of sonic and linguistic patterns symbolizing bird communication. Sound is "natural," given in the melody of bird calls; text is "cultural," found inside sound, suggested by it or crafted for appeal in relation to it.

The distinction between text and melody is evident when Kaluli talk about composition *per se*. *Molan* 'one sings' is used in two senses:

1. Lest it seem this metaphoric basis for sound construction is rather idiosyncratic, it should be pointed out that the 'Are'are people of Malaita in the Solomon Islands are reported to think in precisely the same way about bamboo and music (Zemp 1978, 1979). 'Are'are are an island people whose main music is produced by panpipe ensembles. The entire terminology of panpipe construction, tuning, and performance, and the associated musical notions of intervals, contours, and song forms are all lexically coded with terms that are polysemous with forms of bamboo. Hence water and bamboo, key natural images for these two very different societies, provide metaphoric means for shaping the expression of sonic experience and the theory of its formal organization.

that of vocalizing both text and melody, and that of vocalizing just melody. *Sa-molan* is used for singing to oneself without vocalizing—singing "inside" one's head—or for the sensation of having a song in mind, or for getting words "inside" the head. The most common usage of the verb is "to compose song." Kaluli say that all composition starts with melody "outside" or "around"; it is "in the air" with the sound of birds or actually vocalized as one sings a melody. *Sa-molan* refers to the sensation of words that fit the melody coming to mind. Kaluli say that this is "like a waterfall flushing down into a waterpool." Composition thus involves an "inner" text bonding onto the existing "outer" melody.

Two other concepts in Kaluli compositional terminology further exemplify the idea that sound is a natural, given substance, and that text is a composed, created substance. The first is *gisalo kɔtɔgɔdɔ*, a standard melody to which one may put different texts. I learned of this concept while composing my first *gisalo* song. I sang back a portion for a composer-assistant, who told me, in effect, to put aside melodic complications and use a standard *gisalo* melody, a *gisalo kɔtɔgɔdɔ*, and attach my own text. Later I discovered that this is the conventional way inexperienced composers begin.

The only other speech context for *kɔtɔgɔdɔ* is *kalu kɔtɔgɔdɔ*, used for two people who look alike or who are dressed or decorated identically. As with two people who look the same on the surface but who are quite different in substance, a *gisalo kɔtɔgɔdɔ* is similar to another song only on the sound surface; its "inside" text is substantively different. The implication is that melody can be formulaic, but the creative and newly composed aspect of a song lies in the text.

A related notion is *gisalo nodɔlɔ*, a *gisalo* song copied in terms of major imagery of text but reformulated with new place names to make up a different map *(tok)*. This device is not as common as *gisalo kɔtɔgɔdɔ;* it stands more as an homage to another composer than as a learning device.

My major knowledge of this device came about when a young man from my village was so moved by a *gisalo* sung by a spirit medium that he came to my house and asked to listen to the tape recording in order to learn the song. He explained that should a *gisalo* ceremony materialize, he wanted to use the song and substitute the land, tree, and water names of the longhouse where the ceremony was to be held. A bachelor, he thought the song was so powerful that if he sang it well, a woman would follow him home from the ceremony, that is, consent to elope.[2]

In *gisalo nodɔlɔ,* then, both the melody and a portion of the text containing innovative metaphors and *bali to* imagery are reused; the newly composed element is the map. Through this device, we see how innovative metaphors become the stuff of more conventional symbols, spread and shared over growing sectors of the population. Again, text is the symbolically persuasive core of the song in which the composer makes his mark. The following structural arrangement summarizes:

	MELODY (GISALO)	:	TEXT (SA-GISALO)	::
primary metaphors		(is to)		(as)
water	water pool (*hɔn mogan*)	:	water fall (*hɔn sa*)	::
birds	bird sound (*ɔbɛ gɔnɔ*)	:	bird sound words (*ɔbɛ gɔnɔ to*)	::
space	outside and around	:	inside and down	::
additive metaphor	sing (*molan*)	:	compose (*sa-molan*)	

Abstracting to the paradigmatic level:

	Mythic and		Created and	
Underlying Metaphors	"given"	:	"composed"	::
	Bird	:	Man	::
	Nature	:	Culture	

2. E. Schieffelin (1976:24, 60, 126, 171, 214) discusses the social significance of *gisalo* performances leading to elopement, and the theme of the woman who loses her heart to a dancer.

Intervals, Melodic Movement, and Shape

With only one exception, Kaluli terminology for intervals and melodic contours metaphorically derives from waterfall terms. The two principal intervals for the Kaluli are the descending major second and the descending minor third. These intervals are found in the call of the *muni* bird, the tonal organization of *gisalo* song, and *sa-yɛlab* melodic weeping. Kaluli always name the descending major second *gese* and the descending minor third *sa*.

Gese, from imperative *gesema* 'make one feel sorrow or pity', is used widely in relation to the begging intonation of children's speech (B. Schieffelin 1979) and the communication of sadness. *Gese-* can prefix sound verbs of speaking, singing, whistling, or weeping. In all of these cases it means that there is a descending, plaintive intonation. As a specific term, it marks the descent of a major second.

Sa can stand alone to mean "waterfall," can prefix terms for parts or kinds of waterfalls, and can prefix verbs of soundmaking and textual organization. As it generically stands for "waterfall" in its usual context, it generically stands for the interval of the descending minor third in sound terminology. This is in many ways the most basic and most important interval for the Kaluli. It is found in the calls of the fruitdoves and stands alone as a symbol of sadness, isolation, and loss.

Aside from the specific named intervals of the descending major second and minor third, *gese* and *sa,* the most important concept in Kaluli terminology is that of the tonal center. *Sa-gu* is the onomatopoeic and generic term for "waterfall sound"; in musical terminology it means descent to the tonal center. When the tonal center is held for a long duration in song, it is called *sa-gulu. Gulu* is onomatopoeic for long continual flow at a waterfall. As a verb, *sa-gu-lab* means to sing a line that moves to and ends on the tonal center. *Sa-gu-lab* is also the name for the middle section of *gisalo* songs, in which the tonality recenters by descent to the tonal center. *Sa-gulu* is also the name for the final two lines of *gisalo* songs, each consisting of one syllable droned on the tonal center.

Turning to melodic contours, the most important features are descent and terracing shapes. In the names for waterfall parts, the common term for the ledge, or upper place from which the water drops, is *sa-wɛl*. In melodic terminology, *sa-wɛl* refers to the leading pitch in a line or phrase from which the melody descends. Descent to level melodic shape is called *sa-mogan*. A *mogan* is a still or lightly swirling water pool; *sa-mogan* is the flow of a waterfall into a level waterpool beneath it. This descent to level contour is precisely what is melodically marked by *sa-mogan.*

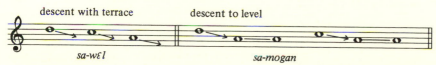

Level melodic contours are themselves named *sa-min;* a *sa-min* is the level area leading to the waterfall drop. *Sa-min* also refers to the slightest degree of melodic ascent in *gisalo,* an ascent of a major second. Such slight ascent is found in generally level melodic shapes, that is, melodic shapes that ascend and hold, or ascend, drop to their initial pitch, and then hold.

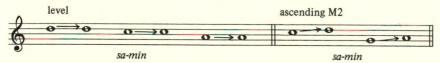

Just as there is no specific name for the interval of an ascending major second, there are no specific names for the larger ascending intervals of the minor third or the perfect fourth. Both the ascending minor third and the ascending perfect fourth are frequent in *gisalo* melodies, but the Kaluli terminology refers only to their contour context and not to their intervalic length.

The term *sa-ga* refers to the branching of a waterway so that one portion remains high on the land and the other drops to a waterfall. In song terminology, *sa-ga* is most frequently used to note the ascent of a minor third or a perfect fourth before descent.

ascent P4 and descent   or   ascent m3 and descent

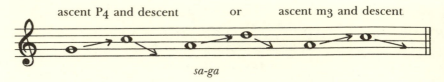

sa-ga

Finally, all *gisalo* songs have contours descending from the tonal center to the minor third beneath and then back to the center. Kaluli term this melodic movement *sa-kɔf.* In waterfall terminology, the *sa-kɔf* is a small waterfall or overflow from a *sa-mogan.* The *mogan* is level, and the overflow is created by a larger waterfall emptying into it. The overflow, like a small waterfall, falls to another level, forms a pool, and evens off.

bounce to tonal center

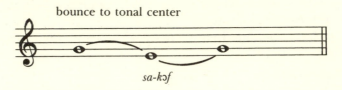

sa-kɔf

To summarize, there are nine basic terms in the Kaluli terminology of melodic intervals and contours of *gisalo.* Two of these name specific intervals, and two others describe motion toward and duration of the tonal center. The other five describe patterns of descent, level, and ascent in melodic movement. Where intervals are not specifically named, they are included explicitly in labels for the major contour context in which they are found.

Rhythm, Meter, and Duration

Compared to the area of melody, there is less in Kaluli theory and talk about the temporal aspects of song. Kaluli use terms deriving from water movement as musical terminology for pacing. In these terms, which are all onomatopoeic, meter and pulse are inextricably related to sensations of resonance and timbre. For instance, the notion of "flow," particularly waterfall flow, is given in standard onomatopoeia as *gulu.* The iconicity of the vowel *u* indicates the sensation of downward movement; *gu* is generic for waterfall sound and *gulu* the most widely used term for waterfall flow. As the term is extended to the domain of temporal organization, Kaluli say that the pace or "flow" of *gisalo* should be an even *gulu.*

Kaluli indicated three levels at which *gulu* applied in the pacing of *gisalo:* the bodily movement of the dancer, the pulse and timbre of the *sob* mussel shell rattle accompanying all *gisalo,* and the pulse and timbre of the *fasela,* the streamers of shiny yellow stripped palm leaves that are a basic part of the dancer's costume.

The bodily motion of the dancer is an up and down, bobbing from the knee movement, which Kaluli say originated with the *wɔkwele* bird, the Giant Cuckoodove. *Wɔkwele* prominently nest in rock gorges near waterfalls; they bob up and down, moving forward slightly or staying in place. Kaluli imitate the call as *wɔk-wu,* the first syllable on the up motion and the second on the down. The onomatopoeia here conforms to the out and down motion and space of sound. Kaluli say that the "flow" of dance should be like the two-part *wɔk-wu* of *wɔkwele,* moving evenly up and down. On every downward movement the *sob* mussel shell rattle clashes lightly.

The *sob* is a rattle whose sound is produced by the shaking of its own substance against the longhouse floor (see figure 15). It consists of about thirty mussel shells (bivalve mollusks, *Virgus beccarianus*),[3] each strung to a web that attaches to a long single string *(kigil).* The excess of string is wrapped around a handle, *olɔ sɛsɛlɔ* ('striped cane'). The dancer's arms are held at his sides, fully extended. In the right hand he holds the *olɔ sɛsɛlɔ,* which manipulates the string and *sob.* A well-strung *sob* has the shells tied to the center web *(asu)* so that all shell bottoms are equidistant from the floor. The dancer does not tense and raise the right hand so as to bounce the shells on the floor. Rather, the shells always touch the floor slightly; on the dancing down motion, as the knees flex, the shells jangle together and brush the floor. Kaluli say that the dancer should not use the wrist to pull the *sob,* it should "flow" with the *gulu* or *wɔk-wu* of the dancer. In effect, the instrument's sound flows indexically to the body's flow.

In the crowded longhouse during a ceremony, the dancer moves down and back through the center aisle. Throughout the movement, the *sob* sounds at his feet, marking his precise motion and placement in space. The darkness of the house limits the visibility of the *sob* itself; the sound, however, distinctly marks the up-and-down motion of the dancer. Its onomatopoeic representation is *gede-gede,* the vowel *e* marking distinct crunching and crackling sounds made at the ground.

Even though the sound is produced by the *sob* shells, it is the *olɔ*

---

3. I am grateful to Barry Roth of the California Academy of Sciences for this identification.

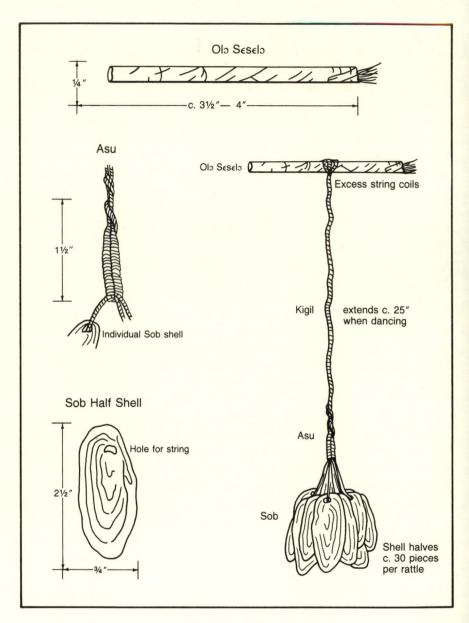

Oᴐ Sɛsɛᴐ

¼″

c. 3½″ — 4″

Asu

1½″

Individual Sob shell

Oᴐ Sɛsɛᴐ

Excess string coils

Kigil

extends c. 25″
when dancing

Sob Half Shell

Hole for string

2½″

¾″

Asu

Sob

Shell halves
c. 30 pieces
per rattle

Figure 15. The *sob*

sɛsɛlɔ that is essential for using the instrument, and one cannot perform *gisalo* without it. *Olɔ sɛsɛlɔ* is the substance that empowers Kaluli to dance "like a *wɔkwele* at a waterfall." *Olɔ sɛsɛlɔ* are not manufactured by Kaluli but are passed on to them by spirit mediums, who get them from *ane mama* (see E. Schieffelin 1976:214 for an analysis of the role of the *olɔ sɛsɛlɔ* in relations between *gisalo* and the spirit world). The small etched piece of arrowmaking cane appears on the medium's chest when he wakes up. He gives it to an appropriate relative of a spirit he has seen, and it is then passed on within the family. The hollow inside of the four-inch-long piece of thin cane contains magical substances, such as a unique form of crystal said not to exist in Bosavi and a bit of feces of the *wɔkwele* bird. Sometimes the open end is stuffed closed with a small feather from an *ɔlon* bird, the Raggiana Bird of Paradise. The *olɔ sɛsɛlɔ* transforms the *sob* from a rhythmic and timbral device to a link between the dancer, *ane mama,* and waterfalls.

In every minute of *gisalo* song, there are about 120 pulses of the *sob;* the variation is generally 112–30. It will be recalled that my discussion of the pacing of *sa-yɛlab* weeping gave evidence that the Kaluli terms *hɛsa* 'gently' and *dinafa* 'carefully' correlate with metronome of $\quad = 120$. In *gisalo* the play of the *sob* and the coordinating downward bob of the dancer have a similar metronome of two pulses per second; the terms *hɛsa* and *dinafa* equally apply.

The final area to which *gulu* pacing applies is the *fasela.* These are streamers of a shiny yellow-to-light-green color, stripped from palm leaves. They are attached in the rear of the dancer's wide bark belt, spring up to the height of the dancer's shoulders and then fall all the way down to the ankles. E. Schieffelin (ibid.:23), discussing the *gisalo* dancer's costume and demeanor, pointed out that Kaluli told him the *fasela* should "break like a waterfall." The *fasela* should not be limp and just fall to the ankles, but must flow, *gulu.* When the dancer bobs upward, the *fasela* flow above the shoulders, and when he bobs downward they flow out and down, like water going over a *sa-wɛl,* a waterfall ledge.

This concern with the motion of the *fasela* in dance movement is most apparent when Kaluli costume for a ceremony. While watching a group of men prepare for a *kɔluba* ceremony, I noticed how two assistants helped the dancer trim, position, and strip the underneath of the *fasela* once the entire set of leaves was placed in the belt. They spent about twenty minutes at it, now and again instructing the dancer to move up and down, so they could test the flow. Attention to detail involved both the visual aspect of the flow and the sound, a continuous shimmering that is distinctly louder on the down motion. The *fasela* should make a *gulu* like an even-flowing waterfall. Kaluli liken the *fasela* and *sob* to a waterfall, and the dancer to a *wɔkwele,* moving up and down and singing in front of it.

Summarizing, then, the Kaluli notion of *gulu,* or 'flow', in pacing: a metric pulse of ♩ = 120; a timbral notion of resonance and continuity of sound while maintaining distinct pulses; prescriptive ideals of *hɛsa* 'gently' and *dinafa* 'carefully'; and symbolic equivalences between dancer, *wɔkwele* bird, and sound/movement location at a waterfall.

Several other terms for moving water are commonly used as rhythmic terminology. In each case the terms code recurring stresses, durative resonant quality, or timbre for the sound. Where the meter is choppy and the resonance uneven or marked by short silences, the applicable term is *kubu,* irregular water splashing sounds. On the other hand, positive evaluative terms are *fo* or *bu,* which in literal contexts mark the pulsating and continuous quality of water rushing over rocks. For a song whose pulse slows down or becomes slow and then comes back up to tempo, the applicable term is *golo,* the sound of variable waterpool swirl.

Vocal Style, Technique, and Performance

In the style and technique of performance, the most important domain for Kaluli is that of vocal production, a constant topic in my discussions with composers, performers, and listeners. Moreover, it was a regular part of discussions I overheard among Kaluli themselves.

Kaluli generally speak of *gisalo mɔlɔ dagan* 'gisalo song voice' and mean several things by this term. First, the sound should be open and unstrained; it should not be nasal or overly head resonant, nor should it be overly breathy or hoarse. Second, the sound should be resonant, clear, enunciated, distinct, and not clipped. Third, the sound should carry "like water rushing over rocks."

In both natural and formal elicitation settings, Kaluli used the verbs for "sing" and "speak" interchangeably when discussing song. *Molab* can mean "sing" in the sense of vocalizing melody and text or "sing" in the sense of vocalizing melody only. *Salab* is a more specific verb, focused on the language use or style of song. It can refer to the "speaking" of a song text or to the style of speaking in song. Selection of these verbs when discussing song is the manner by which Kaluli focus the emphasis on the words, the performance, or the melody plus words as the key topic. When discussing matters of pacing in song, then, Kaluli would talk about *dinafa molab* or *hɛsa molab* 'one sings carefully', 'one sings gently', in a manner that is paced, deliberate, even; when discussing the map in the *tok* of the song, they would use notions like *kɔne salab, kɔnema salab, dihɔgu salab,* meaning that the text was referring to distant, nondistant, or indirect places, respectively.

The most important notion expressed in connection with both *molab* and *salab* concerns vocal register and the pragmatics of song language; this revolves around the verb *gesema* 'make one feel sorrow or pity'. I have discussed the use of this verb for children's begging (following B. Schieffelin 1979), its use to characterize a style of weeping (*gese-yɛlab*, chapter 3), its importance in poetic style (chapter 4), and its use to name the musical interval of a descending major second. When attached to sound verbs, it forms the following paradigm:

(1) *gese-holab*
'one whistles plaintively, evocatively, with descending intonation'

(2) *gese-ganalab*
(used only for *uluna* 'jew's harp', or for fruitdoves)
'it sounds sadly, plaintively, evocatively, with descending intonation'

(3) *gese-yɛlab*
'one weeps plaintively, melodically, sadly, with descending intonation'

(4) *gese-salab*
'one speaks plaintively, (appealing, begging, poetically) with sad, evocative words and intonation'

(5) *gese-molab*
'one sings sadly, plaintively, evocatively, with descending intonation'

Gese-molab and *gese-salab* were the two most frequently used descriptives I heard mentioned in discussions of song. Moreover, *gese-* is used to describe the style of speech and weeping in the story of "the boy who became a *muni* bird." It is the term used most often to refer to the style of talk used by children when they feel sad, lost, abandoned, or denied. The pervasiveness of *gesema* and *gese* in these domains provides more evidence for the explicit connections Kaluli make between expressions of social sentiment, modalities of sound (weeping, poetics, song), birds (particularly fruitdoves), and the myth, "the boy who became a *muni* bird."

Three other sets of constructs are commonly used by Kaluli in discussing vocal performance. The first set relates forms of singing the text to strategies of concealment and *bali to*. The second set concerns the vocal interaction of the lead singer and the chorus. The third involves voice qualities used in performed singing.

Wɔnole salab and *nunugulu salab* are two common ways of singing song texts so that the words are audibly concealed from the audience. These are attention-getting devices as well as strategic poetic resources. *Wɔnole salab/molab* means 'one speaks/sings secretly'; what is heard is either humming or mumbling. Kaluli interpret this to mean the singer is singing "in his own head," thus garbling the message. The inference is that there is deliberate obfuscation for a reason that will become clear once the entire song or a major part of it has been sung. On the other hand, *nunugulu salab/molab* (note the onomatopoeia in *nunu-gulu* 'falling down and droning') refers to speaking/singing text in a way that is phonologically well formed but "out of reach." It is a soft and distant kind of singing/speaking one hears just well enough to know that it is speech. Occasionally one or a few words are audible, which makes the audience even more attentive.

Wɔnole and *nunugulu* vocal production are found in the very opening of songs in which the singer performs without any vocal accompaniment by a chorus. These devices are more common in *gisalo* songs performed by spirits singing through mediums during seances, although they also occur in the *gisalo* songs sung in actual ceremonies. Both of these terms can also characterize secretive or inaudible speech in natural talk.

The second set of typical terms concerns the form of vocal parts. The opening parts of *gisalo* are sung solo, *inɛli molab* 'one sings alone'. The remainder of the song is sung with a chorus. The singer's lines are each repeated by the chorus, but not in a typical call and response form (responsorial or antiphonal). Rather, the chorus begins a split second after the singer, as if it knows the song precisely as well as he does, and ends a moment behind the singer, then picking up the singer's next line a moment after it has begun. The chorus' pitches and text are identical to those of the singer. This form of strict canonic imitation by the chorus is called *tiab,* and the chorus as a group is referred to as the *tiab kalu* 'chorusing men'.

The lead singer, once joined by the chorus, is no longer *inɛli molab* in style but *dulugu molab* 'singing lead'. *Dulugu* (from imperative *duluguma* 'lift up over') refers to the part that stands out; *dulugu salab* is used in daily contexts to mean 'to speak first', 'to hold the floor', or 'to lead the discussion'.

There is no term for singing in unison and indeed Kaluli never sing this way. They take recourse to bird and water analogies when discussing leader/chorus organization, explaining that, like birds and flowing water, they do not sing together, starting and stopping at precise or discrete times. Rather, the important factor is the continuity of flow in the overlapping. The Kaluli term for 'follow' (*fɛsa hanab*) is never used to describe the relationship of the chorus to the singer. The parts are layered, not linear.

Finally, for the actual vocal qualities of the singer, the term *dagan* 'voice/throat' is always used (as in *gisalo molɔ dagan,* above). There are two common problems in vocal production: "cracks" from singing too high and "breaks" from singing too strenuously. The first of these is what Kaluli call *dagano sundab* 'one's voice knots', and the second they call *dagano alo asubidab* (*alo* 'fencepost timber', *asubiduma* 'split'). Having one's voice split like fencepost timber is clearly worse than a random crack or two. An overworked or split voice, which makes the singer sound hoarse and/or out of breath, rates a highly negative *dagano mɔgago* 'bad voice'. It is considered too serious for the usual temporary cure of soft bananas (the preferred food of singers before a performance, said to "soften" the throat).

On the other hand, all positive terminology for voice quality derives from water or bird qualities. *Dagano ebelab* comes from *hɔno ebelab* 'water keeps on flowing beyond the point of vision', commonly used to describe the path of a waterway moving out of one's view in the distance but also directly next to or close to one's immediate body. It is used to describe the continuity, resonance, and carrying power of the voice of a singer whose song "keeps on flowing." *Dagano fodab* comes from *hɔno fodab* 'water rushes strongly and continuously with *fo* sound', commonly used to describe powerful white water breaking over rocks or large bodies of evenly rushing water. It describes the strength of a singer's voice.

From birds (specifically fruitdoves), the most common evaluative remarks about voice quality are *dagano mada kalo ɔngo* or *dagano mada howɛn ɔngo* 'of a voice really like *kalo*' or 'of a voice really like *howɛn*'. By selecting *kalo* (Pink-spotted Fruitdove) or *howɛn* (Orange-bellied Fruit-dove), Kaluli make an evaluation about the plaintiveness of voice quality and the degree to which it is reminiscent of one of these bird's calls, which are really the calls of *ane mama* 'gone reflections', who are in the treetops *kalo* or *howɛn mise* 'in the form of a *kalo* or *howɛn*'.

In sum, the linguistic marking of vocal production and the degree to which Kaluli talk about vocal production in their discussions of song parallel the other aspects of song and poetic conception. In all cases metaphoric relations between sound, birds, and water are drawn. As with weeping, poetics, and song terminology *per se*, Kaluli notions concerning voice quality make explicit links between children's intonation of loss and abandonment, birds, plaintiveness, and sadness. These notions operate on both prescriptive and evaluative levels.

Staging: Sound, Space, Costume, and Darkness

Having noted some salient features of Kaluli conceptualization of musical form, it is essential to point out the importance Kaluli attach to the interdependence of these features with the actual staging of *gisalo*. Staging is the method by which the audience is prepared to treat musical form and style as a meaningful, intentional coding of sentiments. Staging is the focusing by which bird and water metaphors come to their full expression.

Consider the central qualities of the experience of *gisalo:* hearing song that calls to mind a bird at a waterfall and meditating hypnotically on dreamlike images of lands and places; being filled with nostalgic feelings of sadness for deceased friends and relatives; becoming overwhelmed by sentiments of abandonment; and being moved to tears and weeping. These are all dependent upon the articulation of form and staging. As E. Schieffelin argues, it is not just the form of *gisalo*, but the drama, the excitement, and the heightened expectations culminating in its performance that make it so moving to Kaluli (1976: 24):

> The Kaluli regard *gisalo* with enthusiasm and affection. They find it exciting, beautiful, and deeply moving. The dancer in full regalia is

a figure of splendor and pathos. This is not because of the ordeal of burning he must face; rather it is the very beauty and sadness that he projects that causes people to burn him. From the Kaluli point of view, the main object of *gisalo* is not the burning of the dancers. On the contrary, the point is for the dancers to make the hosts burst into tears. . . . To the dancer and the chorus, this reflects rather well on their songs.

The sound of *gisalo* performance has a specific gestalt when heard in the context of the longhouse at night. The longhouse is about sixty feet long, thirty feet wide, ten to fifteen feet high, and four to six feet off the ground. It is constructed with forest woods and barks. The small door-ways at the ends each lead to a veranda and are connected by a long corridor; combined with the humpback shape of the roof, this produces a unique resonance. In the house, sound has an open quality with a slight reverberation. During a ceremony the house is packed with people and filled with sound.

At the same time, the most quiet that one will ever find Kaluli is during a ceremony. Kaluli love to make dramatic noises; they enjoy exuberant display and can fondly greet each other with yelling and whooping. But at the very beginning of a ceremony, an air of hushed anticipation sweeps over the audience. It is the one occasion when Kaluli value quiet.

Gisalo is sung only inside the house. All other varieties of Kaluli song can be sung outdoors, and they often are when women or men are working. These work songs come from previous ceremonies, and there are no constraints on singing them outside of ceremonial contexts, even though they were originally composed for ceremonial performance. *Gisalo*, on the contrary, is never sung for work. Although one may hear a fragment here and there or a man might whistle a portion of *gisalo* outdoors, it is only performed in the longhouse. Furthermore, night is crucial to the staging. Considered the uniquely Kaluli form of song, *gisalo* is sung only by men, at night, in the dark longhouse.

In addition to ceremonies, *gisalo* is sung during spirit medium seances. These, too, take place only in darkness; in fact, full darkness is required, with no light at all permitted in the longhouse. There are no ceremonial preparations for seances, and the songs are all sung by a spirit medium accompanied by an unrehearsed chorus sitting around him; there are no costumes, dances, or burning. Theoretically the songs are not precomposed or rehearsed but rather represent compositions by various spirits of the dead and local spirits of lands that are manifest through the mouth of the medium.

In *gisalo* ceremonies and spirit medium seances, the presence of sound in spatial darkness is highly focused by the quiet attention of the audience. In the ceremony the sound of the singer's voice is always projected in front of the shimmering accompaniment of the *fasela* streamers and the *sob* clashing against the floor at the dancer's feet. Kaluli liken the sound to the call of a *wɔkwele* bird at a waterfall, echoing through the bush. In the seance, on the other hand, the medium lies prone, playing the *sob* at his side. In this way, the jangling of the rattle is more hypnotic and mesmerizing to the surrounding group.

In both contexts the interaction of sound, space, and darkness is crucial to the "hardening," the anticipation, and the climax structure of the events. Being at a ceremony is said to be like being at a waterfall or being off in the bush. The experience of sounds, words, and a hypnotic, dreamlike state brings the forest up close, immersing the listeners in a liminal suspension. In the dark house, as in the forest, it is hearing, not vision that is the dominant sensory mode. While the audience is visually aware of the motion, color, and demeanor of the dancer, the nuances of meaning lie in the texts of the songs and the sounds of the voice, the instrumental pulse, and the bodily motion. In the seances, where darkness prevails, sound is totally focused; the audience is likely to interpret any sound, whether from the medium or from the surrounding bush, as meaningful to a successful understanding of the seance.

For Kaluli audiences and participants, there is a buildup of anticipation, energy, and drama surrounding performance. This is crucial to the sensation of hearing the singer and dancer as a man in the form of a bird or hearing the voices of spirits, who in the visible world appear as birds, through the mouth of the medium. Mediums make use of bird call imitations and forest sound effects to increase the drama of their performances, and this is much appreciated by their audiences. One man told me that being at a seance and hearing spirits through the medium was like "being in the treetops"; the continuity of the forest setting with personal space is a much-desired effect of the staging.

Darkness intensifies sound in space. A crowded longhouse of quiet, excited, anticipating listeners sets the stage for the evocative nature of *gisalo* songs. Like being at a waterfall or being in the forest with the birds, one hears and feels at an intensified level.

The *fasela* streamers springing from the dance belt, along with the *gado* leaves (cordyline), create an outline of shiny yellow-green, almost a body halo, around the dancer. They are constantly in motion, flowing *gulu*, and their sound is as important as their sight.

In the darkness of the house, the bright colors of the costume stand out as if the dancer were in a diffuse spotlight. One Kaluli man said that this focused figure surrounded by scattered light and darkness was "like a bird in the trees." Others compared the streaking light of torches to the way in which light breaks through the forest treeline and spreads about unevenly through the trees.

For Kaluli, staging sets up necessary conditions for the evocative power of song. Song is bird sound and bird words; its melody is the *muni* bird pitches, and its text is "bird sound words." Song is communication from a bird's point of view, communication of one who becomes a bird. Staging is that set of performance settings associated with *gisalo*—sound, darkness, space, costume—that prepares the audience to see and hear the singer/dancer as a bird. The spatial setting and the lighting create the feeling of the forest. The costume and the sound create the image of a bird at a waterfall. Staging, then, is a way in which the metaphor of song melody and language as bird communication is contexted, creating a mental setting where listeners can feel the presence of a bird at a forest waterfall.

An Example of Gisalo: Form, Performance, and Response

The case study of a single *gisalo* song comes from a corpus of thirteen songs sung during a three-hour spirit medium seance on the night of October 1, 1976. That morning, Sɛyo[4] came to our house at Sululib and announced that he would hold a seance if we would go with him to Nagebɛdɛn. Buck and I arrived there with him in the late afternoon and spent the early evening socializing in and around the newly built longhouse. At about 8:30 Sɛyo withdrew to lie down by a firebox at the men's end of the longhouse, relaxing, and at times audibly humming to himself. Women retreated to their area, and men gathered in the rear central hall of the house where light was provided by a few resin torches; rain was sounding noticeably against the palm roof of the house. At about 9:30,

4. The name of this medium is given with a pseudonym, as spirit mediums are currently under pressure from Christian forces in Bosavi to cease the performance of seances.

Sɛyo moved to the rear sleeping platform in the house, and some twenty men sat around him. There was much anticipatory excitement, hushed talking, settling-in noise, whacking the dogs that were running around, telling youths to be quiet, and so forth. At this point the back veranda entrance of the house was sealed off, Sɛyo lay down on his back, and all of the torches were completely extinguished. Then Sɛyo began to make the deep breathing sounds that begin a seance.

The general form of seances is as follows: The medium leaves his body and journeys into the invisible. Throughout the course of the evening, different spirits, including the medium's spirit child, spirits of places, and spirits of the dead, come up through his mouth, sing *gisalo*, and talk with the audience. Each spirit's appearance is marked by a special breath, a *gisalo* song (the map of which provides clues to the spirit's identity; upon recognition, audience members may burst into tears), and statements directed to or conversations with the audience. Sometimes the spirit will refuse to talk and will disappear quickly, other times the conversations will be long. The seance may last all evening or terminate at any point for a variety of reasons.

Seances are the principal context in which Kaluli people gain knowledge about the unseen world and cosmological issues; they are also performance occasions. There is frequently a good deal of joking, and mediums are valued for their dramatic prowess, their skill in entertaining the audience, and the diversity of their repertoire of spirits. Although mediums theoretically claim no prior knowledge of the songs they sing or the things they say, their everyday real-life personalities have much in common with their distinct styles of seance performance.

Throughout the seance at Nagebɛdɛn, the house was completely dark, and Sɛyo kept a lively rapport with the audience. The song discussed here, the second of the evening, was one of three songs that provoked tears and sung weeping.

Overall Aspects of Form

The form of this song is similar to that of most *gisalo*.[5] It begins with the *mɔ* 'trunk', which is composed of two distinct parts. The first, also called *mɔ*, is sung alone *(inɛli molab)* with *sob* accompaniment. The vocal style

5. The terminology employed here varies slightly from that found in E. Schieffelin 1976. This reflects differences between usage as *gisalo* staging terminology and song form terminology in the stricter sense discussed here.

is *nunugulu molab,* meaning that it is sung softly and faintly. The seven
mɔ phrases (a-g) are variable in length and in the number of repeats.

The next section, the second part of the mɔ, is the mɔ plus *talun* or
"trunk" and "verses." It is not sung alone but *dulugu molab* and *tiab;* the
medium's voice "lifts over" those of the joining chorus who sing imita-
tive canon. This section is always characterized by two to five refrains
plus double verse sets. The refrains (same text and melody) are marked
(A¹⁻³); these sing a foundation image. The verses h and i through l and
m have similar melodic and textual form, but the textual content
changes. In this section the medium progresses to singing a full-voiced
gese-molab or "plaintive" vocal style.

The next section, marking the main musical and textual division of
gisalo, is the *sa-gulab,* the "waterfalling" descent to the tonal center. This
begins with a line of *O* intoned on the tonal center of the song (B), then
is followed by three lines that are repeated twice (n).

The next major section, the *dun* or 'branches', is also composed of
two parts. The first part, the *dun* plus *talun* 'branches' and 'verses', contains the major development imagery of the song; it is similar in structure
to the mɔ plus *talun* with refrains (C¹⁻⁵) and paired verses (o and p
through w and x). In the example cited, loud *gana-yɛlab* response weeping
begins at the onset of the third refrain and continues throughout the rest
of the song. The vocal features remain the same but intensify at the onset
of weeping.

Coming out of this section is the short *sa-sundab,* the 'inner tie up'
that invokes a closure to the song. Here there are two sets of repeated
phrases; most *gisalo* have between two and five.

The song closes with the *sa-gulu,* the 'waterfall-droning' at the tonal
center in two lines, *Wo* and *Ye.* The *sob* rattle stops as the chorus finishes,
and, in this song, the weeping continues for another thirty seconds. Kaluli
listeners, remarking on the evocativeness of this song, said the vocal style
at the end became *dagano mada howɛn ɔngo* 'of a voice like the *howɛn* bird',
the Orange-bellied Fruitdove.

Figure 16 summarizes this structure.

Melodic Code

The tonal organization for *gisalo,* as figure 17 shows, is the same as the
pitches of the *muni* bird call and the pitches of *sa-yɛlab* weeping, except
for the addition of a final low pitch. Each section, however, utilizes a
subset of these pitches. The only place where additional pitches are

MAJOR SECTIONS	SUB-SECTIONS	PHRASES	WEEPING	VOCAL ORGANIZATION	VOCAL STYLE
MƆ	*mɔ*	a,b,c, d,e,f, g	Ø	*inɛli-molab*	*nunu-gulu molab*
	mɔ & talun	A^1&h&i A^2&j&k A^3&l&m		*dulugu-molab & tiab*	*gese-molab*
SA-GULAB	*sa-gulab*	B & n		*dulugu-molab & tiab*	*gese-molab*
DUN	*dun & talun*	C^1&o&p C^2&q&r C^3&s&t C^4&u&v C^5&w&x	*gana-yɛlab*	*dulugu-molab & tiab*	*gese-molab (halaido domɛki)*
	sa-sundab	y & z	*gana-yɛlab*	*dulugu-molab & tiab*	*gese-molab (dagano mada howɛn ɔngo)*
SA-GULU	*sa-gulu*	D	*gana-yɛlab*	*dulugu-molab & tiab*	*gese-molab (dagano mada howɛn ɔngo)*

Figure 16. *Gisalo* song schematic

added is the *mɔ;* the occasional B and B̄ here do not alter the tonality or intervalic structure because they are used only in major second and minor third relationships. The *mɔ* uses all of the pitches, and sometimes phrases span a full minor seventh in range (ten semitones). The lowest pitch, E, is used as the tonal center and often appears in line-final position.

All of this changes with the *sa-gulab* and continues in that way for the remainder of the song. The song is "centered" on G, and all phrases end on that pitch, culminating in the final lines of the song, *Wo* and *Ye,* which are droned on that pitch. As figure 17 indicates, during a long portion of the *dun,* only three pitches are in use.

Among the actual melodic contours, shown in the brief excerpts from each song section, all of the named Kaluli forms are in evidence: terracing descent lines *(sa-wɛl),* level lines *(sa-min),* descent to tonal center *(sa-gulab),* symmetrical ascent and descent *(sa-ga),* tonal center bouncing to descent and then back again *(sa-kɔf),* and descent to level lines *(sa-mogan).* The only prominent melodic shape not specified by Kaluli terminology that appears often is the wide, ascending jumps.

Transcription: Sɛyo's Gisalo Song at Nagebɛdɛn

The original pitches are

For comparison and easy reading, the transcription is raised by a fifth (seven semitones). Representative samples of the general *gisalo* melodic shapes are found in these fragments from each section of the song. Phrase letters are given at the left of each fragment. For each section the pulse is given in *sob* rattle beats per minute. Placement of the rattle pulse is indicated above the melodic line. Although the chorus accompanies the singer throughout, singing the same line a split second later, only the final section here, the *sa-gulu,* notes the chorus line in order to show how the song ends. Similarly, although there is *gana-yɛlab* weeping throughout the last sections of the song, only one fragment of the *dun* plus *talun* is presented here to show the musical interaction of the melody and wept-melody lines.

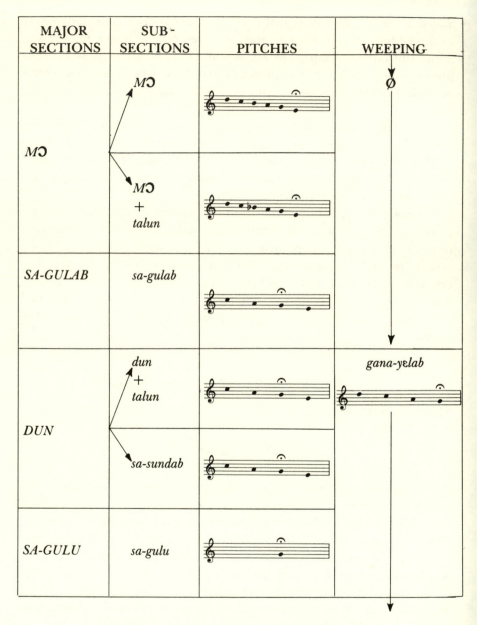

Figure 17. *Gisalo* melodic organization

Mɔ

Mɔ plus *Talun*

i

Wa - bo sa - gu a - bo___

mo - lo - be ya - bo - o - o   Wa - bo sa - gu a - bo - o   o

Sa-gulab

B

o   -   o

n

he - se - la - bo - o

do - go - sin(e) he - se - la - bo - o___   o - wa - ni he - se - la - bo - o___

he - se - la - bo - o

do - go - sin(e) he - se - la - bo - o___   o - wa - ni he - se - la - bo - o___

Dun plus Talun

C

Mu - bi go - go - wo   ne bɔ - bɛ - me - no   ne bɔ - bɛ - me - no

o

ku - gu - nɔ - lɔ   Go - bu - lu ma - lɔ   E

do - wo ne u - lu - li - ya - bɔ - lɔ

hɛ - gi - la - lo u - lu - li - ya - bɔ - lɔ

u - kɛ - yɛ u - lu - li - ya - bɔ - lɔ O____

Dun plus *Talun* with *Gana-yɛlab* weeping

Mu - bi go - go - wo ne bɔ - bɛ - me - no Mu - bi

Weeping

E E bɛ - si - yɔ____

go - go - wo ne bɔ - bɛ - me - no ku - gu - nɔ - lɔ

E E E nɔ - lɔ E

ku - gu - nɔ - lɔ Ku - ša - ki - ni ma - lɔ E

E E bɛ - si - yɔ____ E

ku - gu - nɔ - lɔ Ku - ša - ki - ni ma - lɔ O

E E bɛ - si - yɔ____ E E

Sa-sundab

Sa-gulu

Temporal Aspects of Form

Figure 18 summarizes the metric framework of this song. Seance *gisalo* songs tend to be performed slightly faster than are danced ceremonial songs. But in both cases the pulse indicated by the *sob* is always close to 120 beats per minute. When broken down into sections, it is clear that the opening *mɔ* is the quickest in pace; the song slows at the *sa-gulab,* remains at roughly that tempo for the longest section, the *dun,* and then slows again at the closing *sa-gulu* formula. Overall the song is very close to the Kaluli verbalized ideal about *gisalo* pacing.

The *sob* is not just a metric device. In the *mɔ* the play is softer, with less definite pulsation. After the *sa-gulab,* and particularly through the weeping, the *sob* sound becomes louder and figures more intensely in the actual character of the sound.

The Weeping

The *gana-yɛlab* response in this song is highly musical in its overall pace and melodic control. Even though the weeper is shedding tears and is actually choked up, the pitches of the weeping, precisely those of the *muni* bird call symbol, are consistent over the twenty-three wept phrases (a period of three minutes; nineteen phrases during the song and four as it finishes). The spacing from one wept phrase to the next and the placement of texts within the phrase are also quite consistent. No pitch of any wept portion jars with a sung pitch, and in re-listening to the tapes, one feels that the wept pitches create a musically interactive polyphony with the singing of the medium and the chorus. This contrasts with *gisalo* ceremonies, in which the grieving anger leading to the burning of the dancer promotes less musically controlled weeping and more of a falsetto cry.

Text

The text of Sɛyo's song is the talk of a spirit in the form of a bird staying around the lands of Kokonɛsi longhouse. The map of the song, which is built up through references to places in every phrase of the text, covers a relatively small area of mountains, ridges, hills, streams, creeks, waterfalls, rivers, trees, and flatlands, all known intimately by people who have lived at or are familiar with Kokonɛsi (see figure 19). This is

MAJOR SECTIONS AND TIMES	SUB-SECTION AND TIMES	ACTUAL METRONOME (*sob* pulses per minute)	NUMBER OF *sob* PULSES
MƆ 3'45"	mɔ 1'38"	♩=125	213
	mɔ + *talun* 2'07"	♩=125	255
SA-GULAB 0'22"	sa-gulab 0'22"	♩=122	45
DUN 3'49"	dun + *talun* 3'27"	♩=123	425
	sa-sundab 0'22"	♩=123	45
SA-GULU 0'07"	sa-gulu 0'07"	♩=120	14
TOTALS:	8'03"	♩=124	997

Figure 18. *Gisalo* temporal organization

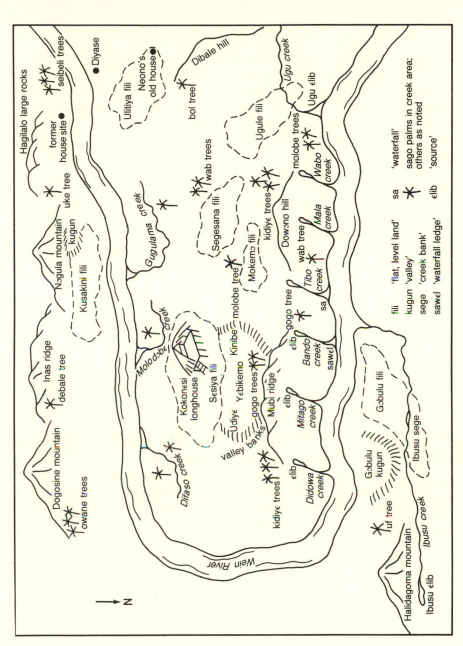

Figure 19. Place names in Sɛyo's song at Nagebɛdɛn

fili 'flat, level land'
kugun 'valley'
sege 'creek bank'
sawel 'waterfall ledge'

sa 'waterfall'
✳ sago palms in creek area; others as noted
ɛlib 'source'

a highly specific textual strategy, because a large portion of the audience at Nagebɛdɛn had a less than intimate knowledge of these lands. One man, Neono, did know them very well. Gradually it became clear that the spirit voice in the song was Dubo, Neono's dead son, hovering over the Kokonɛsi lands that he and his father had once frequented together. The song builds to a textual climax, at which point Neono is moved to tears.

MƆ

Phrase Text		**Gloss**
a)	*Iyɛuwo, iyɛuwo, iyɛuwo*	a) *Iyɛu, iyɛu, iyɛu* (a fruitdove)

b)	⌈ *Molodɔbɛ ilikiyo kinibe*
	   hɔidɛligaba
	
	 ⌊ *O*
	 ⌈ *Mitag-ɛlib lingaba*
	
	 ⌊ *O*
		b) ⌈ Staying at *molodɔbɛ* stream,
		   calling out from *kinibe* valley bank
		 ⌊ O
		 ⌈ Staying at the source of
		    mitag stream
		 ⌊ O

c)	⌈ *Hali-dagoma ilikiyo*
	   ufɛwɔ silikiyo
	 ⌊ *"dowo, dowo"*
	 ⌈ *Hali-dagoma ilikiyo*
	   ufɛwɔ silikiyo
	 ⌊ *"dowo, //cough// dowo"*
		c) ⌈ Staying at *hali* ridge,
		   sitting in the *uf* tree there,
		 ⌊ calling "father, father"
		 ⌈ Staying at *hali* ridge,
		   sitting in the *uf* tree there,
		 ⌊ calling "father, father"

d)	⌈ *Ibusu-sege gedelabe*
	
	 ⌊ *gedelabo, gedelabo*
	 ⌈ *Ibusu-sege gedelabe*
	
	 ⌊ *gedelabo, gedelabo*
		d) ⌈ At the bank of *ibusu* creek,
		    gede
		 ⌊ (the *sob* rattles on) *gede gede,*
		 ⌈ At the bank of *ibusu* creek,
		    gede
		 ⌊ (the *sob* rattles on) *gede gede*

e)	⌈ *Ugu-ɛlib ilikiyo* ⌊ *WO*	e) ⌈ Staying at *ugu* creek's spring ⌊ WO

f) ⎡*Gugulama sagu hɔno*   f) ⎡A waterfall runs *gu* at
                                                               gugulama creek,
    we hole-dabɛno   having called out,
    ⎣*we hole-dabɛno*   someone is listening for
                                          ⎣ a response (2×)

    ⎡*Difaso sagu hɔno*   ⎡A waterfall runs *gu* at *difaso*
                                            creek,
    we hole-dabɛno   having called out,
    ⎣*we hole-dabɛno*   someone is listening for
                                          ⎣ a response (2×)

g) ⎡*"Ne nolo maka" hɔidabɔ*   g) ⎡"I have no mother,"
                                              someone calls,
    "ni imolobe"   "I'm starving"
    ⎣*"ni imolobe"*   ⎣"I'm empty"

Mɔ plus *TALUN*

A¹) ⎡*Nɔgula ilikiyo*   A¹) ⎡Staying at *nɔgula* hill
    ⎣*WO*   WO (calling out from
                                        ⎣ there)

    ⎡*Nɔgula ilikiyo*   ⎡Staying at *nɔgula* hill,
    ⎣*WO*   ⎣WO

h) ⎡*Gi misiya hɔno*   h) ⎡At your high place,
    we hole-dabɛno   having called, someone is
    ⎣*we hole-dabɛno*   listening for a response
                                          ⎣ (2×)

    ⎡*Gi misiya hɔno*   ⎡At your high place,
    we hole-dabɛno   having called, someone is
    ⎣*we hole-dabɛno*   listening for a response
                                          ⎣ (2×)

i) ⎡*Wabo sagu abo*   i) ⎡A waterfall flows *gu* at *wabo*
                                            creek,
    molobe yabo   by the *molobe* tree there,
    ⎣*wabo sagu abo*   a waterfall flows *gu* at *wabo*
                                          ⎣ creek.

⌈ *Wabo sagu aƀo*   ⌈ A waterfall flows *gu* at *wabo*
| | creek,
| *molobe yaƀo* | by the *molobe* tree there,
⌊ *wabo sagu aƀo* | a waterfall flows *gu* at *wabo*
                           ⌊   creek,

A²) ⌈ *Nɔgula ilikiyo*   A²)⌈ Staying at *nɔgula*
     ⌊ *WO*   ⌊ *WO*
     ⌈ *Nɔgula ilikiyo*   ⌈ Staying at *nɔgula*
     ⌊ *WO*   ⌊ *WO*

j)   ⌈ *Kugunɔ hɛdiyɔ*   j) ⌈ Down in the valley,
     | *we hole-dabɛno* | having called out, someone
     ⌊ *we hole-dabɛno* | is listening for a response
                                    ⌊   (2×)
     ⌈ *Kugunɔ hɛdiyɔ*   ⌈ Down in the valley,
     | *we hole-dabɛno* | having called out, someone
     ⌊ *we hole-dabɛno* | is listening for a response
                                     ⌊   (2×)

k)   ⌈ *Dibale aƀo*   k) ⌈ There at *dibale* hill
     | *bol abo-wo* | at the *bol* tree there
     ⌊ *dibale aƀo*   ⌊ over there at *dibale* hill
     ⌈ *Dibale aƀo*   ⌈ There at *dibale* hill
     | *bol abo-wo* | at the *bol* tree there
     ⌊ *dibale aƀo*   ⌊ over there at *dibale hill.*

A³) ⌈ *Nɔgula ilikiyo*   A³)⌈ Staying at *nɔgula* hill
     ⌊ *WO*   ⌊ *WO*
     ⌈ *Nɔgula ilikiyo*   ⌈ Staying at *nɔgula* hill
     ⌊ *WO*   ⌊ *WO*

l)   ⌈ *Gi misiya hɔno*   l) ⌈ At your high place,
     | *"nelɔ" hole-dabɛno* | having called out "for me"
     ⌊ *"nelɔ" hole-dabɛno* | someone is listening for
                                     ⌊   a response (2×)

⌜*Gi misiya hɔno*
⎸*"nelɔ" hole-dabɛno*
⎣*"nelɔ" hole-dabɛno*

⌜At your high place,
⎸having called out "for me"
⎸   someone is listening for
⎣   a response (2×)

m) ⌜*Inas abo*
   ⎸*debabe yabo*
   ⎣*inas abo*
   ⌜*Inas abo*
   ⎸*debabe yabo*
   ⎣*inas abo*

m) ⌜There at *inas* mountain
   ⎸at the *debabe* tree there
   ⎣over there at *inas* mountain
   ⌜There at *inas* mountain
   ⎸at the *debabe* tree there
   ⎣over there at *inas* mountain

SA-GULAB

B)   *O*   B)   O

n) ⌜*Heselabo*
   ⎸
   ⎸*dogosine heselabo*
   ⎸
   ⎣*owaniyɛ heselabo*
   ⌜*Heselabo*
   ⎸
   ⎸*dogosine heselabo*
   ⎸
   ⎣*owaniyɛ heselabo*

n) ⌜Journeying with the sun up
   ⎸   in the east,
   ⎸over east by *dogosine*
   ⎸   mountain
   ⎣lighting the *owani* palms
       there
   ⌜Journeying with the sun up
   ⎸   in the east,
   ⎸over east by *dogosine*
   ⎸   mountain
   ⎣lighting the *owani* palms
       there

DUN plus *TALUN*

C¹) ⌜*Mubi gogowo*
   ⎣*ne bɔbɛmeno* (2×)
   ⌜*Mubi gogowo*
   ⎣*ne bɔbɛmeno*

C¹) ⌜At the *gogo* tree on *mubi*
   ⎸   ridge,
   ⎣come and see me
   ⌜At the *gogo* tree on *mubi*
   ⎣come and see me

o) ⌜*Kugun ɔlɔ*
  ⎸*gɔbulu malɔ,*
  ⎣*E*

o) ⌜At this valley?
  ⎸not the one at *gɔbulu*
  ⎣E

> *Kugun ɔlɔ*
> *gɔbulu malɔ*
> *E*

> Is it at this valley?
> no, not the one at *gɔbulu*
> E

p)
> *Dowo ne ululiyabɔlɔ*
>
> *dowo ne ululiyabɔlɔ*
>
> *hɛgilalowɛ ululiyabɔlɔ*
>
> *ukɛyɛ ululiyabɔlɔ*
>
> *O*

p)
> Father, keep reaching out
>   to me
> father, keep reaching out
>   to me
> keep reaching out to me
>   at *hɛgilalo*
> keep reaching out at the
>   *ukɛ* tree there
> O

> *Hɛgilalowɛ ululiyabɔlɔ*
>
> *ukɛyɛ ululiyabɔlɔ*
>
> *O*

> Keep reaching out to me
>   at *hɛgilalo*
> keep reaching out at the
>   *ukɛ* tree there
> O

C²)
> *Mubi gogowo*
> *ne bɔbɛmeno*

> *Mubi gogowo*
> *ne bɔbɛmeno*

C²)
> At the *gogo* tree on *mubi*
> come and see me

> At the *gogo* tree on *mubi*
> come and see me

q)
> *Nowo ne hɔidɛligabɔlɔ*
>
> *nowo ne hɔidɛligabɔlɔ*
>
> *dowɔno kidiyɛ hɔidɛligabɔlɔ*
>
> *E*

q)
> Mother keep calling out
>   to me
> mother keep calling out
>   to me
> keep calling out to me at
>   the *kidiyɛ* tree on
>   *dowɔno* hill
> E

> *Nɔwo ne hɔidɛligabɔlɔ*
>
> *dowɔno kidiyɛ hɔidɛligabɔlɔ*
>
> *E*

> Mother keep calling out
>   to me
> keep calling out to me at
>   the *kidiyɛ* tree on
>   *dowɔno* hill
> E

r)
> *Segesana wabo*
> *adεyε ne ɔlomemene*
>
> *O*

> *Segesana wabo*
> *adεyε ne ɔlomemene*
>
> *O*

r)
> At the *wab* tree at *segesana*
> *adε* come and help me
>> there
>
> O

> At the *wab* tree at *segesana*
> *adε* come and help me
>> there
>
> O

DUN plus *TALUN*   *GANA-YƐLAB*
                                      weeping by Neono

C³)   ⎡*Mubi gogowo*
      ⎣*ne bɔbɛmeno*   ⟷ 1) *E E bɛsiyɔ E E*

      ⎡*Mubi gogowo*
      ⎣*ne bɔbɛmeno*

                                 ⟷ 2) *E E nɔlo E E*

s)   ⎡*Kugun ɔlɔ*
      ⎢*kugun ɔlɔ*
      ⎢*kušakini malɔ*
      ⎣*E*   ⟷ 3) *E E bɛsiyɔ E E*

      ⎡*Kugun ɔlɔ*
      ⎢*kušakini malɔ*
      ⎣*E*   ⟷ 4) *E E nɔlo E E*

t)   ⎡*Dogosine ululiyabɔlɔ*
      ⎢*owani ululiyabɔlɔ*
      ⎣*O*   ⟷ 5) *E E bɛsiyɔ E E*

      ⎡*Dogosine ululiyabɔlɔ*
      ⎢*owani ululiyabɔlɔ*
      ⎣*O*

DUN plus *TALUN*   *GANA-YƐLAB*

C³) ┌ At the *gogo* tree on
     │   *mubi*
     └ come and see me   ⟷ E E *bɛsiyɔ* E E
     ┌ At the *gogo* tree on
     │   *mubi*
     └ come and see me
                                          ⟷ E E son E E

s)   ┌ At this valley?
     │ is it at this valley?
     │ no not the one at
     │   *kušakini*
     └ E   ⟷ E E *bɛsiyɔ* E E
     ┌ At this valley?
     │ no, not the one at
     │   *kušakini*
     └ E   ⟷ E E son E E

t)   ┌ Keep reaching out at
     │   *dogosine* mountain
     │ keep reaching out at
     │   the *owani* trees there
     └ O   ⟷ E E *bɛsiyɔ* E E

     ┌ Keep reaching out at
     │   *dogosine* mountain
     │ keep reaching out at
     │   the *owani* trees there
     └ O

C⁴) ⎡ *Mubi gogowo*   ⟷   6) *E E nɔlo E E*
     ⎣ *ne bɔbɛmene*

     ⎡ *Mubi gogowo*
     ⎣ *ne bɔbɛmene*   ⟷   7) *E E nɔlo diyaseyo nɔlo E E*

u)   ⎡ *Mokemɔ malɔ*
     ⎢ *mokemɔ malɔ*   ⟷   8) *E E nɔlo mubiyo E E*
     ⎢ *molobe malɔ*
     ⎣ *E*

     ⎡ *Mokemɔ malɔ*
     ⎢ *molobe malɔ*
     ⎣ *E*   ⟷   9) *E E bɛsiyɔ E E*

v)   ⎡ *Bando-sawɛl debolɔ*
     ⎢ *bando-sawɛl*
     ⎢   *ululiyabɔlɔ*
     ⎢ *wabo ululiyabɔlɔ*   ⟷   10) *E E nɔlo mubiyo E E*
     ⎣ *O*

     ⎡ *Bando-sawɛl*
     ⎢   *ululiyabɔlɔ*
     ⎢ *gogowɛ ululiyabɔlɔ*
     ⎣ *O*   ⟷   11) *E E nɔlo mɔmiyɛ nɔlo E E*

C⁴) ⎡At the *gogo* tree on
     ⎢   *mubi*   ⟷ E E son E E
     ⎣come and see me
     ⎡At the *gogo* tree on
     ⎢   *mubi*
     ⎣come and see me   ⟷ E E you're at *diyase* son E E

u)   ⎡Not *mokemɔ*
     ⎢no, not at *mokemɔ*   ⟷ E E you're at *mubi* E E
     ⎢not at the *molobe*
     ⎢   tree
     ⎣E
     ⎡Not *mokemɔ*
     ⎢no, not at the
     ⎢   *molobe* tree
     ⎣E   ⟷ E E *bɛsiyɔ* E E

v)   ⎡At the *debol* tree at
     ⎢   the waterfall ledge
     ⎢   of bando creek,
     ⎢keep reaching out
     ⎢   at the waterfall
     ⎢   ledge of bando creek
     ⎢at the wab tree there   ⟷ E E son you're at *mubi* E E
     ⎣O
     ⎡Keep reaching out
     ⎢   at the waterfall
     ⎢   ledge of bando creek,
     ⎢at the *gogo* tree there
     ⎣O   ⟷ E E son, you didn't come back
                                                       E E

C⁵)   ⌈*Mubi gogowo*
      ⌊*ne bɔbɛmeno*

      ⌈*Mubi gogowo*   ⟷   12) *E E nɔlo segesanayo E E*
      ⌊*ne bɔbɛmeno*

w)   ⌈*Mala sagu malɔ*
      |*mala sagu malɔ*   ⟷   13) *E E nɔlo E E*
      |*udiyɛ malɔ*
      ⌊*O*

      ⌈*Mala sagu malɔ*   ⟷   14) *E E E udiyo bɛsiyɔ*
      |*udiyɛ malɔ*   *nɔlo E E*
      ⌊*O*

x)   ⌈*Tibo-saguwe*   ⟷   15) *E E nɔlo E E*
      | *ululiyabɔlɔ*
      |*tibo-saguwe*
      | *ululiyabɔlɔ*
      |*wabe ululiyabɔlɔ*
      ⌊*O*
      ⌈*Tibo-saguwe*
      | *ululiyabɔlɔ*
      |*wabe ululiyabɔlɔ*   ⟷   16) *E E bɛsiyɔ E E*
      ⌊*O*

SA-SUNDAB
y)   ⌈*Didowa habalebo*
      ⌊*kidiyɛya habalebe*   ⟷   17) *E E bɛsiyɔ E E*

C⁵)   ⌐At the *gogo* tree on
      mubi ridge
   ⌐come and see me
   ⌐At the *gogo* tree on   ⟷   E E son you're at
      mubi   *segesana* E E
   ⌐come and see me

w)   ⌐Not the waterfall at
      mala creek,
     no, not at *mala sagu*   ⟷   E E son E E
     not at *udiyɛ* valley
      bank
   ⌐O
   ⌐Not at *mala sagu*   ⟷   E E you're at *udiyɛ*
     no, not at *udiyɛ*   *bɛsiyɔ* E E
   ⌐O

x)   ⌐Keep reaching out   ⟷   E E son E E
      at *tibo*
     at the waterfall
      there,
     keep reaching at
      the *wab* tree
   ⌐O
   ⌐Keep reaching out at
      tibo creek waterfall,
     by the *wab* tree   ⟷   E E *bɛsiyɔ* E E
   ⌐O

SA-SUNDAB

y)   ⌐Clouds begin to
      cover *didowa*
     shade sets over the   ⟷   E E *bɛsiyɔ* *E E*
      kidiyɛ trees

⌈*Didowa habalebo*
⌊*kidiyɛya habalebe*

z)   ⌈*Hagilalowe*
          haselebo
         ⌊*seibeliya haselebe*   ⟷   18) *E E ulitiyaseyo E E*
         ⌈*Hagilalowe*
          haselebo
         ⌊*seibeliya haselebe*

SA-GULU
D)   ⌈*WO*   ⟷   19) *E E bɛsiyɔ E E*
         ⌊*YE*

          gana-yɛlab   20) *E E mubiyo E E*
          continues after   21) *E E bɛsiyɔ E E*
          song ends   22) *E E mubiyo E E*
                                             23) *E E ulitiyaseyo E E*

       ┌Cloud cover holds at
       │ *didowa*
       │shading the *kidiyɛ*
       └ trees there

z)   ┌Sun is strong
      │ before setting at
      │ *hagilalo*
      │brightly lighting   ⟷ E E at *ulitiya* E E
      └ the *seibeli* trees
      ┌Sun glows strong
      │ before setting at
      │ *hagilalo*
      │brightly lighting
      │ the *seibeli* trees
      └ there

SA-GULU

D)   ┌WO   ⟷ E E *bɛsiyɔ* E E
      └YE

     gana-yɛlab   E E *mubi* E E
     continues after   E E *bɛsiyɔ* E E
     song ends   E E *mubi* E E
                           E E at *ulitiya* E E

Explication de Texte

Mɔ

Several aspects of the *mɔ* (phrases a through g) are typical of *gisalo* songs. The opening line names a fruitdove, which is the conventional signal that the song will be sung from a bird's point of view. Next, map images *(tok)* begin immediately, and they name places close and distant to Kokonɛsi longhouse (close ones in phrase b, distant in phrases c and d, coming back in e, and close again in f). The frequent place movement and the use of verbs of "staying," "calling," and "sitting" develop the theme of a bird's point of view (particularly in c, with the image of the bird in an *uf* tree at *hali* ridge calling "father").

At the end of the *mɔ* (phrase f), there is an evocative change; no longer are the images descriptions of "staying" and "calling," but they use *hole-dabɛno*. This contracts *holɛma* 'call out, with expectation of response' and *dabuma* 'listen'. The audience is now being told that the bird not only is calling out for its "father," but "having called, it is listening for a response." This is a particularly plaintive image for Kaluli, because for one to call and not receive a response is a pathetic indication of loss and abandonment. Finally, in g the whole *mɔ* is wrapped up with the two most pathetic images of loss, lack of kin and lack of food.

All basic Kaluli poetic strategies have been set in motion. There is *sa-salan* in phrase d with the image of the creek name and the *sob,* and it appears throughout in the ways in which the verbs of calling articulate the bird's point of view. There is *bali to* in the image of a bird as a child calling to its father. That someone calls and listens for a response with none forthcoming gives the *hega* ('underneath') that one has indeed been abandoned. There is *gɔnɔ to* in phrase d with *gede* for the sound of the *sob,* and in the *O* and *WO* lines, which move over several pitches with descent and plaintive voice, indicating the bird who sings the song. There is a *tok* immediately, using a conventional strategy.

Mɔ plus Talun

The structuring of the *mɔ* plus *talun* is rigid, in line with the Kaluli idealization of what is required to "harden" the song. In this song the refrains (A[1,2,3]) continue the image of "staying," but now it is from Nɔgula, a mountain from which one can view the whole longhouse area. In the first verses after each refrain (h, j, l) there are no place names, just general names for mountain and valley. Between refrains and each initial verse there is, on the one hand, the shift from an actual place to an imprecise one, and, on the other hand, the shift from "staying" to the more evocative "called and waiting for response." Each phrase then contains elements that interact with the next phrase, making the song simultaneously more explicit and direct and more vague and multiply interpretable.

The second phrases in the verses (i, k, m) add explicit *tok* information, particularly following the vague generic names. At the same time, these also add a dimension of ambiguity because each of the places is in a different direction, all rather distant from Nɔgula or the center of Kokonɛsi. Wabo creek, Dibale mountain, and Inas mountain, each sung with the name of a tree type there, are thus indirect clues despite their specificity.

The *mɔ* plus *talun* builds the basic themes stated in the *mɔ* and develops the map of the song, which gets the chorus and listeners into a tight synchrony with the medium and gathers listener attentiveness through the intertwining of explicit and ambiguous information.

Just as the *mɔ* "hardened" toward its end by changing the image of the bird calling "father" to an image of calling out and waiting for a response, the *mɔ* plus *talun* takes the image of calling out and waiting for a response one degree further in plaintiveness with the addition of *nelɔ*. *Nelɔ* is a child's begging form, accompanied in speech by the whining vocal style of *geseab;* it directly implies "I want" but can also be glossed 'to me', 'do for me', 'give to me'. Following the unmarked *hole-dabɛno* lines in phrases h and j, *nelɔ* fronts the line in l and means "having called out 'for me', someone is listening for a response."

There is also *sa-salan* and *bali to* here. "Inside" the lines remains the implication that the song is sung by a bird (a spirit) whose home is Kokonɛsi. "Underneath" the use of *nelɔ* in phrase l is the new information that the spirit is most likely a child.

Sa-gulab

The *sa-gulab* divides the foundation (*mɔ* 'trunk') from the development (*dun* 'branches') imagery. Phrase n, with no surface connection to previous lines, involves a visual image verb with a place and a tree name. The place name sung is the farthest place from the Kokonɛsi longhouse mentioned in the song. The explicit information in the image is the place, and the imprecise information is that one is journeying north/south. The sense of the line is that one is coming or going toward Kokonɛsi, and the sun is up in the east at Dogosine, indicating much journeying is yet to be

done. This image of early morning light is brought to completion at the
very end of the song, where the *sa-sundab* uses two other image verbs that
indicate passage of time to the end of the day, with the clouds coming
in and sun shining brightly before setting.

Dun plus *Talun*

The *dun* plus *talun* structure is similar to the *mɔ* plus *talun*, with five
sets of refrains plus two verses. This is the longest section of the song,
the place where the text comes to its full "hardening" and climaxes with
a listener being moved to tears. The weeping begins at the onset of (C³).

The verses and refrains are not as tightly structured as they were in
the *mɔ* plus *talun*. While there is some parallelism between texts in the
verses (o, s, and u), there is far more variation related to form being
reshaped in performance, such as phonological change and optional
repetition.

Looking at the actual cohesion and content, the first notable thing
is the way refrain (C) again pushes the sadness of the song one degree
farther. "Come and see me" is a "hardening" of the "calling" *(mɔ)* to
"having called, waiting for a response" (end of *mɔ* and frequent in *mɔ* plus
talun), and finally "having called *nelɔ* waiting for a response" (end of *mɔ*
plus *talun*). This image is found with the place name of Mubi and the tree
name of *gogo*. Mubi is the prominent image associated with the spirits of
the area; it is close-by, overlooking the longhouse, and many birds gather
there.

Phrase o begins the device of stating general and specific map images
and then negating them, thus narrowing the *tok* possibilities. In phrases
o, s, u, and w the device states a land or waterform and then follows with
"no, not the one at *X*," where *X* turns out to be a place going in the
opposite direction of the Kokonɛsi settlement. This is a common and
powerful *halaido domɛki* strategy.

At (C³), Neono begins to weep *(gana-yɛlab)*, creating a sonic polyphony of medium-chorus-weeping. Neono is a Nagebɛdɛn man, married
to a Kokonɛsi woman, Kisi. They lived at Nagebɛdɛn and had a son Dubo,
there. When Dubo was about six or seven years old, they went to live at
Kokonɛsi for the better part of a year. While at Kokonɛsi, Dubo died and
was buried there. After Dubo's death, Neono and Kisi moved back to
Nagebɛdɛn.

The images of someone left alone at Kokonɛsi, a small child as a bird,
calling from the places, streams, and trees there, calling out and waiting

for a response, saying "come and see me," asking for someone to reach out, made Neono think of his dead son, Dubo. This is what moved him to tears. The slight texts of the weeping have place names—Diyase, where Dubo is buried; Mubi, the mountain sung through the refrains of the *dun* plus *talun;* Segesana, the land near several creeks where the family beat sago; Udiyɛ, where Neono had a garden; and Ulitiya, near where Neono and family once lived.

Sa-sundab and *Sa-gulu*

This song follows a common pattern for the construction of the *sa-sundab:*

$$\left[\begin{array}{l}\text{place name plus image verb with } \textit{-o} \text{ ending}\\ \text{tree name plus same verb with } \textit{-e} \text{ ending}\end{array}\right]$$

Such phrases textually frame "as we draw to a close, X is taking place at Y place, at the Z tree there." Visual image verbs relating to sunlight, cloud formations, and sunset are frequently used in these frames; it is also common to find onomatopoeic verbs here. *Sa-sundab* hosts condensed or ellipsed lines, indeed, sometimes just simple strings of images.

While the song has presented a concrete set of images that can be thought about as being a personal history involving Neono and family, it is not really a chronicle of those relations. Closure is invoked by images that do not resolve anything about the sentiments brought up in the song but rather bracket them and call attention to the fact that the song is coming to a close. The formal close is marked by *Wo* and *Ye,* each intoned on the tonal center for the length of an entire line.

Halaido domɛki

Kaluli commentators picked out three factors contributing to the *halaido domɛki* ("hardening") of this song. The first is the progression of verb images, from "calling" to "having called, waiting for response" to "having called *nelɔ,* waiting for a response" to "come and see me" to "reach out to me," "keep calling out," and "come and help me." One clear fact about *gisalo* songs concerns the economy of verbs. There are few verbs used in a song (usually between six and ten), and frequently these are compounds, selected and sequenced by composers in ways that are dramatic. This song is a clear illustration of well-chosen and se- quenced verbs, articulating with each of the sections of the song, and with the general Kaluli compositional axiom that as the song progresses the images should become more plaintive.

A second *halaido domɛki* device found here to build up the section just where Neono begins to weep is the use of kin terms. This song sequentially uses 'father' *(dowo),* 'mother' *(nɔwo),* and culminates with *adɛ.* Each co-occurs with a different verb, and these verbs are the final and most plaintive ones in the sequence just mentioned.

The final textual example of *halaido domɛki* is the use of the negated "Is it X? No, not the one at Y" phrases with *malɔ,* so that the possibilities of the "home" place of the singer of the song remain ambiguous while becoming explicit. Here again we have the Kaluli axioms: be imprecise before being explicit, and add simultaneously nebulous and explicit information.

Musical features also contribute to the "hardening." The *mɔ* was sung *nunugulu,* in a soft distant voice. Once the chorus began to *tiab,* the lead voice became stronger, and the group developed a tight synchrony in the *mɔ* plus *talun.* But, most importantly, the *dun* plus *talun* reveals the medium singing in a stronger *gese-molab* voice, "like a child who has been left behind." Both the development of vocal intensity and plaintive song voice are the register correlates of the *halaido domɛki* in the text.

Another noted feature is the variability (in repeats, melodic and textual changes, and spacing) found in the *dun* plus *talun.* Here the singer gets a chance at center stage; this section hosts optional devices and the greatest degree of reshaping of form through performance style. The quality of voice, the play of the *sob,* and the variations of form here contribute to the *halaido domɛki* by changing the focus from the synchrony of the group (developed in the *mɔ* plus *talun*) to the creative license of the lead voice.

While some Kaluli men told me that singing the intimate place names of the listeners was responsible for making others weep, an equally focused idea was that the "hardening" of a song was the persuasive factor. In this song there is a very explicit example of this second explanation. The weeping begins halfway through the *dun* plus *talun,* and its onset (at phrase C³) is right after the final plaintive verbs are used with the kin and relationship terms, ending with *adɛ.* Listeners agreed that this was the point at which the *halaido domɛki* process of creating aesthetic tension came to its apex.

The process of my coming to understand the situated meaning of this single song was drawn out over nine months. The morning after the seance, which the people of Nagebɛdɛn seemed to enjoy, I walked back to Sululib with Sɛli. Although my command of the language was slight at that point, I generally understood him to make positive comments about the seance and suggestions that Sululib people hear the tape recordings. Over the next two months the recordings were heard several times by Sululib people in casual contexts, and I often listened to them alone in order to keep track of my musical impressions. At the end of December 1976, Kulu and I transcribed and translated the texts of all thirteen songs from the seance; I also interviewed one elderly man and one young woman with Kulu's help. Over these same months, Buck Schieffelin worked intermittently with Sɛyo, interviewing him about mediumship generally and the Nagebɛdɛn seance specifically. At the same time Buck and his assistants made transcriptions of the conversations from the seance; the two of us discussed these materials and compared them to sets we had gathered from other seances and mediums. By March 1977 I knew the materials well enough to work directly with Sɛyo. We spent two days together, listened to all thirteen songs, made additions and corrections to the original transcriptions, and discussed a variety of related issues. Toward the end of June 1977 I played the tapes for Neono, the man who wept during this and other songs. We talked about the texts of his weeping, his feelings about the songs (he wept again as he listened to the tapes), and made the map of the song places. Finally, when Ganigi, an elder of Nagebɛdɛn who had been at the seance, visited Sululib for a week in June, I relistened to the whole seance with him, accompanied by several Sululib men. Our long discussions about the meaning and the power of the songs in the seance as a whole, and this one in particular, fleshed out my notes, which were based on the many informal comments I overheard Kaluli make, or things that I had learned directly through conversations.

While I am confident that these experiences have led to a reasonably detailed and accurate explication of this song, it should be noted that seance songs are not discrete entities. The entire seance itself is a multi-layered and complexly connected social process, and the sets of meanings that people derive and develop through mutual participation at seances have many dimensions. The placement of this song in the series of thirteen, the conversations that bound either side of the song, and the way the spirit of Dubo came through Sɛyo more pointedly in a later song must all be taken into account to explain this song as part of a larger construction.

It is particularly worth noting in this context that the people of Nagebɛdɛn were most enthusiastic about holding a seance. Several people asked Sɛyo to bring up spirits of Nagebɛdɛn people who were recently deceased. Additionally, Sɛyo was aware that Buck and I had recorded another seance the previous week at Sululib, and there was something mildly competitive about his desire to bring us to another longhouse and hold a seance at a place where he would be the center of attention.

This competitive attitude was evident months later when I talked with him about the songs. At that time he laughed often, in an almost mischievous fashion, as we listened to the tapes. He told me how strong the songs were, how they really made people weep forcefully, and how I should play the tapes often for people of my own village. There was an element of self-confidence and bravado to his personal style that paralleled the construction of his songs, which, like the one described here, were generally tightly organized and textually more cohesive than were those of some other mediums. Yet Sɛyo strongly denied that the song was in any way composed by him; he insisted that it was composed by Dubo and simply came through his mouth.

It seems, then, on all counts, that the stage was set at Nagebɛdɛn for a dramatic performance. The people were in a responsive mood to hear the voices of their dead; the medium knew the people and knew their social and individual histories; there were two outsiders whom the medium also wanted to impress; the conditions were right for an optimally dramatic seance with extremely dramatic songs; and indeed, that is what took place.

Conclusion

As is the case with poetics, Kaluli clearly intend to control and structure musical forms for social evocation in performance. At the level of conceptualization, there is a theoretical frame of reference organizing patterns of sound in intervals, contours, and phrases that descend and balance like waterfalls, rush forth like white water over rocks, or gently surge *gulu* like even creek falls. More importantly, these notions about sonic structure, coded in metaphors of water, are explicitly linked to notions about textual structure in a concept of composition "like water falling down and mixing in a waterpool." The creative moment of text coming to mind and flowing into the pool of swirling melody is the act of musical composition.

Turning to performance, *gisalo* exemplifies a complex, multilevel occasion, whether the context is a ceremony or a seance. In the ceremonial situation, there are features of dance, costume, lighting, a large audience, feasting, and reciprocal exchange between two communities surrounding the song performance. In the seance situation, all of these are eliminated and replaced with a dark house, contact with the reflection realm, a chance to hear voices of spirits of the dead and of local places, and a time when one learns about the nonvisible side of things while being entertained by the dramatic prowess of a single person's repertoire of voices, sound effects, and songs.

For *gisalo* ceremonies, the songs are more openly oriented toward making the listeners sad and nostalgic until they are moved to tears. The songs have been thoughtfully composed, deliberately rehearsed, and are finally performed by a dancer whose downcast demeanor and paced solitude, moving up and back the center aisle of the house, creates an image of loneliness and isolation. The act of moving the audience to tears is marked most socially by the instant retribution of burning the back of the dancer, a mark he wears for life. In the long run, however, the burning is neither the central focus of the ceremony nor the central feature of one's memory of a particular performance; rather, the way the songs persuaded the audience to tears is what dominates both the aftermath and the remembrances of *gisalo*.

For seances, fewer of the larger social issues are as dependent upon the success of the songs. Much of the event is taken up by verbal exchanges between the medium (as different spirits) and the audience members. The songs serve as introductory vehicles for each different spirit, and the audience listens to them attending to the map and textual imagery as a series of clues about who is singing the song. The dramatic tension here is different from that which takes hold at a ceremony; at *gisalo* ceremonies members of the host longhouse know the guests will sing the host's lands in order to make them weep; the hosts are prepared to be moved. At the seance there is a larger element of potential surprise, often culminating in weeping like that found in the example here. Unlike ceremonial response, which may be very short, shrieked, and a brief prelude to burning, seance *gisalo* weeping can be highly musical and continuous, creating a polyphony of weeping and song that continues throughout the final portion of a *gisalo* song and even after it has been finished.

In both of these settings, song is an intentional way of constructing messages, beginning at the textual level with "inner" and "underneath" linguistic forms, sound symbolism, and construction of a place name path. It is wrapped in melodic and temporal codes that carry it forth, like a waterfall dropping to a swirling water pool and streaming away. It is then performed in a voice like that of a fruitdove and danced like a cuckoodove bobbing at a waterfall, its voice heard over the constant shimmering of a rattle and its costume arching up and over like flowing water. These bird sounds and bird sound words reorganize experience onto an emotional plane resonating with deeply felt Kaluli sentiments. When textual, musical, and performative features properly coalesce, someone will be moved to tears.

6

━━━━━━━━━━━━━━━━━━━━━━━

In the Form of a Bird: Kaluli Aesthetics

Three sets of constructs—ethnographic, theoretical, and personal—
have run through this study intertwined in an attempt to describe the
richness and relevance of Kaluli cultural patterning of sounds. Some
final arguments will draw each set to a close here, and once again attempt to illustrate their mutual importance. For the ethnography, the
argument is that "becoming a bird" is the core Kaluli aesthetic metaphor. Understanding that metaphor is an exercise in how cultural and
semantic fields are organized in myth, language, expressive codes, and
behaviors. For theory, the argument is that contemporary ideational approaches to culture, represented here by structuralism, cognitive anthropology, and symbolic interpretation, are less interesting as competing paradigms or as single total models than they are as partial stylistic
strategies for coping with the complexity of cultural systems. Finally,
for personal reflection, the argument is that it is spurious to analyze the
content or principles of an aesthetic system without considering the degree of aesthetic intent in the analytic posture. Such intent, in my own
case, involves more concern with co-aesthetic emotion and less of an
attempt to behaviorize, normalize, or test aesthetics by equating it with
"functional beauty."

Sound as Aesthetically Coded Sentiment

Throughout the diverse materials presented in this work a singular emphasis is consistent. That emphasis is the desire to describe in both Kaluli
terms and anthropological terms how ideas generate actions and how
those actions are purposive, expressive forms that constitute an ideology
of emotion in Bosavi. I have tried to convey how the patterning of expres-

217

sive forms embodies and communicates the most deeply felt sentiments in Kaluli social life.

In chapter 2, an analysis of Kaluli ornithological taxonomy revealed how classificatory epistemology is complexly symbolic. Multilayered perceptions of birds indicate an interplay of what Kaluli know from their observational and practical experiences as hunters and naturalists with what they deeply feel about birds as the spirits of their dead. Kaluli ornithology is not a one-dimensional, rigidly ordered and remembered, taxonomic, treelike hierarchy, but a set of images about bird behavior, morphology, and particularly sound, that shifts and refocuses depending on the pragmatic context in which the knowledge is called into action. The coexistence of two major taxonomic constructs, one based on the morphological criteria of shared beaks and feet, and the other based upon sound, indicates the extent to which Kaluli creatively organize their knowledge of birds in relation to ecological understanding and social needs.

Since there is no hard evidence to suggest that the human mind has a propensity to invent unique typologies or to economize on storage space by memorizing fully elaborated transitive taxonomic trees, it is hardly unusual that the Kaluli utilize such diverse cognitive organizations for purposes of organizing information about birds. What the Kaluli data show, in fact, is that cultural knowledge is neither a map nor a summation of a group of taxa but rather the creative ability to organize and think about natural historical and zoological processes in ways consistent with socially structured beliefs about the world.

The Kaluli perceptual and cultural status of birds is perhaps the real foundation of both the myth "the boy who became a *muni* bird" and the expressive modalities of weeping, poetics, and song. Birds are mediators because they are both natural beings and *ane mama,* the 'gone reflections' of Kaluli who have left the visible world upon death and reappeared ɔbɛ *mise* 'in the form of birds'. Sound is the behavior of birds that is both indicative of their natural lives and actions and expressive of their feelings as *ane mama* to those who are living. Hence the concern Kaluli display over which birds say their names, which ones only sound, make a lot of noise, whistle, speak the Bosavi language, weep, sing, or dance.

"Becoming a bird" is the passage from life to death; the spirit representations for different social categories (men, women, old, young), as well as for different temperaments (angry, docile, hostile, cranky), reflect ways in which observations of bird behavior are analogized to human behavior. Bird categories thus come to reflect human categories. This metaphoric potency explains why birds and bird sounds are powerful expressive vehicles for the communication of sorrows of loss in weeping, poetics, and song. "Becoming a bird" is the core Kaluli aesthetic metaphor because it embodies the emotional state that has the unique power to evoke deep feelings and sentiments of nostalgia, loss, and abandonment.

Chapter 3 showed that *sa-yɛlab,* that is, melodic-texted-sung-weeping, is a direct response to death or loss. In the myth it is provoked by loss in the form of a rupture of the social bonds of obligation, reciprocity, and *adɛ* role behavior. The denial of food by his *adɛ* means that the boy has no *adɛ;* if the sister were really his *adɛ,* he would not be hungry or abandoned. This form of loss is analogous to death; the boy becomes a bird. When he opens his mouth, there is only weeping, with the four-pitched, descending *muni* call.

In contemporary Kaluli society, death and loss provoke women to respond identically, and reactions to this weeping compare the performer to a fruitdove, because the weeping has bird sound as its melodic base and sadness over loss as its social base. Which bird the weeper becomes is based on an equation between fruitdove calls and degrees of sadness. To say that a woman has wept *iyɛu ɔngo,* like an *iyɛu,* an Ornate Fruitdove, carries the most aesthetic weight of the three main analogies. In all cases, the strength of weeping derives from being the human sound expression closest to the sonic and emotional state of being a bird. Kaluli find *sa-yɛlab* the most deeply moving form of sound expression.

Chapters 4 and 5 pointed out that the situation is precisely reversed in song. There are two elements to song, sound and text, the Kaluli conceptualizing sound as the "outside" and text as the "inside." The sound is *ɔbɛ gɔnɔ* 'bird sound', and the text is *ɔbɛ gɔnɔ to* 'bird sound words'; these represent the same melody as that found in weeping and the same language as that found in the myth once the boy has become a bird. The sound is thus conventionally associated with weeping and sadness and the language conventionally associated with the talk of one who is lost, abandoned, and reduced to the form of a bird. Bird sound plus bird-sound words equals song.

This metaphoric construction for song is different from the construction of weeping in several ways. Weeping is considered more direct than song because it derives from immediate grief. The language of weeping is very much conversational *to halaido* 'hard words', spontaneously improvised on the spot. Song, on the other hand, is formed by the sound of weeping and the talk of sadness; it is composed and crafted with deliberate ends in mind. Where death and loss move women to weeping, song is intentionally constructed to move men to tears.

This conceptualization of song as bird sound and bird talk is only part of the overall importance of birds as an aesthetic trope. Song is inspired by thinking about birds; when performed, it is sung in a bird voice; men wear bird feathers to make themselves beautiful and evocative; dance is patterned as bird movement; staging in the longhouse involves lighting and darkness that prepare the audience to see the performer as a lone bird. Aesthetic commentary compares the singing to a voice that is *kalo ɔngo* or *howɛn ɔngo,* like *kalo,* the Pink-spotted Fruitdove, or *howɛn,* the Orange-bellied Fruitdove. Moreover, one compares the dancing to movement that is *wɔkwele ɔngo,* like *wɔkwele,* the Giant Cuckoodove. When people are moved to tears by the song and its performance, they are said to have heard "the voice of someone who has become a bird," or "the words inside the song as the call of a bird."

While weeping is a response that Kaluli find natural, and mythically given, it is song that draws upon all aesthetic dimensions to package together elaborate premeditation, composition with sound and text, staging, instrumental and chorus accompaniment, costuming, and dancing. Song is the means through which men create a large social occasion whose purpose is to focus attention on, and invite confirmation of, their skills at provocation and control. It reflects the importance of an elaborate cultural show rather than the importance of the actual death or loss.

These differences between weeping and song as expressive sound forms communicating Kaluli sentiments are resolved by their mutual aesthetic trope. What appears in myth as the scenario of mediation, "becoming a bird," reappears in expression as a pervasive metaphor for form and performance. Mediation additionally is linked to an intimate symbolic dualism. Birds, particularly fruitdoves, embody death and the sonic reflection of *ane mama,* as well as melodies and timbres associated with sadness. Fruitdove calls, then, mediate sentiments of sorrow, loss, and isolation in sounds of weeping, poetics, and song.

There are many routine levels of response—personal, nonverbal, verbal, gestural, group—that Kaluli consider to be indications of emotional confirmation, evaluation, and aesthetic judgment in contexts surrounding weeping and song performance. Kaluli responses are made openly and directly because presence at the scene of evocation demands social response. The explicit purpose of song is to move others to feel sorrow for the performer. The purpose of weeping, where the loss is most profound, is to lament and grieve over death.

At the most basic interpersonal level, Kaluli response to weeping and song is emotional and directly confirmatory. A heartfelt *heyo!* 'sorry' is a most explicit and empathetic "I feel where you are at." This is sometimes accomplished equally well by a soft cluck of the tongue against the back of the upper teeth and the roof of the mouth, accompanied by simultaneously tilting the head to the side, directing eyes downward, and shrugging the shoulders. These responses are seen or heard frequently. Verbal expressives, sounds, and gestures of confirmatory personal feelings and empathy are all common behaviors, indeed, typically Kaluli, at funerary or ceremonial events.

A tremendous variety of nonverbal, obscure, personal, and introspective behaviors exists at the same level of emotion and confirmation. These signal to others that the withdrawn person is inwardly examining or experiencing in body and conscience the profound impact of the weeping or song performance. The extent to which one may hear individuals making verbal comments or explicit gestures of the form interpreted iconically by Kaluli as signals of deep personal sadness is largely determined by the specific individuals present, less by the gravity of the situation. Time and time again, it was clear that very demonstrative and emotional Kaluli individuals could catalyze a chain reaction of commentary or explicit behaviors at these events. These same individuals often took similar roles in situations in which anger or other dramatic emotional states also marked by evaluative verbalizations were at the center of the group experience.

To consider Kaluli aesthetics, therefore, we must consider not only the explicit end—becoming a bird—articulated on the prescriptive and descriptive levels, but also the communal and dramatic nature of Kaluli emotional response.

At this emotional confirmatory level, an individual's willingness to be there and the assumption that he must be there for the purpose of emotional evocation are foremost considerations. In one sense this contexting requires less of Kaluli than does the contexting of dramatic and emotional situations marked by heated argument, anger, or potential violence. In settings for weeping and song, nothing true or false is at stake, no controversy over how things should be done, no question of who is right or wrong or what course of action individuals or groups should take.

Weeping and song do not constitute arguments about the way society or persons should be, but they do present a multiplicity of structures that draw upon culturally ideal and normative scenarios as well as upon their ruptures. In this sense they command persuasiveness in a manner not unlike that which Sol Worth described for caricatures (1974). On the one hand, these expressive codes reference items and events to a lived world of actual people, places, actions, and behaviors. At the same time, they reference the same items and events to abstract qualities and values, precisely described by the Kaluli notion of a *hega* or 'underneath'. The two referencing systems are at times completely intermixed, thus allowing the audience to have a simultaneous sense image of things that are and are not, can be and cannot be, should be and should not be. Weeping and song, in strong contrast to heated argument or arm-twisting rhetoric, do not involve creating tensions and meanings simply by clashing different domains of the literal. Rather, they create that momentary social and personal "inside" sensation in which the weeper or singer can be seen, heard, or felt to *be* a bird.

Gestural, expressive (*heyo!*, sighs, vocalized or whistled expressions of sadness), and more explicitly verbal comments and remarks at funerary and ceremonial occasions must be understood on this emotional level. Kaluli do not attend these events in order to stand back on the sidelines, as it were, and take them in abstractly and rationally. They go with the ability and often with the explicit desire to suspend their thoughts, to reflect on feelings, and to be moved. Indeed, an absence at one funerary event I witnessed was considered major evidence that the nonparticipating man was in fact the witch responsible for the death. Kaluli are supposed to be dramatic, emotional, demonstrative, and reflective. Expression of that emotional side of things is the normal way to behave at events where there is weeping and song; as such, these are the natural contexts in which one hears or sees what I have termed "evaluative" remarks and "aesthetic" responses. Comments of the most explicit verbal form, such as those noting that as a weeper or as a singer and dancer, one is like an *iyɛu,* or *howɛn,* or *kalo,* or *wɔkwele,* are not intended to be abstractions but personal expressions of confirmation of shared experience.

On the other hand, commentaries can be and are made abstractly. When I would sing with people in nonceremonial contexts or play back tape recordings or have discussions about textual imagery with them, there was much response on an abstract level. Playback of recordings made in 1966–68 by Buck Schieffelin brought men to tears in 1977; they responded with aesthetic comments. One day, after returning to the village from recording a local woman singing at a sago camp, I casually played the tapes on my porch. A man got choked up and said, "She's singing my lands," to which several others immediately sighed *"heyo,"* indicating confirmatory sorrow for the sadness they assumed he felt. More formally, I often held discussion sessions where several older Kaluli men sat with me for hours, listening repeatedly to the same song, and recalling the history of its performance, who had wept and why, and how the song "hardened." They enjoyed abstractly analyzing the tape and constantly mixed verbal and gestural forms of evaluation and response.

These are clear indications of the dramatic and excited ways Kaluli attend to and respond to weeping and song. One does not have to test, elicit, cajole, or otherwise search for these kinds of behaviors in Bosavi. Varying degrees of interest, degrees of predisposition to discuss things analytically, and degrees of dramatic personal style exist among the Kaluli when it comes to issues of weeping, poetics, and song composition and performance. Nevertheless, the fact that Kaluli treat sound as aesthetically coded sentiment is culturally pervasive and is responsible for the social reality of dramatic response and evaluation.

[handwritten margin note: If you do, then is your subject the useful, valid one to study,]

At this point an obvious objection to my summary of Kaluli sound and sentiment must be interjected. Is it the case that the variety of sounds and sentiments discussed here are in fact quite limited? What about other domains of soundmaking? What about the sentiments of assertion, violence, energy, anger? Why is the emphasis so strongly oriented toward sorrow and loss? Do birds and bird myths mediate other modalities of sentiment in sound expression?

These are fair objections and contain the challenge to extend the analysis to other kinds of soundmaking and emotional expression in order to be able to argue convincingly that birds indeed mediate all forms of Kaluli sentiment in vocal and instrumental sound expression, as well as in visual and choreographic expression. There are many other important Kaluli emotional states and sentiments as well as many other important bird sounds, myths, and forms of human expression. Yet from the Kaluli point of view, "the boy who became a *muni* bird" is the most important of their bird myths; and tragedy, emotional sadness, and sorrow are most thoroughly embodied in sound forms as aesthetically coded sentiment. Weeping, poetics, and song are not associated with occasions of anger and tension; these sentiments are expressed through other vocal and instrumental sound patterns.

For example, male and female expressive styles are presented, in addition to song and weeping, in a type of communal men's whooping called *ulab* and a type of women's group cheering called *uwɔlab*. *Ulab* means 'saying *u*', and *uwɔlab* means 'saying *uwɔ*'. *U* and *uwɔ* are the sounds made by two prominent Bosavi birds; *u* by the Kapul Eagle *ušulage* and *uwɔ* by the Superb Bird of Paradise *uwɔlo*. Maleness, strength, and exuberance are displayed in the whooping of *ulab*, while femaleness, seductive cheering, and coyness are displayed in the yapping of *uwɔlab*. Not surprisingly, in the spirit realm, Kapul Eagles are the reflections of loud aggressive men, and Superb Birds of Paradise are one of the several birds of paradise that are reflections of beautiful seductive women. Again, we have the paradigmatic relation of metaphor;

$$
\begin{array}{lll}
\text{male} : \text{female} & & :: \\
\text{ušulage} : \text{uwɔlo} & & :: \\
\text{(Kapul Eagle)} \quad \text{(Superb Bird of Paradise)} & & \\
\text{ulab} : \text{uwɔlab} & & :: \\
(\text{♂ whooping}) \quad (\text{♀ cheering}) & & \\
\text{exuberance} : \text{coyness} & & \\
\text{and} \quad \text{and} & & \\
\text{aggression} \quad \text{seduction} & &
\end{array}
$$

This formal organization illustrates culturally constructed relationships between social categories, expression of emotion in vocalization, birds, and patterned modes of sound.

There is much more material along parallel lines, but this example should be enough to point out that the metaphor of "becoming a bird" is the meeting ground of sound and sentiment in Kaluli expression. To summarize:

MODE	Weeping	Song
CONTEXTS	Funerals, occasions of profound loss	Ceremony, seance
FORM	Spontaneous, improvised	Composed, deliberate
MAIN ACTORS	women	men
EXPRESSIVE BASE	Response to death or loss	Fears of loss, abandonment

SOCIAL ENDS	Personal, lament	Social, evocation
METAPHORIC BASE	bird sound bird voice	bird sound bird sound words bird voice bird costume bird dance motion
SOCIAL RESPONSE	Natural expression, the closest sound to being a bird	Cultural staging, the height of manipulating form and performance for persuasion
AESTHETIC TROPE	Becoming a bird	= Becoming a bird

Culture Theory

Having summarized the arguments presented by the ethnographic materials, I will turn to a few final comments about the place of culture theory in the construction of my interpretations here. While these remarks are not intended to launch into new territory without proper preparation, they are nevertheless important in evaluating my approach to the analysis of Kaluli sound expression.

Theories of culture are sometimes taken to be competing paradigms for ethnographic research and analysis. Brandishing terms like "materialist," "structuralist," "evolutionist," and "symbolist," and tossing them about as insults in the contemporary theoretical literature is perhaps the most vulgar representation of this sort of competition. Discussions filled with pretentious claims that X theory has more "power" than Y theory further trivialize the issues. Nevertheless, the extent to which ethnographies are shaped by and inform theories of culture is a serious matter, and all ethnographers have some obligation to explicate the ways in which their descriptions and interpretations fit into the general theoretical concerns of the field.

The analysis here derives rather obviously from those theoretical approaches generally considered ideational (Keesing 1974); structural, linguistic, cognitive, and symbolic studies are the main trends in this domain. The other major group of culture theories, which are adaptive and concerned with material, evolutionary, ecological, and techno-economical studies, have not been brought to bear upon the issues addressed here. Throughout this report I have dealt with cultural analysis at levels of shared meanings, ideas, feelings, concepts, percepts, symbols, thought, knowledge. What I have described are ways that observed or articulated behaviors (some of which are not visible) map onto this ideational realm. In the movement back and forth from formal constructions to actual behaviors, I have tried to map idealized plans onto actual events but have not taken the position that explanation in ethnography is synonymous with the precise prediction of substantive acts or that the proper description and interpretation of social action is merely a reduction of actions to cause-effect statements.

The Kaluli data contain three major domains of observed and articulated social forms. First is myth, which I have approached as a collective creation of mind that compresses shared symbols and more formally crystallizes metonyms into metaphors. Next are things of the natural world and things of cultural form; I have often begun by approaching these items and events in terms of linguistic codability and prominence of verbalization, assuming they are indexes to various types of classificatory, category, or feature salience, and topical focus in discourse. Finally, I have described real instances and case histories of people engaging in the staging and performance of expressive behaviors and responding to them. These have been approached as imaginative and cohesive manifestations, rich both in their particulars and in their relevance to the ordinary ways Kaluli people socially relate to each other through the expression of emotions. Thus myth, cultural semantics as indicated by the ethnography of the lexicon and texts, and symbolic analysis of expressive performances: these are the core images selected as data and analyzed to produce the interpretations here.

These three images, displayed here in a rather dialectical arrangement of formal and informal sections, correspond roughly to the usual data of three ideational approaches: the structural, the cognitive-linguistic, and the symbolic-interpretive. The first of these looks at culture as a para-logical organizing scheme, transforming a small number of underlying mythic elements (like nature/culture) through operations such as opposition, analogy, homology, inversion, and mediation (Lévi-Strauss 1966). The second of these looks at culture as shared concepts coded in linguistic constructs that are internally related by domains. "Cultures are not material phenomena; they are cognitive organizations of material phenomena" (Tyler 1969:3). These cognitive organizations are often studied through naming behavior or lack of it, and this behavior is assumed to be the imposition of cultural order onto perception and conception. The third of these approaches is oriented toward the explication of culture as shared symbols and meanings (or as "an assemblage of texts" [Geertz 1973:448]). It draws upon subjective and hermeneutic interpretation, "thick description" (Geertz 1973), and a broad, humanistic tradition. It is concerned less with formal arrangements of diagrams, laws of thought, rules, or claims about the nature of mind, and more with the intricate and radically contextual significance of public or performed actions in their social settings.

In working through the depth and complexity of the Kaluli materials, I have often been struck by the problems of treating these three approaches as comprehensive or competing in any analytically helpful way. I have been led to see them more as styles that, in their less abstract and rhetorical forms applied to the analysis of actual data patterns, can and should be mutually revealing. While this will be taken as a muddy and inelegant conclusion by those who believe in the exclusivity of theoretical constructs, or others who prefer ethnographies that start with a theoretical viewpoint and constrain the issues to fit that analytic grid, I have freely drawn upon what is useful in each. I believe that a proper analysis of the Kaluli materials demands elaborating patterns and utilizing whatever is necessary to the task; for this I have not chosen a single paradigm but rather have explained what needs explaining, bringing everything necessary into the argument.

I shall try to explain this choice by reviewing some of the issues involved in the competition of these approaches. One major point of contention is formalism and what it purports to represent. Clearly there is a difference between formalism as a means and as a distraction. While proponents of symbolic and interpretive approaches have been highly critical of structuralists and cognitivists on this score, these critiques often attack the manner in which data is expressed and do not deal with some of the broader similarities in the final analyses. Keesing (1974: 84–85) has pointed out Geertz's error of attributing a simplistic reductionism to Goodenough, and Fabian (1975) has similarly shown the processes through which taxonomic modes of thought play a role in symbolic constructions. Formal analyses of the highly diagrammatic or mathematical sort are relatively easy to attack as reductionistic, yet many of these are different neither in assumptions nor in ultimate goals when compared with interpretive analysis.

I will illustrate by turning back to the Kaluli data. In the opening chapter I presented a structural analysis of the myth "the boy who became a *muni* bird" as a preliminary way of indicating how "becoming a bird" is a basic Kaluli metaphor that mediates between social sentiments and sound modalities. An argument can be made that this structural statement was an unnecessary mechanical and formalistic indulgence because the same things could have been said in direct prose. Such an argument, however, attacks the diagrams and not what is really said about metaphor. Fernandez, for example (1974), in an impressive interpretive statement, demonstrates what is apparent throughout the *Mythologiques* of Lévi-Strauss, namely, that metaphors are formal correspondences underlying and upholding framings of social action and plans for performance.

What is objectionable in some structural analyses is not the attempt to express formally notions about the operation of metaphor, but rather the pretention of making a cosmic fuss out of small amounts of data. When a formal analysis of how symbols are connected is scaffolded by a description of how symbols are formulated and performed, objections to formalism are no longer terribly enlightening, and structural statements can assume a valid place in an ethnographic treatment.

I do not mean to imply that there are only minimal differences between the entirety of Lévi-Strauss's work and that of other symbolic anthropologists. Dan Sperber (1975:81) has recently pointed out that the synchronic *en bloc* status Lévi-Strauss often assigns to myths vitiates much of what he says they mean. Geertz and others have similarly pointed out the fallacy of assuming the meaning of things to be solely in their arrangement, rather than in the relations between their arrangement and objects, actions, and thoughts in lived worlds.

How, then, is a myth to be analyzed? In the first chapter I indicated that whatever else one might claim about a structural analysis of "the boy who became a *muni* bird," it is certainly possible to analyze the myth structurally without mangling any of the ethnographic issues or forcing the data into overly reductionistic categories. But does this analysis tell us something unique? I doubt it; it simply shows that a structural analysis can be an adequate stylistic expression of the issues that must be untangled in the study of myth, namely, how metaphors are paradigmatically formed out of metonymic and syntagmatic arrangements. The structural framing summarizes, but it does not inherently explain; explaining the myth requires moving out into the real world of Kaluli concepts and actions in order to deal with the complexity of the social order.

A similar set of tensions emerges in the chapters on birds, weeping, poetics, and song. In these discussions there are many formal descriptions of lexical domains, analyzing term-to-term relations and the features that define their categorical organizations. These, too, can be criticized as unnecessary formalistic games that reduce the data but do not explain it. It is certainly true that methodological exercises of dissecting lexical fields have sometimes devolved into obtuse and pretentious analyses that trivialize rather than illuminate, but this should not doom the possibilities of semantic analysis. Term-to-term relations exist within term-to-object, term-to-action, and term-to-system constraints and organizing strategies. The systematic features of the lexicon in any domain cannot be claimed to be isomorphic with the content, the knowledge, or the epistemological factors that activate the domain. However, the solution to this problem is not more arguments about the weaknesses of cognitive theory but more sophisticated attempts to understand how percept and concept formations relate to lived activities and events. If culture is to behavior as language is to speech, the study object is neither reduced nor simplified; ideal or normative capacities and scenarios must be studied in relation to what people actually say, do, and intend.

A taxonomy of birds, kinds of weeping, or musical and poetic metalanguage does not constitute the totality of what underlies Kaluli bird knowledge, performances of weeping, or constructions of poetry and song. However, these taxonomies and lexical field analyses are necessary parts of a cultural account of how Kaluli construct their world and how they converse about it. Such taxonomies, however logical or partial, are like structural analyses in a basic way: they express arrangements but do not inherently explain them. At the same time I think it impossible to thickly describe and culturally explain these areas without some recourse to the shared organizational features Kaluli articulate about the things in their world and the boundaries of their expression, which means that an understanding of lexically coded concepts should be coupled with studies of actual behaviors, rather than separated from them.

Finally, are symbolic and interpretive analyses really about culture or are they just indexes of behavior? Do they really illuminate the underlying system or are they more concerned with the surface of actions? Do they impede comparison, replicability, and testing by clouding description in a thoroughly subjective language that mimics the pretentions of literary criticism? Is society really like an "assemblage of texts," or has Geertz simply given us a cute metaphor that promotes an indulgence in literary figures of speech rather than the conceptual clarity required to understand what human social life is all about? These questions and others like them in the anti-interpretive rhetoric seem to share a common problem with symbolic critiques of formalist theory; they imply that analysis is an all-or-nothing proposition and leave the sense that interpretation is absent in other approaches that define themselves as more replicable, rigorous, and objective. This is not a particularly insightful critique, because, as Keesing notes (1974:84), there is as much problematic in theorizing that culture is *between* the minds of people as there is in theorizing that it is *in* them or *transcending* them. There is always subjectivity and interpretation in an ethnographic account; the extent to which a report is believable or reliable is judged by a number of criteria and is not a simple matter of methodological verifiability.

After a year of fieldwork, another of analyzing notes, images, and recordings; another of dissertation writing; and another of rewriting, arguing, and reanalyzing, I have grown more and more wary of attempts to delimit which conception of culture is more powerful, correct, or scientific. Ethnography is about describing the complexity of patterning in cultural systems and about explaining how the operation of society depends upon the tacit and overt complicity of its members. It is also about understanding appropriate relations between methods, evidence, and theory. In my search for ways to indicate the shape and complexity of Kaluli cultural patterns, I have humbly found myself in need of the theoretical *bricolage* evident here. It may be easier for ethnographers to accept *bricolage* as the basis of *pensée sauvage* than it is to accept it as the basis of their own constructions, but the act of describing and interpreting the Kaluli cultural patterns presented here has challenged me to draw upon everything necessary to the task. In this challenge I have found a co-theoretical relevance of structures, taxonomies, codes, symbols, and textual explications.

Participation and Reflection

Prior to my arrival in Bosavi, Buck and Bambi Schieffelin told some of their Kaluli assistants that I was a "song man" *(gisalo kalu)* in our own land and that I would come to record and ask questions about their music. By the time my mastery of Kaluli was sufficient to be able to speak to people about musical ideas in any detail, I found myself on the receiving end of many questions. What Kaluli wanted to know was whether or not people wept for song in my society. The experience of formulating responses to such questions had two effects: it made me think about my own musical experiences in some previously unconsidered ways; and it led me to think about why my Kaluli friends had such a desire to question me and converse about aesthetic issues. I don't know whether I learned to be as sophisticated an interpreter of my society as Kulu, Jubi, Gaso *sulɔ*, Mewɔ, and some other men were for Kaluli society, but I am reasonably sure that their questions were not just manifestations of a slight curiosity. Some were deeply interested in talking about song in a rather broad set of ways. They listened with me to tapes I had made among the Samo people (about forty-five kilometers west of Bosavi) during a brief visit to another anthropologist; they played and commented on the Samo drum I brought back with me; they eagerly listened to music from my own and other societies and asked rather impressive questions about its form and meaning.

Two types of music were popular with several men and provided topics of continued interest. Medium-paced blues with a melody line played by clarinet or soprano saxophone had a great appeal. The timbres of the clarinet and saxophone were said to be like those of fruitdoves, and the prominence of the descending minor third interval was regularly noted. A tape of this kind of music, featuring Sidney Bechet on soprano saxophone, was most popular. Some listeners were most impressed that this music originated with and was largely performed by black people. Koto music from Japan was another favorite. A few people went so far as to say that it sounded like water and to ask if this was intentional. In these cases Kaluli could find much in their own ideas about musical form to compare with the recordings, but it was equally true that they utilized the same criteria to discuss other items. Blues played at a fast tempo was considered by most to be too frenetic, and the timbre of many Western instruments and voices was considered unpleasant.

In response to one of my letters home, a musician friend wrote back, "If they are so excited by birds you should tell them about Charlie Parker!" Shortly thereafter I played a recording by Parker, and although the tempo was much too fast to interest anyone, the alto saxophone timbre was considered pleasing. I told Kulu and Gigio that Parker was considered so extraordinary that people called him "Bird," and that after his death the phrase "Bird lives" took on a special meaning for musicians and other people who greatly appreciated his sounds. Their initial reaction was complete disbelief, then Kulu questioned me at some length about the phrase. Parker actually had the nickname "Bird" or "Yardbird" long before he was broadly recognized as the innovator remembered today with "Bird lives," but Kulu wanted to know whether the name was given because of the speed of the sound, "flying" on the saxophone. While Kaluli generally do not attach any positive connotation to the speed of sound, nor liken the pacing of song to bird flight, Kulu wanted to know whether this was the way we thought about song in my land. But what they most wanted to know was whether "Bird lives" actually meant that after Parker's death people continued to *hear* his music. My affirmative reply was met with incredible delight.

More often it was the case that people spoke with me about my own experiences in playing and composing music. I tried to tell them about the jazz nightclub life I knew and to compare it to that of a Kaluli man. As in *gisalo* ceremonies, I related, young women sometimes would come to listen to jazz, lose their hearts to the performer, and go home with him for the night. This rather important feature of the socialization of bar musicians (which gained both notoriety and stereotypic dimensions as a result of the publicity about "groupies" and rock performers in the 1960s) particularly interested the young men. They considered it, despite the differences in potential consequences for elopement and marriage, to be an indication that I understood why song was powerful and an important skill for men to acquire.

As time went on, I began to realize that the ways in which I communicated my own musical experiences not only affected the ways Kaluli spoke with me about song and weeping, but also led them to make certain assumptions about me as a feeling or emotional person. Once I began composing songs and singing more openly with my assistants, I came to understand that the ability to project a sense of dramatic interest in song typified Kaluli verbalizations about aesthetic matters.

It seemed that the best way to make Kaluli understand my real desire to comprehend their songs was to learn how to compose and sing them, an ability that would require a detailed knowledge of a song's structure and elements. Sometimes I would stay up at night, listening repeatedly to recorded songs through headphones while looking at the transcribed texts. The next day, meeting with assistants for discussion and transcription sessions, I would review these songs while we wore headphones, singing along as best I could, sometimes accompanying myself with a shell rattle. My assistants seemed to enjoy this very much and to appreciate my melodic recall when we reviewed one section or another. But whatever their perception of my musical abilities, they were much more impressed when they saw me weep openly after receiving a letter from Buck and Bambi, whose departure had left me alone in Bosavi. If making music, talking about it, and being moved by it are not extraordinary things for Kaluli, it is because these behaviors are so deeply related to the sound and the emotions surrounding weeping. For Kaluli, weeping is a measure and an indicator of one's emotional nature as a person. My musical efforts demonstrated an interest in their songs and a desire to understand them in a personal way, but the sight of me weeping went a lot further to establish for them just what sort of person I might be.

Against a background of experiences like these, the issue seemed to be not whether Kaluli "have aesthetics" in an objective, reverifiable sense, but rather how to describe the quality of experience they feel and the quality of my relation to it. To that end, the writings of Robert Plant Armstrong (1971, 1975) have provided much inspiration for me.

Armstrong argues that aesthetics, "the theory or study of form incarnating feeling" (1975:11), exists at a banal level in anthropology because an adequate theory of the "affecting presence" (the term he prefers to "art") depends on an adequate approach to culture, an approach that cannot be simply a reduction to functions and structures but must concern itself with experience. What he finds in anthropology is a "crypto-aesthetics" that is ethnocentric in its concern with "the beautiful" and its expectation of finding this concern to be "practiced, as opposed to formulated" (1975:14–15). He proposes directing the level of analysis to the being of the affecting presence and the "feelingful" dimensions of its experience as it is "witnessed," a term he uses instead of "viewed," "heard," "seen," or "perceived" to suggest the importance of the relationship between witness and witnessed (1975:19–20).

To address the "being," "feelingful experience," and "witnessing" of the metaphoric base of Kaluli aesthetics—becoming a bird—I turn to a discussion of two photographic images.

The first image has a form that is frequent and conventional in ethnographies. We assume that it represents someone doing what he normally does. With no further information about who is represented there or what he is doing, it is easy to take refuge in the structure of the image—conventional Western portraiture framed in a medium shot—

and to assume that this framing is a significant way to depict a Papua New Guinean dressed in a ceremonial costume holding a drum. Further attention can then be directed to the costume itself, the body painting, the red and white feathers, and the palm leaf streamers.

It is clear, however, that these things are not the meaning of the image, nor is the simple meta-message "the photographer was in Papua New Guinea and saw this costuming." The image could have been made at any number of places, and we have no other internal information to indicate the photographer participated in some event for which the costume was made and used.

Having read the preceding chapters, however, we are in a very different position to assess how the elements contained in the image have been selected and arranged meaningfully. The color symbolism of red, white, and black has been discussed; the use of cockatoo and hornbill feathers for costuming has been analyzed; the "flow" and spread of the streamers for dance has been indicated. Moreover, the general notion that Kaluli ceremonies involve men wearing the feathers of birds, thus making themselves beautiful like birds in song and dance performance, has been explicated. The inversion by which men go to elaborate degrees in composition and staging to move others to tears, while women spontaneously do the same with uncomposed weeping in response to death has also been considered in some detail. The image, then, can be said to depict in this context the elaborate cultural process males create in order to be beautiful and evocative, as well as some of the visual components of that process important to the staging of ceremonial performance.

The second image is clearly not an attempt at iconic depiction, and only the deliberateness of its presentation here might lead one to decide that it is intentional and not a representation of incompetence. Since it does not conform to other typical features of realistic images and documentary photographs, one might further decide that it is an attempt at "art."

Again, having read the preceding chapters, we are in a position to address how the elements arranged in this image are meaningful. In the blur of blacks and whites, some features are noticeable, like the shells and color patterns. Comparing the two photographs, we might surmise that the object of the second image is some distortion of the first, taken with the subject in motion. Costumes have been described as using pliable pieces of cane to hold arm and belt feathers in place, which suggests that the blurs of white are produced by the motion of feathers. This, com-

6. Gaso of Bonɔ dressed in a *kɔluba* costume. Here he is tuning up his drum in preparation for *ilib kuwɔ*, the late afternoon drumming prelude to an evening *kɔluba* ceremony.

7. Frozen in motion while dancing up and down the dark longhouse corridor, a dancer is seen as a "man in the form of a bird," *kalu ɔbɛ mise.*

bined with the descriptions of the flapping motion of the costumes, the bobbing, birdlike motion of the dancers, and the aesthetic ideal of becoming a bird, leads to the interpretation that the photograph is meant to reveal that in ceremonial dance, a man is seen as a bird.

What we have in these two photographs are the opposite ends of the folk models of photography, described by Sekula (1975:45):

> All photographic communication seems to take place within the conditions of a kind of binary folklore. That is, there is a "symbolist" folkmyth and a "realist" folkmyth. The misleading but popular form of this opposition is "art photography" vs. "documentary photography." Every photograph tends, at any given moment of reading in any given context, toward one of these poles of meaning. The oppositions between these poles are as follows: photographer as seer vs. photographer as witness, photography as expression vs. photography as reportage, theories of imagination (and inner truth) vs. informative value, and finally, metaphoric signification vs. metonymic signification.

The first of these photographs clearly fits the attributes of a "realist" image and the second, those of a "symbolist" image. The first image was not theoretically premeditated. On an afternoon before a ceremony, I left my village with a group of men and traveled to another longhouse where they were to dance that evening. At two points along the way they stopped to work on various aspects of their costumes, and I took the opportunity to talk with them and make some snapshots. The pictures were not taken for purposes of analysis, nor did I think much about them as I made them.

The second of these photographs was very premeditated. Two days before the event at which it was made, I spent the day talking with Jubi and asked him to describe what was going to happen. I wanted to get a sense of the anticipatory feelings that accompany the planning and staging of ceremonies. At one point he remarked: "In the middle of the night, while the dancers continue, dancing and dancing . . . you get tired and lie down . . . and then, all of a sudden, something startles you, a sound, or something . . . you open your eyes and look at the dancer . . . it is a man in the form of a bird." I was taken by this description of that hypnotic, tired, dreamy sensation promoted by a long evening of song, as well as the implication that one is emotionally prepared to experience the ceremony in this way.

Jubi's remark was the basis for the second photograph; I decided to

use a metaphoric convention from my own culture's expressive tradition
in photography to make a synthetic and analytic statement about a Kaluli
metaphor. This was the only time I planned and explicitly used photography in a way that required something more than reliable snapshot
reflexes. In a sense, then, the imaging code typically considered to be the
least documentary and the most "artistic" structures what is the most
ethnographic of my photographs. The imaging code considered the most
documentary has the least to do with my imaging behavior as an ethnographer. The more iconic image is explicit and readable, but the noniconic
one is brought into explicitness here as a highly direct synthesis of what
I have otherwise explained largely with words.

On reflection I see the image of a *kalu ɔbɛ mise,* a 'man in the form
of a bird', as a meeting of minds, as an invention of a co-aesthetic relationship more forceful than what I have been able to say about singing Kaluli
songs or other attempts I have made to move emotionally closer to what
I was trying to understand about Kaluli sound and sentiment. Many types
of analytic and interpretive strategies have been utilized here to indicate
how "becoming a bird" is a mediating scheme for Kaluli emotions and
sound expressions. These analyses and interpretations have involved
symbols about symbols, layered representations of representations of
representations. The construction of the *kalu ɔbɛ mise* image, however, is
of another order, a metaphor about a metaphor. Making my own "affecting presence" out of a Kaluli myth takes me back to Armstrong's "being,"
"feelingful experience," and "witnessing" in the process of discovering
how form incarnates feeling.

I cannot understand how one might study aesthetic systems without
a concern for aesthetic intent in the analytic posture or a concern for how
others perceive the analyst's own aesthetic sensibilities. Concentrating on
value-free, objective measurements of aesthetic preferences has done
little to move us toward a more ethnographically informed or humanly
sensitive understanding of other visual, musical, poetic, and choreographic systems. Illuminating experience (and not only function) and
co-aesthetic witnessing can only be accomplished honestly if ethnographers let themselves feel and be felt as emotionally involved people who
have an openly nondetached attitude about that which they seek to understand.

While there were many things I was able to understand about Kaluli
ideals of sound expression as a result of traditional participant observation, I don't think I really began to feel many of the most important

issues, like *halaido domɛki* and the construction of a song climax, until the day I composed a song about Buck's and Bambi's leaving Bosavi that brought tears to the eyes of Gigio, one of their oldest and closest friends. I wept, too, and in that intense, momentary, witnessing experience, I felt the first emotional sensation of what it might be like to inhabit that aesthetic reality where such feelings are at the very core of being human.

During my last few months of fieldwork, I played my drum virtually every day and composed many songs, while plunging deeper and deeper into the analysis of recorded materials in order to grasp why Kaluli responses to song are so strong. Reading back over my diary, I must have become obsessed with the issue of how Kaluli perceptions of me changed and developed as a result of my more open participatory actions in musicmaking. Some of my songs and drumming and dancing lessons were the cause of laughter and embarrassment for Christian Kaluli, who felt that a man from a powerful culture with medicine, missionaries, money, and airplanes had to be crazy to want to learn these things. Yet for me it was the physical sensations of vocalizing and drumming that brought me closer to the performance aesthetic and brought some Kaluli closer to talking with me about its inner dimensions. At that point, too, they began to disappear from my mind and notes as "functionally beautiful art forms" and to take hold as "affecting presences" that I could experience in a feelingful way.

Such experiences were what made it easy for me to loosen up and tell my friends about Charlie Parker, listen to the blues with them, or recount nostalgically my own nights making music in bars. These processes of developing a co-aesthetic relationship with Kaluli are also the grounding of the appreciation informing the sympathetic depiction I have attempted here in explaining the importance of weeping, poetics, and song. That same grounding also stares back at me every time I look at or attempt to discuss the image of a *kalu ɔbɛ mise.*

What I have from my experience in Bosavi, in my body, notes, tapes, recollections, diaries, gifts, and photographs, is of a different order than what I can share through this one photographic image. I feel, however, that the image of a *kalu ɔbɛ mise* stands to this book as an encore stands to a performance. For musicians, an encore is that final blast of energy that keeps you high until the next time you perform. Encores are among the most experience-heightening aspects of playing jazz, and as a listener, I find that wherever the music has taken me, the encore makes sure I stay there.

In the image is a man, a bird, a bird as a man, a man as a bird. My clear intention in placing the image here is to say that having picked these things to pieces, we deserve to conclude by seeing them as one. The image is indeed more immediate and direct in effecting this end than a recording of *sa-yɛlab* weeping or *gisalo* song would be. Even with all the analytic details offered here to prepare an outsider to listen to these sounds meaningfully and metaphorically, the perception of unfamiliar or exotic language and melody always serves to distance a listener and to hinder an immediate response or emotional attachment. Anyway, *sa-yɛlab* and *gisalo* belong to the Kaluli; the encore belongs to me. Not that the rest of the book is a precise mirror of Kaluli collective unconscious; clearly I have mediated, interpreted, translated, recoded, and imposed form and feeling throughout. But encores go somewhat further in both mediation and intention; they are acts of love and appreciation. Additionally, I wish this one to carry the "underneath" that analysis must coexist with synthesis if ethnographers are to witness and feel the emotional dimensions of cultural form and expression.

Appendix:

Kaluli Folk Ornithology

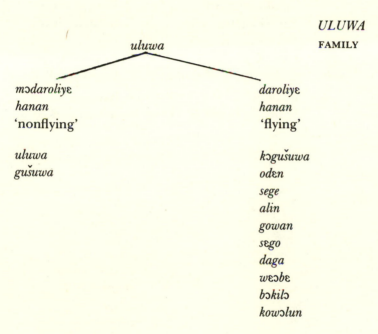

Kaluli	Primary content	Common Names
1. *uluwa*	*Casuarius casuarius*	Two-wattled Cassowary
2. *gušuwa*	*Casuarius bennetti*	Little Cassowary
3. *kɔgušuwa*	*Talegalla* sp. (? *T. fuscirostris*)	Scrubturkey (? Black-billed Scrubturkey)
4. *odɛn*	*Megapodius freycinet*	Scrubfowl

Latin and common nomenclature, following Peckover and Filewood 1976.

5. *sege*	*Aepypodius arfakianus*	Wattled Scrubturkey
6. *alin*	*Goura scheepmakeri*	Great Goura
7. *gowan*	*Phalacrocorax* sp. or spp. (? *P. melanoleucos* ? *P. sulcirostris*)	Cormorant (? Little Pied Cormorant ? Little Black Cormorant)
8. *sɛgo*	*Egretta intermedia*	Plumed Egret
9. *daga*	*Anas waigiuensis*	Salvadori's Teal
10. *wɛɔbɛ*	*Tringa hypoleucos* (also applies to windblown birds at Bosavi airstrip, e.g., *Stercorarius* sp. and *Pluvialis dominica*)	Common Sandpiper Skua, Eastern Golden Plover
11. *bɔkilɔ*	*Gymnocrex plumbeiventris*	Bare-eyed Rail
12. *kowɔlun*	*Rallicula* sp. (? *Rallina tricolor*)	Rail (? Red-necked Rail)

FƆ
FAMILY

alan———————*fɔ*———————*hɛlu*
'large'   'small'

fɔ	*ušo*
hinɛ	*unamo*
tulunei	*umoge*
du	*kišɔbɛ*
bibi	*kalogɔbɛ*
	kɔbalo

13. *fɔ*	*Otidiphaps nobilis*	Magnificent Pheasant Pigeon
14. *hinɛ*	*Trugon terrestris* (? *Gallicolumba salamonis*)	Thick-billed Jungle Pigeon (? Thick-billed Ground-dove)
15. *tulunei*	*Chalcophaps stephani*	Stephan's Ground-dove

16. *du*   *Henicophaps albifrons*   Jungle Bronzewing
    Pigeon

17. *bibi*   *Gallicolumba rufigula*   Cinnamon Ground-dove
    (? *G. jobiensis*)   (? White-bibbed Ground-dove)

18. *uŏo*   *Ptilorrhoa castanonota*   Chestnut-backed Jewelbabbler

    Ptilorrhoa caerulescens   Blue Jewelbabbler

19. *unamo*   *Cinclosoma ajax*   Painted Quailthrush

20. *umoge*   *Drymodes superciliaris*   Scrubrobin

21. *kišɔbɛ*   *Pitta sordida*   Hooded Pitta

22. *kalogɔbɛ*   *Pitta erythrogaster*   Blue-breasted Pitta

23. *kɔbalo*   *Melampitta* sp.   Blackwit
    (? *M. lugubris*)   (? Lesser Blackwit)

                                                  UƆULAGE

                     uŏulage   **FAMILY**

migi ——————————————— *migi*
halaido   *bamo*
'hard beaks'   'flat/wide beaks'

uŏulage	*kɛmos*
salage	*kulubamo*
masan	*himu*
kiboti	*nɔkalo*
bulɛki	*kelebaga*

24. *uŏulage*   *Harpyopsis novaeguineae*   Kapul Eagle

25. *salage*   *Henicopernis longicauda*   Long-tailed Buzzard
    (also includes *Falco*   (Peregrine Falcon)
    peregrinus, a visitor)

26. *masan*   *Aviceda subcristata*   Crested Hawk

27. *kiboti*   *Accipiter poliocephalus*   Grey-headed Goshawk
    (extended to *Accipiter*
    novaehollandiae, an   (Grey Goshawk)
    infrequent visitor)

28. *bulɛki*   *Accipiter melanochlamys*   Black-mantled Goshawk

29. *kɛmos*   *Ninox theomacha*   Jungle Boobook
                (? *Uroglaux dimorpha*)   (? Papuan Hawkowl)

30. *kulubamo* *Tyto tenebricosa*   Sooty Owl
                (Mt. Bosavi only)

31. *himu*   *Podargus* ?*oscellatus*   (? Marbled) Frogmouth
                ? *Aegotheles* sp.   (? Owletnightjar)

32. *nɔkalo*   *Caprimulgus macrurus*   Large-tailed Nightjar

33. *kelebaga* *Eurostopodus mysticalis*   White-throated Nightjar
                Eurostopodus papuensis   Papuan Nightjar

                                                    OBEI
                           obei
                                                    FAMILY
migi————————————*migi*
sambo   *abol*
'long beaks'   'short beaks'

obei   *ɔgowa*
gubogubo   *ɔgowa mitɛfdɔ*
gubogubo-kɛn   *ɛfe-ano*
                               ɛfe-idɛ
                               ɔlon
                               amokɛn
                               mitɛfdɔ
                               wemale
                               uwɔlo
                               sabin
                               yɛgɛl
                               iligo
                               ɛbɛlɛs
                               uasele
                               kɔgɔ
                               waidos
                               kowɔluk
                               sagelon
                               gowalo

34. *obei*	*Aceros plicatus*	Kokomo (Papuan Hornbill)
35. *gubogubo*	*Epimachus fastuosis*-male	Black Sicklebill Bird of Paradise
36. *-kɛn*	*Epimachus fastuosis*-female or immature (both on Mt. Bosavi only)	Black Sicklebill Bird of Paradise
37. *ɔgowa*	*Cicinnurus regius*	King Bird of Paradise
38. *ɔgowa-mitɛfdɔ*	*Cicinnurus regius* x *Diphyllodes magnificus*	King Bird of Paradise crossed with Magnificent Bird of Paradise
39. *ɛfe-ano*	*Diphyllodes magnificus*-male	Magnificent Bird of Paradise
40. *ɛfe-idɛ*	*Diphyllodes magnificus*-female	Magnificent Bird of Paradise
41. *ɔlon*	*Paradisaea raggiana*-male	Raggiana Bird of Paradise
42. *amokɛn*	*Paradisaea raggiana*-female/immature	Raggiana Bird of Paradise
43. *mitɛfdɔ*	*Parotia lawesii*-male	Lawes' Parotia
44. *wemale*	*Parotia lawesii*-female/immature	Lawes' Parotia
45. *uwɔlo*	*Lophorina superba*-male	Superb Bird of Paradise
46. *sabin*	*Lophorina superba*-female/immature	Superb Bird of Paradise
47. *yɛgɛl*	*Manucodia keraudrenii*	Trumpet Manucode
48. *iligo*	*Amblyornis macgregoriae* (Mt. Bosavi only)	MacGregor's Gardnerbird
49. *ɛbɛlɛs*	*Sericulus aureus*	Flame Bowerbird
50. *uasele*	*Arses telescopthalmus* ? *Monarcha* sp. or spp.	Frilled Monarch ? Monarch
51. *kowɔluk*	*Cracticus quoyi*	Black Butcherbird
52. *sagelon*	*Cracticus cassicus*	Hooded Butcherbird
53. *waidos*	*Mino anais*	Golden Grackle
54. *kɔgɔ*	*Mino dumonti*	Orange-faced Grackle

55. *gowalo* *Ailuroedus buccoides*   White-throated Catbird
extended to *A. melanotis* Black-eared Catbird
at higher altitudes

HALINA
FAMILY

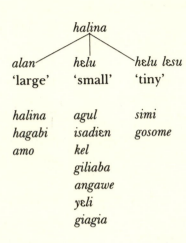

halina

alan   *hɛlu*   *hɛlu lɛsu*
'large'   'small'   'tiny'

halina   *agul*   *simi*
hagabi   *isadiɛn*   *gosome*
amo   *kel*
            giliaba
            angawe
            yɛli
            giagia

56. *halina*   *Prosciger aterrimus*   Palm Cockatoo
57. *hagabi*   *Psittrichas fulgidas*   Pesquet's Parrot
58. *amo*   *Cacatua galerita*   Sulfur-crested Cockatoo
59. *agul*   *Eclectus roratus*   Kalanga (Eclectus Parrot)
60. *isadiɛn* *Alisterus chloropterus*   Green-winged Kingparrot
61. *kel*   *Geoffroyus geoffroyi*   Red-cheeked Parrot
               Geoffroyus simplex   Blue-collared Parrot
62. *giliaba* *Trichoglossus*   Rainbow Lorikeet
               haematodus
63. *angawe*   *Pseudos fuscata*   Dusky Lory
64. *yɛli*   *Lorius lory*   Black-capped Lory
65. *giagia*   *Chalcopsitta sintillata*   Yellow-streaked Lory
66. *simi*   *Microspitta bruijini*   Red-breasted Pygmyparrot
67. *gosome*   *Microspitta pusio*   Buff-faced Pygmyparrot

hi
alan ⎯⎯⎯⎯⎯ *hɛlu*
'large'   'small'

hi-fun	*muni*
hi-susulubi	*iyɛu*
hi-tomolɔf	*kalo*
yoma	*howɛn*
wɔkwele	*susu*
galatɛf	*sowɛgu*
haidase	

68. *hi-fun*	*Ducula mullerii*	Collared Fruitpigeon
69. *hi-susulubi*	*Ducula zoeae*	Black-belted Fruitpigeon
70. *hi-tomolɔf*	*Ducula pinon*	Black-shouldered Fruitpigeon
	extended to *D. rufigaster* and *D. chalconata* at higher altitudes	(Purple-tailed Fruitpigeon Rufous-breasted Fruitpigeon)
71. *yoma*	*Gymnophaps albertisii*	Bare-eyed Pigeon
72. *wɔkwele*	*Reinwardtoena reinwardtsi*	Giant Cuckoodove
73. *galatɛf*	*Macropygia ambionensis*	Brown Cuckoodove
74. *haidase*	*Ptilinopus magnificus*	Magnificent Fruitdove
75. *muni*	*Ptilinopus pulchellus*	Beautiful Fruitdove
76. *iyɛu*	*Ptilinopus ornatus*	Ornate Fruitdove
77. *kalo*	*Ptilinopus perlatus*	Pink-spotted Fruitdove
78. *howɛn*	*Ptilinopus iozonus*	Orange-bellied Fruitdove
79. *susu*	*Ptilinopus superbus*	Superb Fruitdove
80. *sowɛgu*	*Ptilinopus nanus*	Dwarf Fruitdove

	ilai	
alan——————	*hɛlu*	——*hɛlu lɛsu*
'large'	'small'	'tiny'

ilai	*soga*	*nene*
hɔlolo	*mono*	*dolosɔk*
bidɛli-ano	*sɔlɔlɔbɛ*	*dolondo*
tɛfayo	*wɛmis*	*filɛ*
tibodai	*kuma*	*kamonano*
waful	*misak*	*mil*
talo	*wandelobo*	*beɔgolɛ*
sasahi	*ikowab*	*masitob*
mutabi	*sowasowa*	*tifɛn*
bas	*bɔlo*	*suwɛli*
yafalo	*bili*	*kidɛlɛsin*
ilasage	*diligobɛlɛ*	*golabei*
dɛfalɛn	*wasio*	*watua*
gɔgɔbɛ		*fafikon*
higu		*ahandagu*
sosas		
ugɛgɛ		

81.	*ilai*	*Centropus menbeki*	Black Jungle Coucal
		? *Microdynamis parva*	(? Dwarf Koel)
82.	*hɔlolo*	*Cacomantis variolosus*	Brush Cuckoo
		(? *C. castaneiventris*)	(? Chestnut-breasted Cuckoo)
		Chrysococcyx sp. or spp.	(? Cuckoo)
83.	*bidɛli-ano*	*Caliechthrus leucolophus*	White-crowned Koel
84.	*tɛfayo*	*Gymnocorvus tristis*	Bare-eyed Crow
		? *Scythrops novaehollandiae*	? Channel-billed Cuckoo
85.	*tibodai*	*Pitohui cristatus*	Crested Pitohui
86.	*waful*	*Pitohui ferrugineus*	Rusty Pitohui
87.	*talo*	*Pomatostomus isidori*	Rufous Babbler
88.	*sasahi*	*Coracina* spp.-dark	Cuckooshrike (dark)
89.	*mutabi*	*Coracina* spp.-light	Cuckooshrike (light)

(probably includes 5 spe-
cies; *C. papuensis, shisticeps,
morio, montana, boyeri,* and
caeruleogrisea)

90. *bas* — *Artamus maximus* — Black-breasted Woodswallow

91. *yafalo* — *Eurystomus orientalis* — Dollarbird

92. *ilasage* — *Hemiprocne mystacea* — Moustached Treeswift

93. *dɛfalɛn* — *Callocalia vanikorensis* — Uniform Swiftlet
? *C. hirundinacea* — ? Mountain Swiftlet

94. *gɔgɔbɛ* — *Callocalia esculenta* — Glossy Swiftlet

95. *higu* — ? *Climacteris placens* — ? New Guinea Treecreeper

96. *sosas* — ? *Neositta papuensis* — ? Mountain sittella

97. *ugɛgɛ* — *Pomareopsis bruijini* — Torrentlark
Monachella muelleriana — Torrent Flycatcher

98. *soga* — *Dacelo gaudichaudi* — Rufous-bellied Kookaburra

99. *mono* — *Halcyon sancta* — Sacred Kingfisher

100. *sɔlɔlɔbɛ* — *Halcyon torotoro* — Lesser Yellow-billed
Kingfisher

101. *wɛmis* — *Ceyx azureus* — Azure Kingfisher
Ceyx pusillus — Little Kingfisher

102. *kuma* — *Melidora machrorhina* — Hook-billed Kookaburra

103. *misak* — *Melilestes megarynchus* — Long-billed Honeyeater
Meliphaga chrysotis — Tawny-breasted Honey-
eater

? *Meliphaga* sp. or spp. — ? Honeyeaters

104. *wande-* — ? *Nectarinia jugularis* — ? Yellow-breasted Sunbird
lobo — ?? *Meliphaga* sp. or spp. — ? Honeyeater

105. *ikowab* — *Oedistoma iliolophium* — Dwarf Honeyeater

106. *sowasowa* — *Sphecotheres vieilloti* — Figbird

107. *bɔlo* — *Philemon novaeguineae* — Helmeted Friarbird
Oriolus szalayi — Brown Oriole
The former said to be
the male; the latter
the female of the pair.

108. *bili*	*Merops ornatus*	Rainbow Bee-eater
109. *diligobɛlɛ*	*Dicaeum geelvinkianum* ? *Dicaeum* sp. or spp.	Red-capped Flowerpecker ? Flowerpeckers
110. *wasio*	*Melanocharis* sp. or spp.	Berrypickers
111. *nene*	*Crateroscelis murina* (*C. nigrirufa* and *C.* *robusta* at higher elevation)	Chanting Scrubwren (Black-headed and White- throated Scrubwrens)
112. *dolosɔk*	*Pachycephala pectoralis* *Pachycephala soror*	Golden Whistler Sclater's Whistler
113. *dolondo*	*Tregellasia leucops* ? *Poecilodryas* sp.	White-faced Robin ? Flyrobin
114. *filɛ*	*Colluricincla megaryncha*	Brown Shrikethrush
115. *kamo-* *nano*	*Sericornis* spp.	Scrubwrens
116. *mil*	*Sericornis* spp.	Scrubwrens
117. *beɔgolɛ*	? *Phylloscopus trivirgatus*	? Island Leafwarbler
118. *masitob*	*Gerygone magnirostris*	Swamp Warbler
119. *tifɛn*	*Gerygone palpebrosa*	Black-throated Warbler
120. *suwɛli*	*Gerygone* sp. or spp.	Warblers
121. *kidɛlɛsin*	*Rhipidura leucothorax*	Black-throated Thicket Fantail
122. *golabei*	*Rhipidura rufiventris*	White-throated Fantail
123. *watua*	*Rhipidura hyperthra*	Chestnut-bellied Fantail
124. *fafikon*	? *Machaerirynchus* *flaviventer* ? *Microeca* sp. or spp.	? Yellow-breasted Flatbill ? Flycatchers
125. *ahandagu*	*Peltops blainvilli*	Clicking Shieldbill

GLOSSARY OF KALULI TERMS

a	'longhouse'
adɛ	reciprocal relationship term for older sister and younger brother
andoma	'none', 'without'
ane kalu	'gone man', spirit
ane mama	'gone reflection', spirit reflection
ba madali	'for no reason'
bali to	'turned-over words', a key poetic concept encompassing euphemism, metaphor, and obfuscatory language usage; in everyday talk it also involves irony and sarcasm
bɛlɛb	'bat'
Bonɔ	a clan living at Sululib longhouse site in the central Kaluli area
Bosavi kalu	'Bosavi man/person'; any member of the Kaluli, Ologo, Walulu, or Wisesi groups living just north of the slopes of Mt. Bosavi
Bosavi to	'Bosavi language'; the common language of the Bosavi people, marked by four dialects
dagan	'voice'
do/dowo	'my father'
dun	'branches'; in song terminology this refers to verses or development imagery

249

ɛlɛ	'like this/that'
ɛlɛma	imperative 'speak/say like this/that'; contraction of ɛlɛ and *sama*
fasela	palm streamers decorating rear of dance costume
ganalɛma	imperative 'sound'; contraction of *gana* 'sound' and ɛlɛma; appears in text inflected as *ganalab* and *ganalan*
gesema	imperative 'make one feel sorrow or pity'; also appears in text inflected as *geseab; gese* also prefixes verbs of soundmaking to mark plaintive descending intonation and a sad quality, e.g., *gese-molan* 'one sings plaintively, with descending intonation'
gisalo	generically 'song', 'melody', 'ceremony'; specifically 'song', 'melody', or 'ceremony' of the *gisalo* type, which is one of five styles performed in Bosavi, the others being *koluba, heyalo, sabio,* and *iwɔ.*
gɔnɔ to	'sound words/language'; onomatopoeia, most particularly the systematic onomatopoeia of song poetics
halaido	'hard'; a basic Kaluli metaphor for growth, strength, maturity, vitality, and dramatic style (opp. *taiyo* 'soft'; also contrasts with *halaidoma* 'unhard', which indicates something potentially hard that is not or something that is in the process of hardening, like language, physique, aesthetic tension)
halaido domɛki	'making hard'; metaphoric for the 'hardening' process of language acquisition, growth, or aesthetic tension in song and ceremonial performance
hega	'underneath'; in speaking or song texts the reference is to a hidden or underlying meaning or motive

hen wi	'place names', 'ground/land names'
hena sab	'ground living', i.e., terrestrial (opp. *iwalu sab*)
heyalo	one of five Bosavi ceremonies with a distinct song style of the same name; derives from Lake Campbell area
heyo!	exclamation of personal sorrow, yearning, sadness
inɛli molab	'one sings alone'; solo vocalization
iwalu sab	'high-up living', i.e., arboreal (opp. *hena sab*)
iwɔ	one of five Bosavi ceremonies with a distinct song style of the same name; derives from south of Mt. Bosavi; only performed the night before killing pigs
kalu	'man', 'men', 'person', 'people'
kalu ɔbɛ mise	'man in the form of a bird'; spirit reflected as a bird, ceremonial performer transformed into the image of a bird in motion
Kaluli	literally 'real men/people'; members of the central cluster of four culturally identical but dialectically marked groups that collectively refer to themselves as Bosavi people
kelekeliyoba	women's song style performed at the close of an *iwɔ* ceremony at dawn to recite pig names
kesale	'woman', 'women' (opp. *kalu*)
mama	'reflection', invisible manifestation
malolo to	'narrated words'; myths and stories of three types: historical narratives, animal tales, and trickster tales
migi	'nose', 'beak'
mise	'face', 'appearance', 'visage', 'visible form'
mɔ	'trunk'; in song terminology this refers to refrains or foundation imagery
moluma	imperative 'sing'; appears inflected in text as *molan* and *molab*
nosɔk	'cross-cousin'
nɔ/nɔwo	'my mother'

odag	Sonia term equivalent to Kaluli *ilaha;* a large buttressed fig tree that is the home of spirit birds; a prominent image in song lyrics
olɔ sɛsɛlɔ	'stripped cane'; a small piece of etched bamboo forming the handle of the *sob* rattle
ɔbɛ	'bird'
ɔbɛ mise	'in the form of a bird'; a spirit manifest in the visible realm as a bird
ɔbɛ gɔnɔ to	'bird sound words/language'; talk from a bird's point of view; the systematic language of song poetics
sa	'waterfall'; prefixes waterway terms or waterfall terms, e.g., *sa-mogan* 'waterfall pool'; all *sa* prefixed terms are polysemous and utilized as song terminology, e.g., *sa-mogan* 'melodic descent to level contour'; in this context *sa* itself indicates 'descending minor third'; *sa* also prefixes verbs of soundmaking to indicate that the outer sound has an inner component, a text, e.g., *sa-holan* 'one whistles with words in mind' versus *holan* 'one whistles'
sabio	one of five Bosavi ceremonies with a distinct song style of the same name; performed by young men in duo or quartet as an afternoon prelude to a ceremony of larger scale; introduced from the Fasu area northeast of Bosavi
sama	imperative 'speak/say'; refers to *parole,* the act of speaking and ways of speaking in a particular context; also appears inflected in text as *salan* and *salab*
sob	mussel-shell rattle use for the performance of ceremonial or seance *gisalo*
Sonia	language west of Bosavi; *gisalo* songs utilize much lexical borrowing from Sonia as a mystifying device
Sululib	ground name (literally 'source of Sulu stream') that is the home of members of clan Bonɔ in the central Kaluli area

talun	verse lines of development imagery in the major sections of *gisalo* songs
tiab kalu	'chorus men'; formal or informal group of singers who accompany the performer or medium by chorusing song lines in identical form a split second after the lead in overlap
to	'words', 'language', 'dialect'
to halaido	'hard words/language'; grammatical and appropriate language
tok	'path', 'road', 'gate'; in song poetics the sense is more of a 'map' formed by the sequence of place names in the text
tolɛma	imperative 'speak/say words/language'; contraction of *to* and *ɛlɛma;* refers to *langue,* the systematic form of language or linguistic competence
wi	'name'
wi ɛlɛdo	literally 'with two names'; reciprocal and mutual food name used by two people as a term of affection indicating a special shared relationship mediated by once sharing the food substance from which the name derives
wɔnole	'secretly', 'stealthily'
yɛlɛma	imperative 'weep'; contraction of *yɛ* and *ɛlɛma;* generic term for crying that contrasts with five specific variants; also appears in the text inflected as *yɛlab* and *yɛlan*

REFERENCES

Armstrong, Robert Plant
    1971 *The affecting presence: An essay in humanistic anthropology.* Urbana: University of Illinois Press.
    1975 *Wellspring: On the myth and source of culture.* Berkeley: University of California Press.

Bell, Harry
    1974 Mt. Bosavi as an ecological island. ms.
Berlin, Brent
    1976 The concept of rank in ethnobiological classification: Some evidence from Aguaruna folk botany. *American Ethnologist* 3(3):381–99.
Berlin, Brent, Dennis Breedlove, and Peter Raven
    1968 Covert categories and folk taxonomies. *American Anthropologist* 70(2): 290–99.
Bird, Charles
    1976 Poetry in the Mande: Its form and meaning. *Poetics* 5:89–100.
Bolinger, Dwight
    1950 Rime, assonance, and morpheme analysis. *Word* 6:117–36.
Brown, Paula, and G. Buchbinder, eds.
    1976 *Male and female in the New Guinea highlands.* Washington, D.C.: American Anthropological Association.
Bulmer, R. N. H.
    1967 Why is the cassowary not a bird? A problem of zoological taxonomy among the Kalam of the New Guinea highlands. *Man* (n.s.) 2(1):5–25.
    1969 Field methods in ethnozoology with special reference to the New Guinea highlands. Department of Anthropology and Sociology, University of Papua New Guinea, roneo.

Champion, Ivan
    1940 The Bamu-Purari patrol, 1936. *Geographical Journal* 96(3):190–206; 96(4):243–57.

Chenoweth, Vida

1968 Managalasi mourning songs. *Ethnomusicology* 12(3):415–18.

Clarke, William C.

1975 Man, land, and poetry. University of Papua New Guinea Inaugural lecture, Department of Geography. Port Moresby: University of Papua New Guinea.

Darwin, Charles

1965 *The expression of the emotions in man and animals.* Chicago: University of Chicago Press (originally published in 1872).

Diamond, Jared M.

1972 *Avifauna of the eastern highlands of New Guinea.* Cambridge: Nuttall Ornithological Club.

Diffloth, Gérard

1976 Expressives in Semai. *Oceanic Linguistics* (Special publication No. 13, Austroasiatic Studies I). Pp. 249–65. Honolulu: University of Hawaii Press.

Douglas, Mary

1973 *Natural symbols.* New York: Random House.

Empson, William

1930 *Seven types of ambiguity.* London: Chatto and Windus.

Ernst, Tom

n.d. Ph.D. dissertation on Onabasulu social organization. Department of Anthropology, University of Michigan. In preparation.

Fabian, Johannes

1975 *Taxonomy and ideology: On the boundaries of concept classification.* Lisse: Peter de Ridder Press.

Feld, Steven and Bambi B. Schieffelin

1982 Hard words: A functional basis for Kaluli discourse. In *Georgetown University roundtable on languages and linguistics 1981:Text and talk,* ed. Deborah Tannen, pp. 351–71. Washington, D.C.: Georgetown University Press.

Ferguson, Charles

1973 Some forms of religious discourse. *International Yearbook for the Sociology of Religion* 8:224–35.

Fernandez, James

1974 The mission of metaphor in expressive culture. *Current Anthropology* 15(2):119–45.

Fitzgerald, Dale

1975 The language of ritual events among the GA of Ghana. In *Sociocultural dimensions of language use,* ed. Mary Sanches and Ben Blount, pp. 205–34. New York: Academic Press.

Fox, James

1974 "Our ancestors spoke in pairs": Rotinese views of language. In *Explora-*

tions in the ethnography of speaking, ed. Richard Bauman and Joel Sherzer, pp. 65–85. New York: Cambridge University Press.

Freund, Paul
1977 Social change among the Kasua, southern highlands, Papua New Guinea. Ph.D. dissertation, Department of Anthropology, University of Iowa.

Geertz, Clifford
1973 *The interpretation of cultures.* New York: Basic Books.

Hides, Jack
1973 *Papuan wonderland.* London: Angus and Robertson Ltd. (originally published in 1936).

Hymes, Dell
1962 The ethnography of speaking. In *Anthropology and human behavior,* ed. T. Gladwin and W. D. Sturtevant, pp. 13–53. Washington, D.C.: Anthropological Society of Washington.
1974 *Foundations in sociolinguistics: An ethnographic approach.* Philadelphia: University of Pennsylvania Press.

Jakobson, Roman
1960 Linguistics and poetics. In *Style in language,* ed. T. A. Sebeok, pp. 350–77. Cambridge, Mass.: MIT Press.
1968 Poetry of grammar and grammar of poetry. *Lingua* 21:597–609.
Jakobson, Roman, and Linda Waugh
1979 *The sound shape of language.* Bloomington: Indiana University Press.

Keesing, Roger
1974 Theories of culture. In *Annual review of anthropology,* v. 3. Ed. Bernard Siegel et al., pp. 73–98. Palo Alto: Annual Reviews.
Kelly, Raymond C.
1977 *Etoro social structure.* Ann Arbor: University of Michigan Press.

Leach, Edmund
1976 *Culture and communication.* New York: Cambridge University Press.
Lévi-Strauss, Claude
1963 *Structural anthropology.* New York: Basic Books.
1966 *The savage mind.* Chicago: University of Chicago Press.
1969 *The raw and the cooked.* New York: Harper and Row.

Majnep, Ian, and Ralph Bulmer
1977 *Birds of my Kalam country.* Auckland, New Zealand: Auckland University Press.
Merriam, Alan P.
1964 *The anthropology of music.* Evanston, Ill.: Northwestern University Press.

1967 *Ethnomusicology of the Flathead Indians.* Chicago: Aldine.
Montagu, M. F. Ashley
1959 Natural selection and the origin and evolution of weeping in man. *Science* 130:1572–73.
Mukařovský, Jan
1964 Standard language and poetic language. In *A Prague school reader on aesthetics, literary structure, and style,* ed. Paul Garvin, pp. 17–30. Washington, D.C.: Georgetown University Press.

Nettl, Bruno
1956 *Music in primitive culture.* Cambridge: Harvard University Press.

Peckover, William, and Win Filewood
1976 *Birds of New Guinea and tropical Australia.* Sydney, Australia: A. W. Reed.
Pratt, Thane K.
n.d. Birds of Mt. Bosavi, southern highlands district, Papua New Guinea. ms.

Radcliffe-Brown, A. R.
1964 *The Andaman islanders.* New York: Free Press of Glencoe (originally published in 1922).
Rand, Austin, and E. T. Gilliard
1967 *Handbook of New Guinea birds.* New York: Natural History Press.
Rosenblatt, Paul, R. Patricia Walsh, and Douglas A. Jackson
1976 *Grief and mourning in cross-cultural perspective.* New Haven, Conn.: Human Relations Area Files Press.
Rule, Murray
1964 Customs, alphabet, and grammar of the Kaluli people of Bosavi, Papua. ms.

Sapir, Edward
1929 A study in phonetic symbolism. *Journal of Experimental Psychology* 12: 225–39.
Schieffelin, Bambi B.
1979 How Kaluli children learn what to say, what to do, and how to feel: An ethnographic approach to the development of communicative competence. Ph.D. dissertation, Department of Anthropology, Columbia University.
1981 A developmental study of pragmatic appropriateness of word order and case marking in Kaluli. In *The child's construction of language,* ed. Werner Deutsch, pp. 105–20. London: Academic Press.
Schieffelin, Edward L.
1972 Gisaro: Ceremonialism and reciprocity in a New Guinea tribe. Ph.D. dissertation, Department of Anthropology, University of Chicago.
1976 *The sorrow of the lonely and the burning of the dancers.* New York: St. Martin's Press.

1978 The end of traditional music, dance, and body decoration in Bosavi, Papua New Guinea. Boroko: Institute of Papua New Guinea Studies, discussion paper, 30/31/32.

Sekula, Allan
1975 On the invention of meaning in photographs. *Art Forum* 13(5):37–45.

Simon, Artur
1978 Types and functions of music in the eastern highlands of West Irian. *Ethnomusicology* 22(3):441–55.

Sinclair, James
1969 *The outside man: Jack Hides of Papua.* London: Angus and Robertson Ltd.

Sperber, Dan
1975 *Rethinking symbolism.* New York: Cambridge University Press.

Tiwary, K. M.
1975 Tuneful weeping: A mode of communication. *Working Papers in Sociolinguistics,* No. 27.

Tyler, Stephen
1969 Introduction. In *Cognitive anthropology,* ed. Stephen Tyler, pp. 1–23. New York: Holt, Rinehart, and Winston.

Werner, O., and Joann Fenton
1970 Method and theory in ethnoscience or ethnoepistemology. In *A handbook of method in cultural anthropology,* ed. R. Naroll and R. Cohen, pp. 537–78. New York: Natural History Press.

Wheelwright, Philip
1968 *The burning fountain: A study in the language of symbolism.* Bloomington: Indiana University Press.

Wood, Michael
n.d. Ph.D. dissertation on Kamula social organization. Department of Anthropology, Macquarie University. In preparation.

Worth, Sol
1974 Seeing metaphor as caricature. *New Literary History* 6:195–209.

Zemp, Hugo
1978 'Are'are classification of musical types and instruments. *Ethnomusicology* 22(1):37–67.
1979 Aspects of 'Are'are musical theory. *Ethnomusicology* 23(1):5–48.

DISCOGRAPHY

Kaluli Music

Music of the Kaluli 1982, Institute of Papua New Guinea Studies
Kaluli Weeping and Song 1982, Barenreiter-Musicaphon

These two stereo recordings have been edited from field tapes made in 1976–77; they document Kaluli ceremonial song styles, instrumental sounds, and music of everyday work and recreation. The second disc contains the actual *sa-yɛlab* and *gisalo* performances analyzed in this book.

INDEX

Adamson, C. I. J., 7

adɛ: and food, 28; *gesema* interactions, 25–27; in myth, 20–21, 39; in poetic language, 35, 42, 133, 156–58; role obligation, 29; socialization, 25–27

aesthetics: "affecting presence," 233, 236–38; bird metaphor, 217–20, 224–25, 236–38; commentary, 220–23, 231–33; and emotion, 220–23, 233, 236–38; evaluation, 221–23; participation, 236–38

'Are'are (Solomon Islands): music theory, 165n

Armstrong, Robert Plant, 233, 236

Asia Pacific Christian Mission, 9; evangelization, 9

bali to 'turned-over words': and bird names, 65–66; and 'hardening' structure, 142, 144; lexical substitutes, 65–66; in poetic language, 132–33, 138–44; metalinguistics, 138–39; metaphors, 142–43; plaintive phrases, 143–44; Sonia language, 139–40; and spirit images, 65–66; vocal delivery, 144

Baseo, 107

bats, 84

Bechet, Sidney, 231

"becoming a bird": aesthetic metaphor, 217–23, 236–38; costume, 220, 234–35; dance, 220, 234–35; and *muni* myth, 218–19;

and performance, 220, 234–35; photographic metaphor, 236–38; and sound, 218–20; and spirit reflections, 218, 220, 224; in weeping and song, 220, 224–25

Beli, 106, 123–24

Bell, Harry, 44n

Bibiali, death and mourning of, 106–8; relation to Hane *sulɔ,* 121–29

bidɛli-ano bird: voice and sound symbolism, 79–80; and weeping, 81

Bird, Charles, 132

birds: as *ane mama,* 30–31, 45, 61, 66, 84, 218, 224; arboreal/terrestrial split, 46, 58–59, 83; auditory hunting, 61; *bali to,* 65; and children, 30–31; classification, 30, 218; color symbolism, 62–63, 66–71; costume, 66, 68, 70–71; covertness, 59; curses, 63; facial tatoos, 67; and human speech, 76–80; identification, 45; in Kaluli thought, 30; and *muni* myth, 219–20, 223; personal names, 66; and sadness, 219–20; sayings, 63, 76; and seasons, 60–61; sexual dimorphism, 47, 66; and song, 219–20; sound, 71–82, 84–85, 218, 224; and space, 61–62; spells, 63; symbolism, 45, 218, 224; taboos, 52–53, 62; taxonomic ambiguities, 46–47, 51–52, 57, 60; taxonomy, 46, 58–60, 82–83; and text,

metalinguistics: *bali to,* 138–39; *gɔnɔ to,* 144–45; *langue* and *parole,* 133–34; *sa-salan,* 133; structure, 134–38; syntactic modification, 137–38

Mewɔ, 231

Montagu, Ashley, 87

Mt. Bosavi, 3–4

Mourning dove, 23

Mourning warbler, 23

muni bird: bird myth, 20–21, 39–43; as a child, 30–31; and fruitdove family, 31; and *gisalo,* 36–37; as mediator, 39–43; and sadness, 31, 41; and sound, 31, 41; and weeping, 32–33, 39, 89, 92–94, 124

myths: about birds, 22–23; dogs and animals, 23; Newelesu cycle, 23; performance style, 22; structural analysis, 38–43, 225–26, 228–29

nene bird: and children, 79, 81; voice symbolism, 79, 81

Neono, 193, 210–13

obei bird: and *ane mama,* 68; and birds of paradise, 54; and cockatoo, 68–69; sexual dimorphism, 54–56; symbolism, 65, 68

obei bird family, 54–56

ɔbɛ gɔnɔ to 'bird sound words': and 'hard words', 34–35, 131; and *muni* myth, 130, 133; as poetic language, 34–35; and song language, 130, 161; and 'sound words', 148

Ofea, 98

O'Malley, Jim, 7

onomatopoeia: and bird classification, 72–73; and song poetics, 132, 136, 144–50

Osolowa, 98

Parker, Charlie, 231–32, 237

photography: analysis, 233–38; and fieldwork praxis, 233–38; realism, 234–35; symbolism, 235–36

place names *(hen wi):* in Hane sulɔ's weeping text, 122–27; in *sa-yɛlab,* 105–6. See also *tok*

poetics: *adɛ,* 212; aesthetic tension, 132–33, 138; *bali to,* 138–44, 208–9; as bird language, 34–35; and children, 35; and conversation, 34–35; general features, 130–33; *gɔnɔ to,* 144–50, 208; 'hardening', 208, 212; in *gisalo* songs, 208–12, 215; intention and interpretation, 131–32, 139–40, 161–62; and *muni* myth, 34–35, 155–58; *sa-salan,* 132–38, 208–9; and song, 36; Sonia language, 35; *tok,* 150–56, 208–10; verb paradigm, 159–61; 'words inside *gisalo',* 132

Pratt, Thane, 44n

Radcliffe-Brown, A. R., 87

research methods: bird classification, 44–46; classification by sound, 71–73; covertness tests, 59; recording bird sound, 62; variation and stratification, 60, 82–84. *See also* fieldwork

Roth, Barry, 171n

sabio: performance contexts, 36; song features, 35–36; tonal organization, 37

sa-salan 'inside speaking': and bird voices, 136; and children's speech, 137; in poetics, 132–38

sa-sundab 'inner knotting': in song, 137–38

sa-yɛlɛma 'sung-texted-weeping': aesthetics and evaluation, 128–29, 219; *bali to,* 106–7, 121, 124–28; for Bibiali, 107–28; at funerals, 96–98; and *iyɛu* bird, 219; linguistic structure, 104–5, 127, 219; and loss, 98–99; and *muni* bird, 89, 92–94, 102, 129, 219, 223; musical structure, 99–104, 127–28; performance, 100–102; terminology and contexts, 92–93; texts, 103–7. *See also* weeping

Schieffelin, Bambi B., 9–12, 86–87, 230, 233, 237

Schieffelin, Edward L., 3, 6–7, 9–12, 25, 27–30, 60, 62, 86–87, 94, 99, 151, 167n, 173, 178, 181, 182n, 213–14, 222, 230, 233, 237

Publications of the American Folklore Society

New Series

General Editor, Marta Weigle